BODILY AND NARRATIVE FORMS

# Bodily and Narrative Forms

THE INFLUENCE OF MEDICINE
ON AMERICAN LITERATURE,
1845-1915

Cynthia J. Davis

STANFORD UNIVERSITY PRESS
STANFORD, CALIFORNIA

Stanford University Press
Stanford, California
©2000 by the Board of Trustees of the
Leland Stanford Junior University
Printed in the United States of America
CIP data are at the end of the book

Library of Congress Cataloging-in-Publication Data
Davis, Cynthia J.
  Bodily and narrative forms : the influence of medicine on American literature, 1845-1915 / Cynthia J. Davis.
    p. cm.
  Includes bibliographical references and index.
  ISBN 0-8047-3773-8 (alk. paper)
    1. American literature—19th century—History and criticism.
  2. Literature and medicine—United States—History—19th century.
  3. Literature and medicine—United States—History—20th century.
  4. American literature—20th century—History and criticism.
  5. Body, Human, in literature.   6. Medicine in literature.
  7. Diseases in literature.   8. Narration (Rhetoric).   I. Title.
PS217.M44D38      2000
810.9'. 356—dc21                                                99-057776

This book is printed on acid-free, archival-quality paper.

Original printing 2000

Last figure below indicates year of this printing:
09   08   07   06   05   04   03   02   01   00

Designed and typeset in 10/13 Minion by John Feneron

*For John and Tanner Reagle and Katie Davis*

# Acknowledgments

I am indebted to many people and institutions for helping to make this book possible. My deepest thanks go out to the numerous individuals who contributed to various stages of this multi-staged manuscript. While at Duke University, I learned a great deal from Jan Radway, Jane Tompkins, Marianna Torgovnick, Michael Moon, Jennifer Thorne, and Cathy Davidson, all of whom encouraged me to turn my initial, rather fuzzy interest in the intersection between literature and medicine into a more rigorous and sophisticated analysis. Cathy in particular has provided unfailing support over the past ten (ten!) years: my debt to her is as great as my esteem for her.

A number of my colleagues at the University of South Carolina have helped me to work through issues in the book; for their insightful readings of various chapters, I want to thank Nina Baym, Judith James, Dianne Johnson, Jim Miller, Joel Myerson, Bill Richey, and especially Kate Brown, whose careful and clarifying reading of Chapter 3 made all the difference. Other members of my department, especially Don Greiner and Robert Newman, provided moral support throughout the entire process. Robert also provided a much-appreciated semester off, during which I finished revising the manuscript. Lisa Moreno, Evelyn Westbrook, Prathima Anandan, and Beth Diehls all deserve credit and thanks for proofreading various portions of this manuscript. I am greatly obliged to Dick Hoppman for doing an impressive amount of research to help a stranger find the perfect book cover illustration. Finally, I'd like to thank Silvia Tandeciarz, Katy Goelzer, and Kathy West for offering long-distance friendship and invaluable commentary.

Parts of this manuscript have already appeared in print. I drew on Chapter 2 to write "Margaret Fuller, Body and Soul," which appeared in

*American Literature* 71 (March 1999): 31–56. A much earlier version of my thinking on Fuller was recently published as "What 'Speaks in Us': Margaret Fuller, Woman's Rights, and Human Nature," in *Margaret Fuller's Cultural Legacy*, edited by Fritz Fleischmann (Peter Lang, Spring, 2000). An article excised from the first chapter's discussion of Oliver Wendell Holmes, Sr., will shortly appear in *Nineteenth-Century Contexts*; also imminent is an essay on the formal aspects of American literary realism, which draws on the third chapter's discussion of Howells and style. This latter will appear in *Approaches to Teaching Literary Realism and Naturalism*, edited by Thomas Dean and Louis J. Budd (MLA, Fall 2000).

A generous Research and Productive Scholarship grant from my university enabled me to conduct the research for this book. I completed the Gilman chapter thanks to a grant from the university's Professional Women on Campus organization. I am grateful to the University of South Carolina for both grants and for generously supporting the research interests of junior faculty. I need to acknowledge the Houghton Library at Harvard University for permission to publish extracts from the Oliver Wendell Holmes and William Dean Howells collections. Extracts from the Blackwell family and Charlotte Perkins Gilman papers are published here with the permission of the Schlesinger Library, Radcliffe College. I am grateful to the librarians at both the Schlesinger and the Houghton for their patient responses to my frequent requests for manuscripts and assistance.

I could not have done the research at either Cambridge library had not my in-laws, Allan and Nancy Clapp, kindly opened their home to me. Nancy even served as my research assistant during one enjoyable day at the Houghton, and both Al and Nancy generously offered food, shelter, support, and occasional comic relief. Their son, John M. Reagle, has made this project not only possible but bearable thanks to his steady, comforting presence and his confidence in me. My parents, Jill and Tanner Davis, have always believed in me, and their pride in my accomplishments has proven one of the nicest rewards of this project. Most rewarding of all, though, was the birth of my son only days after I completed the manuscript. Though he didn't contribute directly to the writing of this book, he was the prize I kept my eye on throughout.

# Contents

| | |
|---|---|
| Introduction | 1 |
| 1. Medical Insight: Oliver Wendell Holmes and *Elsie Venner* | 13 |
| 2. "Where Soul Is Termed Sentiment": Sentience and Transcendence in the Works of Louisa May Alcott, Harriot K. Hunt, and Margaret Fuller | 49 |
| 3. Irregular Yet Balanced: Elizabeth Stuart Phelps's and William Dean Howells's Woman Doctor Novels | 89 |
| 4. Form Follows Function? Charlotte Perkins Gilman, Re-presentation, and the Literature of Estrangement | 122 |
| 5. Black Aesthetics: The Race Novels of Frances E. Watkins Harper, Charles W. Chesnutt, and Pauline E. Hopkins | 154 |
| Notes | 197 |
| Works Cited | 227 |
| Index | 249 |

# BODILY AND NARRATIVE FORMS

# Introduction

*Bodily and Narrative Forms* examines how emergent medical beliefs joined aesthetic imperatives to lend bodily representations their particular shape and substance in the years between 1845 and 1915. During the era of medicine's professionalization, a number of medical and scientific constructions of embodied identity were put forward; this book pays particular attention to the transformations resulting from these constructs' complicated encoding within and as literary forms. Its reputation for regimentation and homogeneity notwithstanding, the medical profession as it consolidated during the nineteenth century never uniformly advanced a single understanding of embodiment. Instead, it offered a number of often contradictory conceptions of the relationship between body and self—conceptions that also informed contemporary works of literature.

By carefully exploring these specific conceptual frameworks, *Bodily and Narrative Forms* contributes to a more accurate, complex cultural history of how the body and form were conceived in this country's period of industrialization. I say "and form" because it is clear to me—in fact, it is my central claim—that attempts to grapple with these diverse medical understandings through narrative means were not restricted to narrative content alone but necessarily involved formal features as well. Accordingly, in the five ensuing chapters I examine how these features functioned to mediate, facilitate, or obstruct any direct transcription of medically inspired ideas about bodily form into narrative form. As I demonstrate, the exigencies of literary form frequently proved as, if not more, decisive in determining the contours of bodily representations than an author's preconceptions about embodied subjectivity and how it ought (and ought not) to be defined and lived.

*Bodily and Narrative Forms* takes its starting date from the founding of the nascent American Medical Association and spans the decades in which, according to historian Paul Starr, American medical science struggled for authoritative status. What has intrigued me most about the years between my two boundary dates (1845 and 1915)—and about the earlier decades, in particular—is that this era, often cited for its medicalizing and essentializing of identity, actually represents a time of turmoil for the medical profession, a time in which scientific authority was in crisis and mainstream doctors and their prescriptions were considered unreliable, even suspect.[1] What I uncover or, better, recover in studying this time period is a variety of medical beliefs and practices, each of which was challenged either by members of the lay public or by other members of the healing professions. These conflicts prove that medical definitions of embodied identity were—contrary to received knowledge—both complicated and unstable. And literary works directly or indirectly informed by these medical debates tend to only further complicate matters.[2]

The main premise of *Bodily and Narrative Forms* is that these literary works engage in these debates structurally and not just thematically. That is, it is not only in *what* these texts represent that we can trace writers' attempts to negotiate emergent or existing medico-scientific understandings of embodiment, but in *how* they represent these understandings, the formal devices they deploy. When read alongside resonant medical frameworks, the texts I address in this study are clarified as attempts to grapple—both thematically and formally—with an increasing tendency to turn to embodied existence as both essential referent and source. Yet as these literary examples attest, this referentiality remained more of a problem than a reliable solution. Attempts to directly transport clinical suppositions into literary form were rendered all the more problematic when confronted by the relatively fixed parameters, ideological sedimentation, and generic (i.e., neither idiosyncratic nor particularly manipulable) conventions that help to structure narrative.[3]

Of course, such attempts are inherently problematic because the human body and beliefs about its significance are inscribed in literary texts not as natural entities but as denatured signs, making literature a rich site through which to explore any instability in their fashioning. In *Bodily and Narrative Forms*, I examine literary translation without assuming that the relationship between context and text is ever simple or simply direct.

Aesthetic expression is never reducible to ideology, although the two are not altogether independent. As Terry Eagleton has maintained,

> The text does not merely "take" ideological conflicts in order to "resolve" them aesthetically, for the character of those conflicts is itself overdetermined by the textual modes in which they are produced. . . . the work is "processing" ideological conflict under the form of resolving specifically *aesthetic* problems, so that the problem-solving process of the text is never merely a matter of its reference outwards to certain pre-existent ideological cruxes. It is, rather, a matter of the "ideological" presenting itself in the form of the "aesthetic" and *vice-versa*—of an "aesthetic" solution to ideological conflict producing in its turn an aesthetic problem which demands ideological resolution, and so on. (*Criticism and Ideology* 88)

In short, aesthetic expression is neither identical to nor isolable from ideological context; we should consider the two instead as engaged in a dialogue shaped by the complex and specific properties of aesthetic forms. Though the authors I discuss write in part to come to terms with bodily ideologies, what solutions they offer in their writings are specifically aesthetic in nature rather than in some crude sense ideological.

The system of ideas that particularly concerns me in this book has to do with embodied existence as defined by medical and scientific communities. One of the most productive methods I've found for thinking through the relationship between these bodily constructs and their literary translation is to examine bodily and literary forms as analogous entities. Aesthetic properties, boundary issues, motivating energies, the possibilities of full presence or of latent or manifest meaning—all lend substance to both types of forms. Comparing them along these lines has helped me to map the intricate structure of the relationship between context and text. In the chapters that follow, I frequently explore homologies or structural similarities—hence my comparison in Chapter 1 of the inclination to define a doctor's role as detached observer rather than sympathetic consult and, concomitantly, an emergent preference for narrative detachment over intrusion. Likewise, in Chapter 3 I examine similarities between theories of the body as a closed energy system and a narrative compulsion toward comparable compensatory closure. In each of *Bodily and Narrative Forms*' chapters, my aim is not merely to establish an homology but to examine the extent to which the paired structures actually converge. I resist the easy seduction of an analogy by drawing deeply in each chapter on archival resources, including personal correspondence, public lectures, journal entries, and the like. These sources firm up what might otherwise appear to be merely provocative links between bodily theories and literary forms and provide a more concrete foundation for my attraction to "form" as an applicable term for both the human and the narratival.

When signifying the latter, "form" as I use it in this study may occasionally refer to generic or subgeneric choices, or to different literary schools, movements, or modes; it may elsewhere refer to various rhetorical and aesthetical devices including point of view, voice, style, and tone. In general, I want "form" to indicate that I am addressing not just what a story means but how it works, how it is structured. Throughout this study, I consider literary form in four overlapping ways: as symptom, stress, strategy, and stumbling block. Formal features and devices may, in other words, symptomatically convey things left unexpressed within the content of the narrative. They may also serve to add stress to things already accentuated therein. Often simultaneously, we can consider form in Kenneth Burke's terms as "a strategy for confronting or encompassing [a] situation" (54), whether that situation be strictly literary or more broadly historical. Finally, formal mandates can be seen as impeding the effective communication of an author's apparent intent or a narrative's ostensible purpose.

Throughout, this project considers the works under discussion as, in a Bakhtinian sense, dialogized cultural forms.[4] Particularly, it views them as providing specifically literary formats for working out and through certain issues and, as Fredric Jameson has proposed, for "inventing imaginary or formal 'solutions' to unresolvable social contradictions" (*Political Consciousness* 79). Jameson's emphasis on the formal nature of these solutions supports my sense that a novel's cultural work—specifically, its attempts to contest or, alternatively, perpetuate emerging medical constructions of embodied subjectivity—may be carried out not just thematically but formally. In *Bodily and Narrative Forms*, my aim is to elucidate this formal work, its processes and tactics, its successes and failures. To do this, I take seriously the notion that form has a "content" different from its "expression" and often "distinct from the ostensible or manifest content of the work" (Jameson 99).

Yet another way to discuss the potential functionality of form is through what Wai Chee Dimock has termed "formal referentiality." Form, Dimock proposes, needs to be placed in context and understood "in terms of a system ... that relates to homologous systems outside the novel's province" ("Economy" 80). The risk here is that if this approach is understood too simplistically, it might yield potentially reductive readings of sophisticated works. But there are compensatory benefits, among which Dimock lists the possibility of reconstructing the novelistic preconditions which "make the very creation of form possible," as well as the potential "to think, more generally, about the grounds for equivalence that govern both the narrative arrangements inside fiction and the social arrangements outside it" (81). This is precisely the kind of reconstructive thinking that motivates *Bodily and Narrative Forms*.

It seems necessary to situate a book about form itself dialogically. *Bodily and Narrative Forms* at least implicitly responds to three occasionally overlapping strands of literary analysis: formalist, new historicist, and feminist. Taking these strands in order, I have tried to make a case for a reformulated formalist poetics that recognizes the extent to which imaginative conventions and codes are not inherent, isolate properties of a given, bounded text but produced within specific historical and political contexts at specific moments in time. At the same time, I am concerned that the transition from older, more strictly formalist critical approaches to newer, historicist approaches has led to a neglect of the intermediary function of form in the complicated interchanges between text and context. Doubtless as a corrective measure, new historicists often textualize context with too little regard for the literariness of the literary artifact and with too much regard for how narrative content (and content alone) reflects social context. In my own historicizing study, I have sought to resuscitate form as an intervening third term, one that complicates any direct translation of history into literature (and back again). Finally, I want *Bodily and Narrative Forms* to build on poststructuralist feminist interpretations of the body as text by simultaneously considering the text as "anatomic structure" (Burke 76). My project embraces a larger impulse in current feminist literary criticism to push past an initial interest in thematics toward a deeper commitment to analyzing form. Thanks to the important work of some dozen or more feminist critics, virtually any discussion of women's literature today must deal directly with aesthetics.[5] I would like my book not only to engage in these ongoing conversations but to encourage new ones.

*Bodily and Narrative Forms* also warrants location vis-à-vis works in the fields of medicine and literature and, more generally, alongside social and intellectual histories of medicine. Prior studies exploring the influence of medico-scientific epistemes upon literary works have generally neglected the role bodily ideologies play in structuring the latter as well as the former.[6] Alternately, the histories of medicine and embodiment to which I am indebted often tend to concentrate on gender as the primary, even exclusive, category of analysis.[7] While acknowledging the gendered component of the corporeal definitions put forth during this time period, I also demonstrate that these definitions were never exclusively or irreducibly gendered—that they never could be, given the complexity of bodily frameworks. At times, these historians risk oversimplifying the diverse ways in which nineteenth-century doctors read bodies by highlighting gender as the key to meaning; they also risk perpetuating this highlighting in their own late twentieth-century texts. Then as now, gender operates as a formidable strategy of containment, but in these historical studies what is at risk of being contained are the diverse, particular, and multi-faceted ways in which the body comes to matter.[8]

The readings that make up *Bodily and Narrative Forms* combine to suggest that even where gender was at issue in medical and literary representations of embodied subjectivity, it was never the only issue. As a means of testifying to the heterogeneous and complicated ways in which physical existence was both lived and understood, the chapters of *Bodily and Narrative Forms* are organized around five carefully selected debates concerning embodiment, staged either within the diverse medico-scientific community or between members of this community and a more skeptical public. The five chapters are arranged in a loosely chronological fashion, with the first two mutually informative chapters covering materials ranging from the 1840s to the 1860s, the third chapter addressing texts and documents produced in the 1870s and 1880s, the fourth chapter covering texts written from the early 1890s through 1915, and the fifth chapter focusing on works published in the first decade of the twentieth century. In general, each chapter begins with a discussion of the debate at hand, then analyzes how the concept or concepts of embodiment under debate are reconfigured when rendered in narrative form.[9] In addition to exploring century-old formal constructs, each of the chapters also implicitly tests certain recent literary critical assumptions.

The groundwork of *Bodily and Narrative Forms* is laid out in its first two chapters, where I am specifically concerned with the potentially disparate ways in which sentimental and realist stories frame the relationship between body and self. These initial chapters combine to question whether the conventions of realism are really more conducive to graphic displays of the physical and whether they are inherently antithetical to more subjective, sentimental ways of knowing. They also raise questions about whether sentimental formulas necessarily allowed greater room for excess and transcendence and whether the equation between white, middle-class women and sentimentalism invariably holds.

Chapter 1, "Medical Insight: Oliver Wendell Holmes and *Elsie Venner*," begins by discussing the increasing enthusiasm within the newly organized medical profession for defining the doctor's role as "objective eye," especially in light of a concomitant concern over the wisdom of repudiating a more sympathetic iconography—i.e., the tear or touch. It then examines Holmes's signal role in the founding of the American Medical Association and his Harvard lectures on anatomy and physiology, unearthing evidence of the doctor's fascination with the powers of surgical vision. In his clinical treatises, Holmes explicitly dissociates the insightful intrusions of the medical gaze from frequently more empathic and fumbling medical interventions. His first novel, the protorealist *Elsie Venner* (1861), pits this acutely penetrating clinical gaze against the potentially lethal, mesmerizing stare of the renegade eponymous heroine. Yet in the end, a desire to craft a sentimental coda to his clinical tale raises problems for Holmes, his doctor-narrator, and the viability of his visual model. Fearful that too aberrant a portrayal of his serpentine heroine will jeopardize the realism of his story (not to mention its popularity), at the penultimate moment Holmes's doctor-narrator abandons his pose as detached, disembodied observer to weep sympathetically for the recently departed Elsie. In striving to make this exchange a seamless one, Holmes smooths over the elsewhere bumpy transition between sentimental and realist modes, conjuring up a fictional world in which clinical realism and authority might be confirmed by either the disinterested gaze (diminishing physicality) or the sentimental tear (foregrounding it)—though not necessarily at the same time.

The second chapter, "'Where Soul Is Termed Sentiment': Sentience and Transcendence in the Works of Louisa May Alcott, Harriot K. Hunt, and Margaret Fuller," examines the midcentury tendency to describe a woman (doctor or patient) as an overflowing heart and the debate over whether this represented her healthiest modus operandi. The chapter focuses on the friction ensuing when a desire to represent woman as emotional and hence healthy rubs up against conventional generic and gendered depictions of her as emotional and hence susceptible to disease. In particular, it examines the tactics of three white, middle-class women writers—chronic invalid Louisa May Alcott, "irregular" doctor Harriot K. Hunt, and migraine sufferer Margaret Fuller—who either revised or rejected highly wrought sentimental formulas. Although as traditionally defined, sentimentalism connotes images of excess rather than mimesis, I am especially interested in the ways in which some of its stock excesses—specifically, pain and prostration—came too close for comfort to these writers' own first-hand knowledge of bodily suffering. Their familiarity with the sickroom led these women to distrust a formula in which abasement (emotional or physical) was entertained as one viable route to transcendence, since for each woman such abasement approximated (dead) end more than means. Suspicious of the symbolic equation of physical frailty and a greater spirituality, these writers omitted the former from their published works in order better to accentuate the latter. In order to do so, however, each had to distance herself from not just conventional sentimental forms but her own deeply personal experience of embodiment, as well as the engulfment both so frequently entailed.

Chapter 3, "Irregular Yet Balanced: Elizabeth Stuart Phelps's and William Dean Howells's Woman Doctor Novels," traces the pressures that conventions of closure place upon given forms, textual and corporeal. It takes up the postbellum conflict between those who felt that the body operated most efficiently as a closed energy system and those who worried that this system of checks and balances was both punitive and enfeebling. My particular focus is on how theories of equilibrium and disequilibrium contribute to the designation of certain bodily forms as more healthy and certain narrative forms as more realistic than other notably more "happy" ones. This concern with equilibrium is crucial to the emergent practices of both literary realism and clinical pathology, as my discussion of the debate ensuing from Dr. Edward H. Clarke's 1873 *Sex in Education* documents. Clarke's argument—that educating the female mind depletes her womb—was informed by Herbert Spencer's theory of the body as closed energy system. In her contribution to an 1874 collection of essays rebutting Clarke's thesis, Phelps insists that we are more than biology and hence more than those who study biology say we are. In this rebuttal, Phelps extends her critique beyond Clarke's theory of the body as closed energy system to his text presented as such. Later, in her novel *Doctor Zay* (1882), Phelps attempts once again to re-open Clarke's conclusions. She also, ambitiously, seeks to unsettle the proportionate realism of Howells, whose 1881 "woman doctor" novel prescribes a Clarkean antidote for its female subject's perceived imbalance: marriage. What Phelps seeks to realize in *Doctor Zay*, by contrast, is a realistic but "happy ending" (for both doctor novel and doctor heroine) that somehow still maintains the happy surplus that in Phelps's formulation always exceeds a given form. The novel's efforts to satisfy both goals simultaneously amounts to a real balancing act—one that is, I argue, ultimately incarnated in *Doctor Zay's* form at the expense of Dr. Zay's form. One aim of this chapter is to explore whether American literary realism deserves its reputation for overlooking stylistic concerns. It also re-evaluates the merits of the realists' denigration of excessive endings and imbalanced, allegedly artless closure.

Chapter 4, "Form Follows Function? Charlotte Perkins Gilman, Representation, and the Literature of Estrangement," begins by situating Gilman within the determinisms of her day. Throughout her public career, Gilman waged war against psychological constructions of the self—especially those of her one-time doctor, S. Weir Mitchell, and the man she would later scorn as an "absurd Sexolator," Sigmund Freud—for their attention to sublimated motivation over obvious cause and for their pathologizing of woman's nature. Viewing human nature as inherently healthy, Gilman insisted that disease never emanated from within but was always imposed from without—in particular, where women were concerned, from domestic constraints. It is this late-century dispute over whether an invalid's symptoms originated within her inherently sickly nature or outside the patient's originally, innately healthy frame that informs my discussion of Gilman's corpus. Gilman's disdain for hidden causes may explain why, while advocating a mimetic literature that "truthfully re-presents" human life, Gilman scorned works in which the artist seemed to be exclusively "engaged in exhibiting to us his own interior—which is not always beautiful." Her scorn makes all the more ironic readings of her classic tale "The Yellow Wallpaper" as evincing a perverse form of "interior exhibitionism," and as approximating hysterical simulation more than it does "truthful re-presentation." Even though the story could be interpreted as documenting and decrying the domestic determinism Gilman railed against in other venues, such a reading is muddled, I argue, by the story's uncanny format, with its persistently sublimating *unheimlich* (or unhomelike) undercurrent. Decades later, Gilman would return to essentially the same ground in her utopian novel *Herland*. But there, a generic emphasis on the future, the sociological, the explicit, and the natural forestalls the possibility of uncanny representation. What reading these two narratives jointly teaches is that didactic efficacy and "truthful re-presentation" depend as much upon formal choices as they do upon specific content—bearing out Gilman's own dictum that "what the thing does makes it what it is." In this chapter, I challenge the assumption that readings that unearth (or stories that contain) a latent subtext are inevitably more complex than their more manifest cousins.

The final chapter, "Black Aesthetics: The Race Novels of Frances Watkins Harper, Charles W. Chesnutt, and Pauline E. Hopkins," expands the project's dimensions by explicitly considering how race—and in particular, "race novels"—complicate overly simplistic biological equations of identity with form. I start by revisiting the clash between the pseudoscientists of the racial nadir—who were quick to label African-American forms intrinsically deficient aesthetically—and leaders of the racial uplift movement, who boldly proclaimed, in various ways, the inherent beauty of black bodily (and literary) forms. This pseudoscientific emphasis on crude animality and primitive sensuality provides an important context for the efforts of three turn-of-the-century African American authors—Harper, Chesnutt, and Hopkins—to craft novels discrediting such reductive, essentializing frameworks while still retaining "aesthetic" value (the stress here lies on the word's etymological links to the sensate body). In the process, each of these writers attempts to revise the prejudicial script which inscribes in black forms a desire for a beauty that they also, inherently, lack. More than just exploring the material effects of these works' ideology, this chapter investigates the ideological effects of their materiality. In other words, I examine the implications of Harper's assumption in *Iola Leroy* that there is room enough within the expanse of sentimental forms for both ethereal and natural representations of black aesthetics; of Chesnutt's search in *The Marrow of Tradition* for a way to blend extant forms into a new yet still aesthetically pleasing and realistic whole; and, finally, of Hopkins's decision in *Of One Blood* to resort to the *super*natural as ultimate guarantee of and safest space for conveying the beauty of blackness. Rather than rehearsing the still-prevalent critical divide between aesthetical versus ideological evaluations of African-American literature, these three novels prove that it is, precisely, in the aesthetics of form that some of the most cogent polemical points can be conveyed. In keeping with this point, this chapter sets out to interrogate the popularity of cultural and political interpretations of black-authored texts, especially where this hermeneutics is accompanied by a resistance to more formalist or aesthetic readings.

My final thoughts on my own attempts to conjoin aesthetical and ideological approaches appear in a brief appendage to this final chapter, where I outline both the benefits and risks of a poetics devoted to resuscitating form as at once aesthetic, historical, and political. My hope is that *Bodily and Narrative Forms* will not only offer a more detailed and complicated picture of the period in which these novels were written but also stir new interest in these often overlooked or underappreciated works. I would also like my approach to serve as a model for subsequent studies interested in examining the complex interchanges between context and form.

At the heart of *Bodily and Narrative Forms* lies my abiding interest in both medicine and literature, as well as in how the two fields intersect. In April of 1994, my teenaged sister Katie was diagnosed with a rare and, as it turned out, lethal form of childhood cancer. She died almost exactly a year later. During her illness and afterwards, I was writing this book. Looking back over this difficult time, it seems to me now that my declining interest in largely thematic juxtapositions of literary and medical phenomena and my increasing preoccupation with the mediating, often frustrating forces of form had something to do with what was happening to my sister. I think that it grew out of daily having to face the way a body might determine someone's fate but not her self, the truth that a person might mean more than her disease-ridden frame and yet not, in the end, be any different from it. Clarifying for me the complex ways in which bodies might matter and the too simplistic ways they have been taken to matter, my sister's struggle could not help but indirectly restructure how form came to matter in and to this study. I would like to believe that all of our scholarly projects are undertaken for reasons that matter as deeply.

# 1

## Medical Insight

*Oliver Wendell Holmes and 'Elsie Venner'*

In the midst of an introductory lecture to his 1861 anatomy and physiology class at Harvard University, Oliver Wendell Holmes, Sr., paused to celebrate the revolutionary implications of the microscope:

> Up to the time of the living generation of observers, Nature had kept over all her inner workshops the forbidding inscription, *No Admittance!* If any prying observer ventured to spy through his magnifying tubes into the mysteries of her glands and canals and fluids, she covered up her work in blinding mists and bewildering halos, as the deities of old concealed their favored heroes in the moment of danger. Science has at length sifted the turbid light of her lenses, and blanched their delusive rainbows. (*Border Lines* 30–31)

What most excites Holmes about microscopic insight is that it enables the once-blinded scientist to penetrate through the effluvia that previously enshrouded Nature's inner workings, allowing him to venture where no man had gone before. For Holmes, the microscope's ability to unveil these secrets has clarifying consequences for science as well, elevating it above the mists of obscurity and uncertainty threatening to bog down the emergent discipline.

With the advent of clinical medicine, as Michel Foucault has argued, "the relationship between the visible and invisible—which is necessary to all concrete knowledge—changed its structure, revealing through gaze and language what had previously been below and beyond their domain. A new alliance was forged between words and things, enabling one *to see* and *to say*" (*Birth* xii). In other words, the bodies opened up by and to the clinical gaze yielded not just new sights but a new discourse, whose truth value, in turn, was anchored in the visual revelations of the operating table and the microscope. While the medical gaze originally developed as a "plurisensorial structure" (*Birth* 164)—encompassing not just visual but auditory and tactile powers—over time, these sensations were ideologically severed from the bodies in which they originated even as the language in which scientific discoveries were conveyed was being purged of emotion, intuition, and conjecture. Such erasures, however, were not just gradual but uneven; they were by no means accomplished when Holmes began extolling microscopic insight. As such, the celebration of the clinical gaze at midcentury was symptomatic less of power or knowledge than of desire—in particular, a desire for an inscrutability capable of deflecting not just public scrutiny but the rampant skepticism with which mainstream medical practices and prescriptions were being met at this time.[1]

Although as the site of the senses his body was the physician's best hermeneutic tool, it would also prove an obstacle to the impersonality and objectivity considered integral to clinical diagnoses. As Foucault concedes, in actuality the clinical gaze "is a gaze of the concrete sensibility, a gaze that travels from body to body" (*Birth* 120). The desire to suppress the origin of this journey culminated in the mythologizing of the doctor-patient encounter "as a simple, unconceptualized confrontation of a gaze and a face, or a glance and a silent body" (*Birth* xiv–xv). The empirical and non-reciprocal nature of such confrontations depends upon the medical eye remaining both the "depository and source of clarity" (*Birth* xiii); were it to be clouded by doubt, by emotions, its clinical authority would risk being undermined, subjecting the clinician to the sort of scrutiny he sought to employ with others and avert from himself.

This fantasy of disembodied surveillance, this eagerness to observe and objectively represent previously obscure corporeal truths, are also central problematics of the emergent literary mode of realism.[2] Yet too few studies of the clinical gaze and/or clinical realism sufficiently flesh out the intimate relationship between the gazer and the gazed upon, not to mention the one between this increasingly detached realistic approach and the more involved, subjective, sentimental mode it sought to displace.[3] In this chapter I explore these constitutive relationships by paying special attention to the observer's physicality, so often elided when doctor-patient interactions and the production of clinical narratives are discussed. The following close analysis of the writings of doctor and author Oliver Wendell Holmes pursues the trace of this physical presence by mapping the sites and "sights" upon which emergent American realist and medical practices overlap, as well as by noting where, at least at this early moment, they diverge.

The correlation between realism's and medicine's naturalizing narratives is both long-standing and well documented. Flaubert, one of realism's fathers, himself had a father who was a doctor, and, of course, the author's arguably most realistic work, *Madame Bovary*, makes the practice of medicine a central concern. The connection between the genre and medicine is pronounced for other prominent realists as well: as Lars Åhnebrink writes in *The Beginnings of Naturalism in American Fiction*,

> Claude Bernard"s *Introduction à l'étude de la médecine expérimentale* (1865) did much to establish medicine as an exact science.... Upon this book Zola founded *Le Roman expérimental*, which demanded a literature governed by science and in which he used the same methods as a scientist. By substituting for the word "doctor" the word "novelist," he could make his meaning clear and give to the work of art the rigidity of scientific truth. (269–70)

In the United States, Holmes's career as both physiologist and novelist provides an early example and excellent arena in which to explore the materialism and commitment to verisimilitude central to both fields, as well as the ways each venerates a specific type of observation and observer. Holmes's insistence that the medical point of view was fundamentally a realistic one inverts the familiar contention that the realist perspective is a clinical one. As Mark Seltzer attests in his *Bodies and Machines*,

> The frequent associations of later nineteenth-century realism with a sort of dissection, vivisection, or surgical opening of the body are well known. But the association of realism with these technologies of the body points also to the realist imperative of making everything, including interior states, visible, legible, and governable ... the requirement of embodiment, of turning the body inside out for inspection, takes on a virtually *obstetrical* form in realist discourse. (95–96)[4]

Seltzer's requirement of embodiment applies not to the realist but his subject matter, not to the seer but the seen—a dichotomy also increasingly considered essential within medical science and one that is (we should note as Seltzer does not) invariably gendered.

Realism's disengaged narrator and corporeal subjects also deserve to be understood at least in part as responses to sentimentalism's intrusive narrators and etherealized characters. And herein lies the rub for Holmes: although his medical training convinced him of the truth of emergent scientific understandings of human nature and the power of cognitive, referential language, by literary bent Holmes had a weakness for sentimentalism, or, to be more precise, for an emotional, convivial prose in which his "I" was pronounced—indeed, this "I" stood as the very signature of his famous columnist persona, "The Autocrat of the Breakfast Table." *Elsie Venner* (1861), Holmes's first novel, was composed at a time when American literary realism as a formal movement had yet to officially commence (although rumblings could be heard in the wings). Written in the golden years of sentimentalism yet compelled by a "realist imperative," Holmes's *Elsie Venner* stands a confused conglomeration of residual and emergent modes. Indeed, the novel might provocatively be understood as a testament to the pressure of more conventional sentimental narrative forms upon realist ideologies of human form. For even as it is visibly committed to physiological depictions and clinical observations, *Elsie Venner* is also informed by a desire to explicitly instruct and deeply move, aims that do not always sit well with more mimetic modes of representation.

In a toast delivered at the 1853 meeting of the American Medical Association, the assembled doctors saluted Holmes's skills at deftly melding the clinical and the fictional: "The union of Science and Literature—a happy marriage, the fruits of which are nowhere seen to better advantage than in our American Holmes!" ("Toast"). Yet in Holmes's own fiction, this union was not always so "happy"; the joining of evolving medical and literary understandings of form—both written and corporeal—did not always run smooth. It did not run smoothly in *Elsie Venner*, where Holmes actively deploys the gaze to efface the physician's body while simultaneously foregrounding the patient's. Yet in the end, he swaps this method for a more hands-on, comforting, and conventional approach. As I will demonstrate, Holmes's efforts to craft a clinical tale and legitimize a clinical perspective are ultimately hampered by the mandates of residual, more empathic forms of narrative (and of medicine) whose attractions Holmes, for all his clinical enthusiasms, could not finally resist.

Composed at a time when mimetic modes were not the best way to ensure sympathetic responses to medical insights and medicalized subjects, in its penultimate pages *Elsie* ultimately and hurriedly trades mimesis for mediation, resorting to the emotional subjectivism the author so abhorred when evinced in medical texts. Among other things, the novel's conclusion foreshadows future difficulties with scripting convincing realist closure, difficulties *Elsie* and other protorealist works, including Rebecca Harding Davis's *Life in the Iron Mills*, effectively evade through their hasty retreat to residual sentimental paradigms.

In the sections that follow, I elaborate upon Holmes's involvement and investment in the organization of American medicine, and, specifically, upon his identification of the medical man with or as the clinical eye. This context will help to clarify the overdetermined visual economy that informs Holmes's *Elsie Venner*. It will, however, do little to clarify why his narrator would choose, in the story's final chapters, to trade disembodied aloofness for weepy intrusiveness, especially when these tears restore to visibility the residue of embodiment that Holmes's visualized metonymies effectively efface elsewhere in the narrative. Indeed, this intrusion would seem to retroactively undermine the reliability of the preceding, seemingly detached observations even as it signals the very impracticality of such detachment at this particular historic moment. In order to better understand this modal switch, it will be necessary to turn from a broader medical context to a closer examination of the exigencies of representational modes.

In 1884, Doctor J. Marion Sims, who began his tenure as president of the American Medical Association in 1875, reflected in his autobiography on the history and progress of his profession. Looking back at the state of medicine in the United States at midcentury, Sims confesses that "the practice of that time . . . was murderous. I knew nothing about medicine, but I had sense enough to see that doctors were killing their patients, that medicine was not an exact science, that . . . it would be better to trust entirely to Nature than to the hazardous skill of the doctors" (150). Sims here tempers Holmes's 1861 celebration of medicine's conquest over Nature by conceding Nature's more typical triumph over medical science in these earlier decades. It was Sims's skepticism about the medical profession, not Holmes's optimism, that was widely shared by the populace, leading numerous potential patients to turn for relief to homeopathy, Thomsonian "irregulars," midwives, or even their pastors and family members before or instead of consulting a "regular" doctor about what ailed them.[5]

Sims was not the only member of the profession to indulge in self-criticism. In 1848, Nathaniel Chapman, the first president of the newly formed American Medical Association, told those gathered at its annual convention that "the profession to which we belong has become corrupt, and degenerate, to the forfeiture of its social position, and with it, of the homage it formerly received spontaneously and universally" (*Transactions* 7). Chapman may have overestimated the former homage. As numerous historians have documented, medical science at midcentury was more often than not deemed nescience; well up until the end of the century, "regular" doctors' attempts at healing (dramatized, for instance, during the periodic cholera epidemics throughout the century[6]) were haphazard and often disastrous. It was actually only in the first decades of the twentieth century—boosted by genuine end-of-the-century advances in technology and therapeutics, especially in the fields of bacteriology and germ therapy—that medical practitioners finally achieved what Paul Starr deems "professional sovereignty." As Starr attests, "in a remarkably short period physicians began to achieve the unity and coherence that had so long eluded them. From a mere eight thousand members in 1900, the AMA shot up to seventy thousand in 1910, half the physicians in the country. By 1920, membership had reached sixty percent. From this period dates the power of what came to be called 'organized medicine'" (110). It was not until the early 1900s, then, that the profession of medicine could comfortably confer upon itself the status of a "science," connoting theoretical, objective knowledge (as opposed to experiential, intuitive, or subjective comprehension) of Nature.[7]

Not coincidentally, the organizational impulses of the American medical profession and the larger scientific community were virtually simultaneous. In 1846, the same year that the National Medical Convention was held, Orson Munn began publishing his *Scientific American*, the Smithsonian Institution and the Yale Scientific School each opened, and Louis Agassiz arrived in America (Bruce 3). The following year, the

American Association of Geologists and Naturalists, meeting in Boston under the leadership of Agassiz, decided to broaden its boundaries and rename itself the American Association for the Advancement of Science. Dedicated to preaching and advancing what Robert V. Bruce refers to as the "gospel of science" (225), the AAAS found its prestige enhanced by the cultural fascination with Darwinism and technology. Although membership was never that high in the antebellum period—in fact the Association was suspended during the Civil War and many thought the National Academy of Sciences (founded in 1863) would supplant it—it experienced a rebirth in the postbellum period and by 1900 had 1,700 members (288–89, 313–15).[8]

Although not all scientists were doctors, virtually all doctors wished to be considered scientists. In fact, one of the markers of the medical profession's gradual ascendancy during the latter half of the nineteenth century (proceeding, admittedly, in fits and spurts, with numerous setbacks in between) was an increasing tendency to collapse these two titles. In the late 1830s, however, as Sims's recollections indicate, such a conflation could not be taken for granted. Faced with widespread and not unwarranted public distrust of the profession's attempts to assert its expertise, the Medical Society of the State of New York in 1839 initiated the first attempts to call a meeting of all national medical colleges and societies. Not one state responded to its invitation (Stevens 29). Seven years later, after an interval that saw the invention of anæsthesia—a term Holmes claimed to have coined—and a mounting crisis over lax medical education and licensing, the moment appeared riper. In 1846, a National Medical Convention was held in New York, out of which the American Medical Association—whose first meeting was held in Philadelphia in 1847—was born.

At that meeting, Nathan S. Davis, who would go on to be an influential spokesperson for the AMA, countered the skepticism shared even by some members of his audience by arguing that

Of all the voluntary social organizations in our country, none are at this time in a position to exert a wider or more permanent influence over the temporal interests of our country than the American Medical Association. This assertion may startle the mind of the professional reader and call forth a smile of incredulity, nay of contempt, from the nonprofessional; but let both follow me to the end and judge. (qtd. in Fishbein 21)

As Davis's comments indicate, the AMA represented to its founders a therapeutic intervention in the lives not of patients so much as regular physicians, who sought to defend their professional viability from what one state legislator referred to as every citizen's "inalienable right to life, liberty, and quackery" (qtd. in Larson 20).

In the same year that the National Medical Convention was held, Elizabeth Blackwell was applying to medical schools and the country's first medical school for women only—Boston Female Medical School—was but two years from opening. Nevertheless, the issues troubling the doctors attending that first conference were not, at least according to the official transcripts of the meeting, explicitly gendered ones. Nor was the problem apparently one of lack of organization or direction. In his genealogy of the new organization delivered during a lecture at the Massachusetts Medical College in 1847, Holmes argued that "Our medical community was already thoroughly organized; an ethical code, in most respects identical with that adopted by the National Convention, had been in action here for a long series of years; a general state of harmony and an enlightened public sentiment were already prevalent" (10).

Although Holmes most certainly exaggerated his final claim, a statement he made earlier in this lecture more accurately illuminates the underlying motivations of the new Association:

If the feeling in which this [the American Medical Association] originated were truly stated, it would be found that it was a result of the institution of *inferior medical schools*, situated in the wrong places, and managed by the wrong men, and the consequent cheapening and vulgarizing of education, until the degree of doctor of medicine has, in some parts of our country, ceased to be an evidence of a decent amount of knowledge on the part of those who possess it. The honorable and thoroughbred practitioner found himself shouldered by ignorant novices claiming to be his equals, who had never devoted half the allotted period of pupilage to study, who had never touched a scalpel, who had never seen a hospital, and in the face of an easy public, apt to take men at their own valuation, and having no proper means of discriminating between them. (8–9)

The ability to "discriminate" lies at the heart of Holmes's definition of a "regular" (or as he puts it, "thoroughbred") doctor and a regulated profession. According to Holmes, the motivating impulse behind the organization of American medicine at the national level was to differentiate between practitioners of divergent socio-economic and educational status.[9]

Although the simultaneous emergence of the female medical professional is not directly cited by Holmes in his list of organizational impulses, this is not to say that gendered concerns were absent. In *Sympathy and Science*, her groundbreaking history of women and medicine, Regina Morantz-Sanchez argues that American medicine was defined from the outset via a dialectic between her titular terms. She contends that in the main, the scientific definition of medical practice was adopted and advocated by male practitioners and the sympathetic by female. The early literature of the AMA, however, suggests that both definitions were not only present at once but that they held simultaneous if uneven appeal for elite male members of the profession.

In fact, tensions between these co-existing definitions of medicine form the lurking subtext of many of the first convention's founding documents, including its newly stipulated code of medical ethics, dedicated to elaborating a physician's rights and responsibilities. Therein, the code's drafters contend that, "being required to expose his health and life for the benefit of the community, he [the doctor] has a just claim, in return, on all its members, collectively and individually, for ... all possible tenderness and regard to prevent needlessly harassing calls on his services and unnecessary exhaustion of his benevolent sympathies" (*Transactions* 84). Such sympathies, we see in this early formulation, are considered a part of a doctor's make-up but are easily at risk of being overtaxed, either by the patient or by the physician: "professional duty requires of a physician, that he should have such a control over himself as not to betray strong emotion" (84). If the doctor does not maintain this control he may end up like "many medical men, [who] possessed of abundant attainments and resources, are so constitutionally timid and readily abashed as to lose much of their self possession and usefulness at the critical moment" (85). Clearly, the drafters saw a doctor's craft as balancing precariously on the line between rights and duties, control and emotion, self-possession and self-abasement—or, put another way, on the line between "science" and "sympathy."

This line, of course, also functioned ideologically to delineate conventional gendered and generic dichotomies—i.e., to divide masculinity from femininity, realism from sentimentality. Traces of these dichotomized terms ineluctably inform the drafters' rhetoric. Indeed, the code of ethics suggests that such divisions were so tentatively sketched that crossover and convergence were commonplace. For instance, the code's authors seem at times more invested in linking sympathy and science than in distinguishing between them, as in this elaboration of the duties of physicians to their patients: "[physicians] should study ... in their deportment, so to unite *tenderness* with *firmness* and *condescension* with *authority*, as to inspire the minds of their patients with gratitude, respect and confidence" (93).

Among our received notions of the nineteenth century is that the "cult of true womanhood"—ideological offshoot of the capitalist socioeconomic structures that helped to divide work from home, production from reproduction, masculinity from femininity—counted among its most loyal promoters both the domesticated bourgeois woman and the physicians who often prescribed domestification, or at least bed rest, for her (see Welter; Ehrenreich and English). One would assume, then, that in their attempts to situate themselves above these female patients and beyond the increasingly antagonistic definition of the profession as necessarily sympathetic, "regular" doctors would strive to dissociate themselves from "domestic" values, sympathies, and practices. At least initially, however, many of these doctors were attempting the tricky maneuver of ideologically distancing themselves from conventionally feminine attributes while simultaneously attempting to access their most classic sites: i.e., the home and the female body.[10] This quandary helps to explain why regular doctors might have intentionally or unintentionally adapted a sympathetic language to facilitate their entrance into arenas that might have otherwise proved unsympathetic toward them.

The AMA's code of ethics is one site where these physicians' desires for ingress into hitherto "feminine" realms surface metaphorically, so that a doctor's duties are elaborated upon in rhetorical images that resound with women's traditional domestic responsibilities. For instance, in the code's description of the "Duties of Physicians to Their Patients," doctors come remarkably close to resembling the legendary angels in the house, the preservers of "the privacies of personal and domestic life" (93):

"For the physician should be the minister of hope and comfort to the sick; that, by such cordials to the drooping spirit, he may smooth the bed of death, revive expiring life, and counteract the depressing influence of those maladies which often disturb the tranquility of the most resigned, in their last moments" (94).[11] After all medicinal attempts to heal the patient's body have failed, the physician is encouraged to employ his own comforting physical presence to heal his or her "drooping spirit." A bedside manner that includes "smoothing the bed" highlights the physician's own corporeality while also demonstrating the porous boundary between sympathetic and scientific definitions of the profession in its organizing moments.

As the century progressed, however, professional attention to the comforts of bedside manners waned. In a nearly direct inverse relation, the more patients came to be seen strictly through a pathologizing lens as bodies, not souls, the less the doctor's own corporeal presence was represented as integral to curative interventions. As healing became more professionalized and specialized, the clinician's role came increasingly to be defined as observer rather than participant. And, as Foucault has suggested, "the observing gaze refrains from intervening: it is silent and gestureless" (*Birth* 107).

This gradual abstraction is presaged within the 1847 code of ethics. By the end of the document, the sentimental rhetoric that enabled its authors initially to wax eloquent over the doctors' abilities to "soothe and tranquilize" gives way to talk of "true science," "veracity," "positive facts," and "sound logic" (*Transactions* 88), stripping the doctor at the level of language, at least, of the emotion that may still have been evident in his practice. As the authors of the code conclude, "the right of free inquiry, common to all, does not imply the utterance of crude hypotheses, the use of figurative language, a straining after novelty for novelty's sake" (89). These references to "crudeness" and "straining" suggest that physicality ought to be eliminated from doctors' words just as, ideally, it would soon cease to define their bedside manners.

This disembodied, objective linguistic standard was not intended to pertain exclusively to the founding documents of the AMA. According to the code's authors, all genres of medical writing should strive to be both factual and impartial. Indeed, objective medical discourse was linked to matters of health, both public and professional: "physicians are peculiarly enjoined, by every consideration of honour and of conscientious regard for the health and lives of their fellow beings, not to advance any statement unsupported by positive facts, nor to hazard an opinion or hypothesis that is not the result of some deliberate inquiry into all the data and bearings of which the subject is capable" (88). Through such dictates, these AMA documents issue an early yet clarion call for empiricism, for a referential language that would substantiate the practitioner's claims to scientific accuracy and "sovereign authority"—in word if not yet in deed.

↬

Before the first meeting of the American Medical Association disbanded in 1847, several new committees were established and enjoined to present reports at the next annual meeting. Among these was the Committee on Medical Literature chaired by Oliver Wendell Holmes, who must have seemed an obvious choice. Holmes, whose life virtually spanned the nineteenth century (1809–94), managed in that span to produce a great deal of writing. In addition to drafting important medical essays, including his pathbreaking "Contagiousness of Puerperal Fever" (1843), Holmes also enjoyed literary pursuits, publishing his first volume of poetry in 1836. By 1847, the year of the first national medical conference as well as his appointment as Parkman Professor of Anatomy and Physiology at Harvard University Medical School, he had already established his reputation as a poet, wit, and scholar among his fellow "Boston Brahmins" (an appellation he himself coined). Ten years later, when his "The Autocrat of the Breakfast Table" column began to appear in the newly launched *Atlantic Monthly*, Holmes's fame would spread beyond his hometown. His whimsical columns for the magazine would eventually be collected in the three-volume *Breakfast Table* series, and it is upon this series as well as his poetry ("Old Ironsides" is still recited by Boston school children) that Holmes's literary reputation remains staked. Other highlights include two "lives," one of John Lothrop Motley and one of Ralph Waldo Emerson, and three novels: *Elsie Venner* (1861), *A Mortal Antipathy* (1885), and *The Guardian Angel* (1891).

While frequently sentimental and loquacious in his poetry and *Atlantic Monthly* columns, in his medical writings Holmes's tone rings different. His praise for objectivity in clinical treatises is elaborated upon in the 1848 Committee on Medical Literature Report, published as an appendix to the convention documents that year and authored by Holmes alone. Echoing other voices concerned with literary paucity and derivativeness, Holmes uses this report to encourage his colleagues to forge a uniquely national literature:

It cannot be denied that the great *forte* of American Medical scholarship has hitherto consisted in "*editing*" the works of British authors. . . . The American constitution must be studied by itself—it differs from the European in outline, in proportions, in the obvious characters of the skin and hair—why should it not differ in the susceptibilities which, awakened, become disease? . . . Here is the true field for the American medical intellect. (*Transactions* 38–39)

For Holmes, America's uniqueness is grounded in corporeal distinctiveness: it is the difference of our bodies that should compel us to produce a different sort of literature. Holmes thus establishes a correspondence between corporeal referent and its written representation, grounding a distinctly American form of writing in a distinctly American form.

Since a doctor's role is to unveil Nature, Holmes deems it fitting he should do so in transparent language:

The physician should remember, that his style has no more occasion for pomp of oratory and glitter of epithet, than his costume for the gold lace and feathers which belong to the military chieftain. Nothing is more offensive than an attempt to tell that which should be said plainly and decently, in high flown language. It vitiates the taste of the student who listens to it or reads it, and exposes the profession to derision from those who cannot value the important truths disguised by such ill chosen finery. (37)

Once again Holmes correlates language and corporeality, but here the relationship hinges not on nationality but on nudity: medical language, figured as a body, is unclothed the better to disclose its insights. In the process of stripping a doctor's language of its emotional and sartorial trappings, all traces that might identify the author are also conveniently removed. A series of intricate metonymies displaces the physician's own body, its emotions and excesses, onto his language, then banishes from that "body-language" all the flaws that may not be as readily removable— much to the profession's chagrin—from the physician as embodied subject. The clinical vision employed by physicians to read bodies was not expected of lay readers confronting a physician's body-language, since the truths of the latter should be readily apparent to the naked eye.

Vision preoccupied Holmes throughout his lengthy career. In addition to several scholarly essays on the topic and its myopias, Holmes wrote the preface to Edward H. Clarke's *Visions: A Study of False Sight (Pseudopia),* published in 1878 (Clarke also authored the notorious *Sex in Education,* which Holmes sympathetically reviewed in the *Atlantic Monthly* in 1873).[12] Holmes's fascination with the microscope has already been noted; he was also an enthusiastic fan of the stereoscope as enlightened entertainment for the masses.[13] Elsewhere in the same introductory lecture in which he praises the former, Holmes credits Bichat—the father of pathological anatomy—with having "succeeded in reducing the structural language of nature to syllables" and expands upon his admiration for

The microscopic observers who have come after him [as they] have analyzed these [syllables] into *letters,* as we may call them,—the simple elements by the combination of which Nature spells out successively tissues, which are her syllables, organs which are her words, systems which are her chapters, and so goes on from the simple to the complex, until she binds up in one living whole that wondrous volume of power and wisdom which we call the human body. (*Border Lines* 26–27)

Here, the body becomes text legible to the scientific eye through the powerful lens of the microscope. Tellingly, in this passage the microscope is not simply an apparatus distinct from the scientist but an adjective used to describe him.

Repeatedly throughout this introductory lecture, Holmes imagines the doctor/surgeon as possessing optical powers capable of deciphering the body's hidden meanings, "enabling him to see with the mind's eye through the opaque tissues down to the bone on which they lie, as if the skin were transparent to the cornea, and the organs it covers translucent as the gelatinous pulp of a medusa" (*Border Lines* 32–33). So taken with this ability was Holmes that he decided to organize his entire anatomy course around the theme of "illustration," claiming that "all the objects of anatomical research are visible ones," and stating that his intentions for the year were "to render visible everything which the eye could take cognizance of, and so turn abstractions and catalogs of names into substantial and objective realities" (32–33).[14] For Holmes, this concretizing power—available with or without the aid of the microscope—represents that which distinguishes the medical practitioner. Yet even while the medical scientist might be capable of making the abstract concrete, for Holmes the chief virtue of science itself is its abstract, disembodied nature: "Science, of all things, should be freest from servile adherence to territorial limits; Science ... like the atmosphere, cannot exist in one place, without diffusing itself gradually over others" ("Introductory" 17). While its objects of study may be reduced to specific anatomies, science itself should remain as diffuse and rootless, as omnipresent as the atmosphere.

So defined, medical science epitomizes the essence of what Burton J. Bledstein deems "The Culture of Professionalism," which flourished from mid-century on. In order to achieve the status of profession, according to Bledstein, a field must of necessity transcend specific ground-spaces in order to extend its practice and its authority to include "every worldly sphere." Intriguingly, at the same time that the professional disassociates himself from any delimited sphere, it becomes his simultaneous occupation to identify[15]

> every category of person who naturally belonged to a specific ground-space: the woman in the residential home, the child in the school, the man in his place of work, the dying person in the hospital, and the body in the funeral parlor; the immigrant in the ghetto, the criminal in the prison, the insane in the asylum, the Indian in the reservation, the Negro in his segregated area, the Irishman in the saloon, the prostitute and the pimp in the red-light district. (56)

Put simply, professionalism's lack of adherence to place hinges on putting others in their place. Anticipating Michel Foucault's influential study of the emergence of a *scientia sexualis* for which the classificatory impulse was fundamental, Bledstein demonstrates the ways in which professions attain ostensible transcendence—and power—by identifying nonprofessional bodies as specific and concrete entities (see also Foucault, *History of Sexuality*, esp. 53–73).

For Holmes, the categorizable others against whom his profession was to be defined were primarily "irregulars," in particular, homeopathic practitioners.[16] But they also included women, and not just female healers and midwives. After all, the dynamics of the gaze inform numerous relationships. For example, Holmes was by no means averse to what he saw as a little harmless "girl watching," a penchant he confesses to in one of numerous digressions in "The Autocrat." In this column, worth quoting at length, Holmes complains that

> There is [an] unfortunate way of looking, which is peculiar to that amiable sex we do not like to find fault with. There are some very pretty, but, unhappily, very ill-bred women, who don't understand the law of the road with regard to handsome faces. Nature and custom would, no doubt, agree in conceding to all males the right of at least two distinct looks at every comely female countenance, without any infraction of the rules of courtesy or the sentiment of respect. The first look is necessary to define the person of the individual one meets so as to recognize an acquaintance. Any unusual attraction detected in a first glance is a sufficient apology for a second,—not a prolonged and impertinent stare, but an appreciating homage of the eyes, such as a stranger may inoffensively yield to a passing image. It is astonishing how morbidly sensitive some vulgar beauties are to the slightest demonstration of this kind. When a *lady* walks the streets, she leaves her virtuous indignation countenance at home; she knows well enough that the street is a picture-gallery, where pretty faces framed in pretty bonnets are meant to be seen, and everybody has a right to see them. (194–95)

In Holmes's intentionally humorous yet revealing schema, men get to look, women get looked at, and ladies allow themselves to be looked at— the "right to look," although generously afforded in the end to "everybody," is depicted earlier on as belonging exclusively to "all males."[17]

Holmes's belief in this gendered visual dichotomy is both evidenced and complicated by his views on female doctors. In 1879, in yet another introductory lecture, Holmes confesses to his students that "I myself, all things considered, very much prefer a male practitioner, but a woman's eye, a woman's instinct, and a woman's divining power are special gifts which ought to be made useful. If there were only a well-organized and well-trained hermaphrodite physician I am not sure I would not send for him-her" (qtd. in Tilton 332–33). There are several aspects of this passage worth noting. First, Holmes not only essentializes but dichotomizes "vision," "instinct," and "divining power," so that each gender is afforded its own unique visual and emotional methodology. Second, he acknowledges that a physician may successfully incorporate both "masculine" and "feminine" approaches to therapeutics into his/her practice, a point he (according to habit) illustrates via a specific body-type: this time a hermaphrodite. Yet to Holmes's clinical audience the image of the hermaphrodite would not conjure up a viable professional but instead a maladjusted patient in need of the former; further, the way Holmes sets up his conditional sentence leaves unfinished but not unpredictable the fact that since there is no such "well-organized," "well-trained" "him-her," he'll have to make due with the extant male-dominated profession.

Holmes's views on women and medicine are complex: as a doctor-character in his novel *A Mortal Antipathy* argues, "I am for giving women every chance for a good education, and if they think medicine is one of their proper callings, let them try it. I think they will find that they had better at least limit themselves to certain specialties, and always have an expert of the other sex to fall back upon. The trouble is that they are all so impressible and imaginative that they are at the mercy of all sorts of fancy systems" (qtd. in Morse 187).[18] As I discuss in the next chapter, the qualities Holmes considered liabilities—impressibility and imaginativeness—were seized upon by many female practitioners as both birthright and professional boon. Holmes, who openly admired one of his Paris medical lecturers even though she was a woman, generally believed that those he referred to as "the ovarian sex" were born not to doctor but, if anything, to nurse (Tilton 333).

Ultimately, Holmes's chief objection to women as clinicians is more complicated than the patriarchal truism that women were meant to be seen, not to see: a woman's eye, Holmes suggests, casts far too sympathetic a glance to qualify her for the rigorous practice of medicine. Rather than read the truth objectively, a female gaze was destined to respond emotionally; the most natural function of a woman's eye was not to pierce but to weep. As *Elsie Venner* makes clear, when actively looking (not necessarily for love) and not content to be looked at, a woman and her "eye" can only destroy, not feel and, most emphatically, not heal.

⁓

When his colleagues toasted Holmes as "the Union of Science and Literature," they weren't kidding. After a reader dismissed Holmes's first novel, *Elsie Venner*, as "medicated" (which, in modern parlance, would translate as "medicalized"), Holmes took such pride in the anecdote that he began his second preface to *Elsie* by relating it. Holmes's friend S. Weir Mitchell would later echo this reader's verdict when he characterized Holmes's subsequent novel, *A Mortal Antipathy*, as "daringly medical" (qtd. in Tilton 352). As Lawrence Rothfield maintains in *Vital Signs*, novelists who employ clinical presuppositions do so in order "to define the relation of self to body as a medical one" (xiii) and to foreground disease as integral to "the developing life of an embodied self" (4). Holmes, who proudly acknowledged what his critics condemned as his "too physiological point of view" ("Response" 3), supposed just these things in his fictional works, especially in *Elsie Venner*.

Yet at the same time, Holmes remained reluctant to purge his physiological viewpoint of all traces of subjective emotion. Although *Elsie* may be "medicated," it is not necessarily mimetic. The novel's descriptive passages are not consistently couched in the unadorned language Holmes and others associate with truth-telling, nor does the narration always maintain the distance associated with a realist perspective. In addition, the story's serpentine protagonist bears little resemblance to the typical characters populating realist fiction. In short, Holmes's "clinical" tale—above all else, *Elsie*'s point of view identifies it as such—more closely resembles a pastiche of realistic and sensational modes and devices.

In his preface to *Elsie* Holmes explains his plot as an attempt to "justify morality from nature or human nature":

Was Elsie Venner, poisoned by the venom of a crotalus before she was born, morally responsible for the "volitional" aberrations, which translated into acts become what is known as sin, and, it may be, what is punished as crime? . . . on presentation of the evidence, she [should be seen as] a proper object of divine pity and not of divine wrath, as a subject of moral poisoning. (x)

In so arguing, Holmes connects stirring pity for his deviant protagonist to a detailed examination of her. Yet this potential sympathy is diluted in the narrative through the distancing effect of the visual and biologized epistemologies employed therein. In *Elsie*, Holmes attempts to demonstrate the powers of a detached point of view while still reaping the benefits of a fully engaged reading. But if to sympathize is, ideally, to collapse the boundaries between pitier and pitied so that the two are momentarily identified, rousing such feelings for Elsie was destined to prove a difficult task. How many readers, after all, would want to identify with a protagonist who enjoys sleeping with snakes?

Holmes himself acknowledges that readers were more apt to be revolted than affected by Elsie's plight:

> An obvious objection to this story was that it was abnormal, exceptional, improbable, or impossible,—but it answered my purpose for its time. The *natural* sequence to it was to show how in the *normal* order of things a series of inborn instincts and propensities may act the same part as the poisonous alien element in the hypothetical story, and this is what I am now doing. *Here we come upon the ground of direct observation.* I describe the facts of inherited qualities as we who study families see them. I carry my subject through such exposures as our experience of life has shown us to be of too frequent occurrence [sic]. I hope to find, as I have found heretofore, many among my own profession who fully recognize the truth of the general laws I illustrate. (Notebook n.p., emphasis added)

This description of purpose exemplifies the correlation between realist writing and the clinical gaze: as Holmes stipulates, his story commenced from a desire "to show" a "directly observed" scientific principle to his readers. And what these skills of "direct observation" most effectively demonstrate are the "normalcy" and "naturalness" of the author's writing process over and against the abnormal, unnatural nature of his protagonist. Holmes's description confirms Lawrence Rothfield's supposition that a "novelist's authority . . . depends upon the hegemony of his or her epistemic model—upon our willingness to accept this range of possibilities, this sphere of actions, as in some way more true to life, more authoritatively realistic, than any other way of imagining the real" (185). In *Elsie*, Holmes stakes both his truth claims and the potential hegemony of his model on the penetrating powers of a clinical viewpoint, evincing little concern for characterization, plausibility of plot, or any of the other conventions typically associated with realist modes. While he suggests that *Elsie* is in one respect a true story, its truth is something he expects lay readers to miss and only doctors, equipped with enhanced visual powers, to perceive.

What Holmes advocates more than anything else, then, is a realism grounded less in mimetic representation than in "medicated" perspective. It mattered less whether the novel's plot or characters were deemed plausible than that the plausibility of its point of view was accredited. Giving a clinical twist to James's famous dictum, the story's claims to accuracy lie more in what and how the narrator sees than in what he shows or even tells. In Holmes's *Elsie*, realism does not rest in mirroring an external Nature so much as in exposing an interiorized, feminized nature and a doctor's skills at facilitating this exposure. It is only after this interior has been fully probed that, Holmes insists, one could begin to sympathize with the subject. In fact, Holmes optimistically proposes that dissection is the one true prerequisite for a sympathetic reading.

This proves optimism even for Holmes because, although up to the penultimate moment *Elsie* works to champion emergent ideologies of realism and masculinity over the reigning epistemes of sentimental cultures, its ending resorts to visibly sentimental gestures. This sudden switch to a sentimental narrative mode in the last chapter might be understood as an attempt to model a response a reader would hopefully emulate. Yet if so, it concedes the limitations of clinical dissection and perception even as it inverts the evolution of organized medicine, which purports to supplant the subjective with the objective gaze. It is one thing, the story of *Elsie* suggests, to weave a realist narrative out of the dialectic between medical vision and medicalized subjects; it is quite another (as the response—both anticipated and actual—to *Elsie* would prove) to expect audiences to sympathize with such a construct, built as it is, after all, out of such distancing materials.

⌒

The Elsie Venner who first made her appearance in a serial in the *Atlantic Monthly* in 1859 is remarkable for her strangely sibilant "s" and a succinctly serpentine sinuosity.[19] She owes these distinctive traits to her poisoning, prenatally, when her pregnant mother was bitten by a snake. Indeed, it is left unclear whether the mother dies as a result of childbirth, the snake's poison, the shock of the snake-like appearance of her daughter, or, most probably, all of the above. Elsie's father Dudley, lamenting both his wife's untimely demise and his daughter's snakiness, allows his young child to grow up relatively unsupervised, excepting the help of her old black nurse, Sophy, and the occasional professional advice of the town physician, Doctor Kittredge. Elsie expresses an early preference for

# Medical Insight: Holmes and *Elsie Venner*

running wild through the mountains, often spending the night in caves on the aptly named "Rattlesnake Ledge" that hovers over the Venner mansion, where numerous cousins of the snake that struck the late Mrs. Venner reside.

As the story opens, a young man, Bernard Langdon, is forced to leave medical school for pecuniary reasons and take a job teaching at a rural academy, the same one Elsie sporadically attends when she is not otherwise distracted. Fascinated by Elsie—a strikingly beautiful girl who is described as possessing diamond eyes, a low forehead, a slight lisp, and a penchant for bedecking herself in gold coil jewelry and a pin that resembles Cleopatra's asp—Langdon decides to get to the heart of her mystery. In addition to consulting Kittredge and rereading Keats's "Lamia," he writes for advice to his old medical school professor (the "I" who narrates the story, and who, like Holmes, is a professor of anatomy at a distinguished university).

In the meantime, Elsie has likewise taken an interest in her new teacher, but hers is of a far more passionate nature. Her increasing love for Bernard infuriates her swarthy, vaguely Latin American cousin Dick, who has wanted to marry Elsie ever since she bit him when the two were children and especially since he realized that she was the sole heir to a great fortune. Dick conspires to murder Bernard but is driven out of town when Dr. Kittredge and his trusty manservant foil his plot. Love is in the air in Rockland: Bernard eventually falls for the granddaughter of the local Reverend and the widowed Dudley Venner is smitten with young Helen Varley, the soft-spoken schoolteacher who both works with and befriends Bernard. Elsie is the only one to love and lose, and when she realizes Bernard is indeed lost to her, her health rapidly declines. Before she dies, however, Elsie is miraculously returned to her true—read essentially feminine—nature through a fit of weeping and a hug from her father. After her death, the necklace that had been a permanent fixture on Elsie's neck is removed by the loyal Sophy, revealing to the astonishment of all that the mark (of a snake bite? of Cain?) which the necklace allegedly concealed had vanished without a trace. Not long thereafter, the rattlesnakes inhabiting the town's mountains also vanish, after an earthquake which destroys Rattlesnake Ledge (and kills Sophy).

*Elsie* is a novel open to numerous interpretations: among others, it might be read as a Darwinian allegory where the chain of being extends from serpent to true woman; a biologistic revision of the Edenic story in a time when medico-scientific epistemes were replacing religious ones; an American rendition of Keats's "Lamia" (see Hallissy); a morality tale about the perils of female sexual aggression; and, given the novel's appearance on the eve of the Civil War, a cautionary tale on the fate of mixed-race offspring: Elsie's "dark" mother's nationality is identified—Spanish—but her race is not.

Anne Dalke has suggested that rather than sex or race, economics becomes the central motivation of the novel, claiming it impels all but Elsie's actions and hence explains Elsie's necessary death in a world driven by the bottom line (59). Certainly, one economy operating in *Elsie* is a sexualized one, whereby the triangularized bonds between medical practitioners—Bernard and Kittredge, Bernard and the narrator—are cemented over Elsie's body and their collaborative, ultimately successful efforts to define its meaning. This sexualization is noted by Gail Parker, who claims Holmes confuses "phallicism" and "professionalism," mental and sexual energy in his literary and medical work; although Parker sees these tensions as antagonistic and unreconciled in the novel, it is my belief that they ultimately shore each other up, reconciled if tentatively through the operations of the doctors' penetrating visual hermeneutics. In this chapter, however, my aim is not to pinpoint *Elsie*'s (and Elsie's) meaning *per se* but to make visible the visual mechanics through which meaning is made.

One of the most noteworthy aspects of this Victorian novel is that its primary relationship is neither husband-wife nor lover-beloved but doctor-patient. It is the story's three male doctors who represent the best readers of the troubling, pathological text that is Elsie Venner: Elsie, both novel and character, text and body, is a disturbing read largely because, as snake-woman, she is marginal to normative gendered identities. In fact, the crisis of the novel is precipitated by a phrase that connotes gender ambiguity and the dissolution of discrete gendered spheres: "either sex." At the beginning of the novel, the doctor-narrator bemoans the fact that he has let Bernard "go off into the country with my certificate, that he is fit to teach in a school for either sex! Ten to one he will run like a moth to a candle, right into one of those girls'-nests, and get tangled up in some sentimental folly or other, and there will be the end of him" (20). Mixing his metaphors, the professor paints an image of his young student as a blinded moth headed straight for the snake's "nest" of some mesmerizing girl. The "end of him," as the narrator goes on to spell out, refers not to Bernard personally so much as professionally: "Oh, yes! country doctor,—half a dollar a visit ... no home, no peace, no continuous meals, no unbroken sleep, no Sunday, no holiday, no social intercourse, but one eternal jog, jog, jog, in a sulky. . . . All this of two words in a certificate!" (20–21). Those two words, "either sex," and the gender confusion they conjure up, are implicated in the potential downfall (amorously and professionally) of a promising young doctor who would have been better served, the narrator declares, had he kept his eyes fixed firmly on his textbooks. There, he would have learned to study girls strictly through a clinical gaze as patients, forsaking as too dangerous the ardent gaze of potential lovers.

In order to recontain this threat, the narrative works to reinscribe what were considered essential but threateningly tenuous gendered *sites* (i.e., both the "essence" of womanhood and the realms—domestic and bodily—in which that essence was presumably secured) as and through gendered *sights*, whereby a medical and pathological way of seeing are sharply differentiated, the former belonging to the male diagnostician, the latter, to the female patient. The emotions—running the gamut from love to hate—that saturate Elsie's "mesmerizing" eyes are read as signs of dis-ease and disorder in this medicated novel whose plot and characters are shaped via the equally penetrating but far cooler clinical gaze.[20]

The famed division between participant and observer that informs— in theory more than practice—American literary realism suggests that the former acts, the latter watches, and a different type of power and agency is afforded to each.[21] But in *Elsie* as protorealist novel, seeing is doing; observing is the central mode of participation in the novel. This is something that Elsie herself comprehends and that represents much of her threat to the novel's credentialed observers: as Elsie confesses to a mesmerized Helen after an instance in which she uses her hypnotic gaze to draw the teacher to her side, "I thought I could make you come" (78). Here and elsewhere, Elsie's visual faculties intervene in the actions of others, compelling the doctors in the novel to react with potent visual interventions of their own—interventions that work ineluctably to rob Elsie of her powers of perception and, as a result, of her agency.

Holmes's novel was written at the same time as Darwin's *Origin of the Species* (1859). One of the most intriguing aspects of Darwin's understanding of natural selection, and in particular sexual selection, is that it is the woman gazer—"an apparently unconcerned beholder of the struggle" (69)—who does the job of selecting the "fittest" mate, thereby increasing the chances that both will survive. Females of the species, therefore, wield the powers of life and death not simply through their reproductive capacities but, crucially, through their capacity as seers. In his novel, Holmes incorporates this female capacity to see and select, but as a destructive rather than potentially (pro)creative force and hence as best annihilated. Due to the invasion of the snake's venom, "a woman's eye"—traditionally the "window to her soul" through and in which one sees her purported sentimentality, softness, and loving nature—has been transformed into an "*evil eye*, . . . so bad that [it] might produce strange effects on very sensitive natures" (223).[22] When first described, Elsie is distinguished, along with her "peculiar undulation of movement," by her "black piercing eyes, not large" set within "a face that one could not help looking at for its beauty, yet that one wanted to look away from for something in its expression, and could not for those diamond eyes" (77–78). Black diamonds, Elsie's eyes sparkle with—and this is what renders them so mesmerizing—an unchecked passion. True, she selects the fittest (as her love for the superior Langdon would indicate), yet this selection only endangers rather than enhances his chances for survival.

Up until the novel's end, the clinical eye remains exclusively diagnostic, while Elsie's diseased gaze reads others only to captivate, weaken, or destroy. As such, it is distinctly unladylike. Recalling Holmes's visual definition of lady—she who allows herself to be looked at—it is clear that Holmes does not identify the upper-class Elsie as such but rather finds her in Helen Darley: "The meek teacher's blue eyes met the luminous glance [of Langdon]. She too was of gentle blood. . . . If she had not lifted her eyes to his face so softly and kept them there so calmly and withdrawn them so quietly, he would not have said to himself, 'She is a *lady*'" (74–75). The calm, soft, and quiet gaze of the lady Helen contrasts sharply with the passionate, intense, "disenchanting" (105) diamond-hard gaze of the unwomanly Elsie.[23] Despite the fact that Elsie is to-the-manor-born and Helen is of only modest, impoverished antecedents, it is Helen, or more particularly, Helen's "looks," that single her out as a lady, Elsie's "looks" that single her out as a snake. After all, one is supposed to be enchanted by the way a woman looks (appears), not disenchanted by the way a woman looks (peers).

In fact, one of the primary reasons Elsie's stare is diagnosed by the novel's medical men as poisonous is that it has the power to produce discomfort and even disease in others.[24] This is exemplified most clearly in Elsie's effect on Helen. Elsie's eye, which "glitters always, but warms for none" (176), makes Helen increasingly nervous until Bernard diagnoses borderline hysteria and resolves to do his best to intervene between teacher and "pupil" (in both senses of the word). The ophidian Elsie seems to have this debilitating effect on other women as well: every governess she had as a child was forced to leave "because she made them nervous. One of them had a strange fit of sickness; not one of them ever came back to the house to see her" (146). Not only does this suggest that Elsie's eye, as opposed to medical gazes, enfeebles those it looks upon, it suggests that it is not just Elsie's gaze, but gazing on Elsie—not one came back *to see her*—that induces hysteria.

This may explain why, even after her death, when those eyes are permanently sealed, what Elsie most frequently garners is not the sympathetic but the voyeuristic gazes of her neighbors, which work to recompense the many times that Elsie, when living and lethal, stared them down: "All was ready for the sad or curious eyes which were to look at her"; "some searching eye might detect a trace of that birthmark which it was whispered she had always worn a necklace to conceal"; "the young girls from the school looked at her, one after another" (456); and so on. Elsie, in life seizing and manipulating the unwomanly power of the gazer, is in death immortalized as the woman gazed upon, a result foreseen in her personal physician's sole prescription regarding his volatile patient: "Watch her" (147).

In its ability to pierce the very marrow of those she gazes upon, Elsie's snaky stare both approximates and perverts the medicalized one Holmes celebrates. To ward off this threatening proximity, the narrative works to differentiate Elsie's penetrating but enfeebling gaze from the medical profession's purportedly restorative one by stripping the former of its powers and in the process objectifying both it and her. In the process, Elsie's visual capacities are pathologized by rooting them in an overdetermined, diseased female physiology. While Elsie's venomous powers serve both to call attention to and ultimately poison her supple, serpentine body, the physicality of the novel's physicians is either skillfully erased from sight or strongly correlated to the clarity and healthiness of their vision.

Bernard Langdon's body, for example, is not concealed but made prominent; his is, in fact, the body described in the most meticulous detail in the novel. To describe Langdon is quite literally to dissect him, and the tool for this dissection is "the critical eye":

His limbs were not very large, nor his shoulders remarkably broad; but if you knew as much of the muscles as all persons who look at statues and pictures with a critical eye ought to have learned,—if you know the *trapezius*, lying diamond-shaped over the back and shoulders like a monk's cowl, or the *deltoid*, which caps the shoulder like an epaulette,—or the *triceps*, which furnishes the *calf* of the upper arm,—or the hard-knotted *biceps*,—any of the great sculptural landmarks, in fact,—you would have said there was a pretty show of them, beneath the white satiny skin of Mr. Bernard Langdon. (32)

From its knowledge of anatomy, the "critical eye" here is clearly the medical eye, the one that most appreciates because it can identify the very musculature of the medical student's physiology. Here the vitality of the young doctor-to-be is corroborated by his vibrant physical presence, just as Elsie's essential sickness is verified by the apparent unnaturalness of her eerily supple frame. If the physician, especially as romantic hero, cannot at this juncture be convincingly disembodied, he can at least possess a body that advertises his personal and professional health.

Nonetheless, when Bernard is first introduced, it is his eyes that attract the narrator's attention: "Those large, dark eyes of his would sink into the white soul of a young girl as the black cloth sunk into the snow in Franklin's famous experiment" (17). As the story unfolds, his visual powers only become more pronounced, exemplifying the gradual metonymic displacement of physician's/physical body by the clinical eye. Bernard's ability to penetrate to the very souls of his female students leads to his epithet: he is compared to a "woman-tamer" (10, 34) or "sex-subduer"

(37), thus countering Elsie's mesmerizing powers with an equal and reactive force of his own. Studying Elsie, Bernard employs his "medicated" vision not only to diagnose her disease but to deflect and defuse her own equally searching glance. It is, for instance, through surreptitiously examining Elsie while she is engaged with her books in his classroom that he initially arrives at his diagnosis of her deviance:

> The more he saw her, the more the sadness of her beauty wrought upon him. She looked as if she might hate, but could not love. She hardly smiled at anything, spoke rarely, but seemed to feel that her natural power of expression lay all in her bright eyes. A person accustomed to watch the faces of those who were ailing in body or mind, and to search in every line and tint for some underlying source of disorder, could hardly help analyzing the impression such a face produced on him. The light of those beautiful eyes were [sic] like the lustre of ice; in all her features there was nothing of that human warmth which shows that *sympathy* has reached the soul beneath the mask of flesh it wears.... There was in its stony apathy, it seemed to him, the pathos which we find in the blind who show no film or speck over the organs of sight; for Nature had meant her to be lovely, and left out nothing but *love*. (183)

These observations transfigure Elsie's gaze from a means of sight to a site of self-expression, from active force to passive mirror. Bernard's obstetrical vision detects the essential lack of "sympathy" or "love" in Elsie's eyes which would make what one reads in them a potentially sentimental or romantic text, the reflection in those mirrors a potentially pleasing one. And, if not sympathetic they must, in Bernard's view, be "inhuman"; he can offer no other alternatives. Significantly, Elsie's once-dangerous looks are ultimately equated with the opaque and empty stare of the blind, rendered ineffectual by his own more potent powers of in-sight.

The first time Langdon ventures beyond merely observing Elsie to interceding in her actions occurs when Elsie tries and essentially succeeds in mesmerizing Miss Letty Forrester, the girl whom the young medical student will eventually marry. Noticing the hypnotic effect Elsie's gaze has upon Letty, Bernard

> turned toward Elsie and looked at her in such a way as to draw her eyes upon him. Then he looked steadily and calmly into them. It was a great effort ... but he was determined to look her down, and he believed he could do it.... All this took not minutes, but seconds. Presently she changed color slightly,—lifted her

head, which was inclined a little to one side,—shut and opened her eyes two or three times, as if they had been pained or wearied,—and turned away, baffled, and shamed, as it would seem, and shorn for the time of her singular and formidable or at least evil-natured power of swaying the impulses of those around her. (309–10)

As a result of this encounter Bernard's own "formidable" visual powers are intensified while Elsie's are diminished. In fact, soon thereafter, when Elsie looks at Bernard her eyes

seemed to lose their cold glitter, and soften into a strange, dreamy tenderness. The deep instincts of womanhood were striving to grope their way to the surface of her being through all the alien forces which overlaid them.... she did not know how to mask the unwonted feeling which fixed her eyes and her thoughts upon the only person who had ever reached the spring of her hidden sympathies. (393)

This transformation and the role of the clinical gaze in inducing it testify to the introspective, dissecting powers of observation. But they also typify the dialectic between objective perspective and sentimental response that Holmes tried to instantiate not just within, but also in regards to, his novel. At least within the confines of the narrative, medical vision is afforded the power both to delve into human nature and simultaneously to unleash the sympathy hidden in its depths.

It is important that the ability to unleash these emotions is attributed to the clinician in Bernard, not the lover: the young scholar is universally forgiven for not being able to return the affection of such a cold-blooded, inhuman creature. The most Bernard can offer Elsie is pity, which unlike the purportedly dissolving force of empathy or love only augments the desired hierarchical distance between male doctor and female patient. As Bernard says of Elsie, "I pity her, she is so lonely. The girls are afraid of her, and she seems to have either a dislike or a fear of them. They have all sorts of painful stories about her. They give her a name which no human creature ought to bear.... There is not one of them that will look in her eyes" (214). Such passages in *Elsie Venner* work to intertwine science and sympathy even as they disentangle the latter from femininity. For the ladylike and truly feminine Helen and her "overwomanized" students not only refuse to look Elsie in the eyes, when they do look they respond with an instinctive repulsion, withholding the sympathy that, according to existing gender ideology, should come naturally to them. Bordering on hysteria, Helen requires a healing, not a "life-draining" gaze, which is what she describes Elsie's as being: "she seems to take the life out of me when she looks at me" (127). Helen only begins to feel for Elsie when, nursing the dying girl, she recognizes the "true, womanly nature" hidden in the "depths of her being," (432), a recognition that comes too late to do Elsie any good.

The only woman who does offer Elsie sympathy—and hers is combined with a marked fear—is Sophy. Elsie's relationship with her nursemaid is "the nearest approach to sympathetic relations that Elsie ever had," yet it doesn't provide much comfort. The narrator describes it as "a kind of dumb intercourse of feeling, such as one sees in the eyes of brute mothers looking on their young" (419), a description that speaks as much to what Edwin Hoyt prettifies as Holmes's "gentle racism" as it does to the author's interrogation of whether women's gazes were indeed inherently more compassionate.

In contrast to the female characters, the novel's medical personae are capable of unconditional pity; indeed, their powers of sympathy are represented *as a direct result* of their acute powers of perception. As Bernard confides to his friend Phillip,

do you know the pathos there is in the eyes of unsought women, oppressed with the burden of an inner life unshared? I can see into them now as I could not in those earlier days. I sometimes think their pupils dilate on purpose to let my consciousness glide through them; indeed, I dread them, I come so close to the nerve of the soul itself in these momentary intimacies. (230–31)

Sympathy facilitates science: the wider these unsought women open their eyes for his examination, the better he is able to clinically diagnose what ails them. For all its clear benefits, the danger here is that by representing sympathy (and science) as the exclusive properties of clinicians, the narrative essentially predicts a lay reader's lack of compassion for or understanding of Elsie (and *Elsie*).

While Bernard may have represented Elsie's one real chance of being cured (read, her last hope of attaining "true womanhood"), this cure is withheld precisely because love is not intended to be a "regular" mode of healing in this clinical novel. Although Doctor Kittredge advises Elsie's father to encourage his daughter to socialize with young men, proclaiming that "she will not love any one easily, perhaps not at all; yet love would be more like to bring her right than anything else" (195), he does not hold out much hope that Elsie will find love, nor does he intend that lover to be in any way related to the medical profession. As Kittredge advises his younger colleague, Langdon, "Keep your eyes open and your heart shut. If, through pitying that girl, you ever come to love her, you are lost" (214).

Kittredge appears to have taken his own advice. Physical descriptions (or, more accurately, the lack thereof) serve to foreground the senior physician's detached and probing gaze. Throughout the novel he is portrayed as "a shrewd old man, who looked pretty keenly into his patients through his spectacles, and pretty widely at men, women, and things in general over them" (98). Kittredge is Elsie's primary physician, but their encounters involve very little consultation or even conversation; his practice is based explicitly on observation rather than intervention. He devotes his time with Elsie to looking "steadily, thoughtfully, tenderly" (148) at the girl whose looks are considered lethal; "his eyes were fixed steadily on the dark girl, every movement of whom he seemed to follow" (99). As did Bernard, the older doctor eventually engages in a visual duel with Elsie in order to assert his mastery over her:

the doctor ... lifted his head and dropped his eyes a little, so as to see her through his spectacles. She narrowed her lids slightly, as one often sees a sleepy cat narrow hers ... so that her eyes looked very small, but bright as the diamonds on her breast. The old Doctor felt very oddly as she looked at him; he did not like the feeling, so he dropped his head and lifted his eyes and looked at her *over* his spectacles again. (100–101)

In a battle of wills expressed through a battle of gazes, Elsie proves no match for the physician, who gets the last glance both here and elsewhere.

Ultimately, Elsie's error lies in her stubborn refusal to turn herself into a text open for perusal and in trying instead to appropriate the medicalized powers of both reading and altering bodily and emotional states. As Dr. Kittredge reassures a town minister, "God opens one book to physicians that a good many of you don't know much about,—the Book of Life. ... it is printed in bright red type, and the binding of it is warm and tender to the touch" (325). The flesh here is made word, but it is regular physicians exclusively who are represented as capable of speaking its language and deciphering its meaning. In the end, despite her best efforts, Elsie is inexorably transformed via the triplicate force of the narrative's clinical gazes from self-author to objectified text, an evolution completed when, once safely back in medical school, Bernard delivers a paper about Elsie entitled "Unresolved Nebulae in Vital Science" (481). Thus classified and conveyed via clinical language to an appreciative audience, Elsie's (and *Elsie*'s) reception as a valid, even engrossing subject of study—at least for a medical audience—is inscribed and anticipated within the narrative at the same time that Bernard's professional viability is legitimized (it is this paper that earns him his medical degree).

Intriguingly, the legitimacy of the novel's clinical gazes resides in their diagnostic rather than their curative powers. The medical point of view is equipped to perceptively interpret Elsie's inner nature, yet what is uncovered there is a text so aberrant vis-à-vis normative femininity that the most sympathetic gesture any reader could make might very well be to shut her "bright book of life" as soon as possible (325). In fact, it is possible that Bernard directly brings about her death (a mercy killing?) through a sprig of white ash which he sticks in a basket of flowers sent by the school "in sympathy" during her illness and which proves a deadly poison to Elsie. Sympathy, then, contra the claims of many newly trained female doctors, is here represented as having no power to cure, and science is apparently better employed as a hermeneutic than a therapeutic tool. Or rather, its therapeutic intervention occurs at the level of the social rather than the individual body: in the wake of Elsie's death, equilibrium is effectively restored to both town and narrative.[25] It cannot be entirely coincidental, during this bumpy period in American medical history, that the narrative valorizes the power of medicalized vision over the power of medical intervention, diagnosis over cure, strategically grounding its authority in the former at a time when the latter's success could not be guaranteed and, if incorporated into the narrative, would code it as more romantic or "heroic" than realistic.

Read as an allegory for the medical debates about sympathetic or scientific methodologies, the novel polices the degree of emotion doctors are allowed to express. They can be sympathetic but not, at least while performing their professional duties, sentimental; they may be committed professionally to science but not romantically to their patients. The novel also strictly regulates female emotions: if a woman is not sentimental she must be unwomanly. Indeed, it would seem that Holmes's true woman is not just sympathetic but lachrymose. As one of a number of counters to Elsie's cold, piercing gaze, Holmes offers "Alminy," "a good soul, with red cheeks and bright eyes . . . her bright eyes were moist" (34). This moistness attests to the girl's emotionalism and is represented in the narrative as utterly appropriate, as the proper condition of a woman's eye. Given that Elsie's "unwomanly" attempts to appropriate the penetrating gaze of the physician is precisely what signifies her disorder, it thus makes sense that it is only when she stops staring and starts weeping that she is finally cured (if, finally, dying). Above all else, it is Elsie's gaze that is transformed in these last moments: her once cold eyes become warm and soft during her crying bout, suggesting to all those watching by her bedside that the woman in her has at last vanquished the snake, a victory encoded within her retinae: "the likeness she bore to her mother [came] forth more and more, as the cold glitter died out of the diamond eyes" (441). One way to interpret this outcome is as the result of the process of "interiorization," through which the individual interiorizes "the inspecting gaze" so that she is transformed from the one surveyed to the one who oversees herself (Foucault "Eye" 155). In other words, what happens to Elsie on her deathbed may not be that she relinquishes the clinical gaze so much as she redirects it, turning it inward, in order to finally uncover the woman the doctors had already detected lurking inside her seemingly snaky exterior. If so, then this conclusion not only verifies the novel's essentializing medical diagnoses but equates women's self-knowledge with weeping self-abandon.

Of Elsie's few mourners (even her father feels more relieved by her death than sorrowful), none is as touched by Elsie's passing as the novel's third doctor, the narrator. The most experienced and, not incidentally, the most invisible and incorporeal of all the physicians in the novel, he remains anonymous therein, a player only in the novel's opening and closing passages, although we are reminded of him as a result of his occasionally intrusive "I" and his pervasive, observant eye. Throughout the majority of the narrative, as a sort of long-distance medical consultant, he remains detached from the story, telling it both in retrospect and at second hand. At the narrative's end, however, his gaze is no longer clinical but moist—he relinquishes his role as a distanced narrator and is instead incarnated as an interested actor in his own tale.

In the final pages of *Elsie*, the narrator abandons his retrospective stance and enters the narrative via an encounter with the now married and prosperous Doctor and Professor Langdon, who is accompanied by his new bride. During this meeting, the narrator spies on the latter's wrist a familiar chain. The narrator and narrative concludes, "My eyes filled with tears as I read upon the clasp, in sharp-cut Italic letters, *E.V.* They were tears at once of sad remembrance and of joyous anticipation; for the ornament on which I looked was the double pledge of a dead sorrow and a living affection. It was the golden bracelet,—the parting gift of Elsie Venner" (486–87).

Never having physically encountered Elsie yet aware of her from Bernard's account, the narrator occupies the reader's structural position. Thus his tears suggest that we who do not know Elsie personally can still remember her fondly, especially now that she is safely reduced to a sentimentalized memento mori—a charm if not a charmer—upon which all can gaze without danger and perhaps even with pity. This intrusion of the professor's tear and body in *Elsie*'s final chapter imposes a conventionally sentimental ending on an otherwise "medicated" narration in a time when sentiment sold. Holmes, as popular author as well as respected doctor, would have been well aware of sentimentalism's potential profit, both in fiscal and affectional terms. Additionally, this tearful moment operates structurally as an attempt to foreshadow and dictate response to both Elsie and *Elsie*. As Holmes claimed in his preface, what he desired most of all was for readers to respond sympathetically to an essentially scientific conundrum, and his narrator as first and model reader epitomizes this response. Indeed, his tears invite a generic reading experience—a shared sentiment across genders, professions, and so on—in a novel that otherwise posits reading as a specialized activity, the province of a select few.

Structural similarities, however, exist not only between the narrator and the reader. The narrator's tears suggest additional, uneasy parallels between the narrator and the protagonist, both of whom ultimately trade a piercing gaze for a weepy one. Both sets of tears signal closure: Elsie's the end of self, the narrator's the end of narrative. Yet even the possibility of identification between the narrator and Elsie risks dismantling the hierarchies the narrative relies upon, even celebrates. More to the point, in order to retain its clinical status, "the observing gaze refrains from intervening" (Foucault *Birth* 107), and yet, intervening is precisely what Holmes's observer does in the end. The tears in his eyes obscure his ability to remain a detached observer, his body in the street and in the narrative hinder his ability to remain impersonal, abstract(ed).

This doctor's tears appear all the more exceptional given that the narrative's other doctors conspicuously refrain from displaying emotion in public. For example, Bernard confesses to a friend, "do you know I am the sort of man that locks his door sometimes and cries his heart out of his eyes,—that can sob like a woman and not be ashamed of it? I come of fighting-blood on one side, you know; I could be savage on occasion. But I am tender,—more and more tender as I come into manhood" (230). While Bernard concedes that there is a place for a doctor's tears, he stipulates that that place exists exclusively behind closed doors. Similarly if more strenuously, Dr. Kittredge warns against the dangers of public displays of emotional distress:

> The old Doctor was a model for visiting practitioners. He always came into the sick-room with a quiet cheerful look, as if he had a consciousness that he was bringing some sure relief with him. The way a patient snatches his first look at his doctor's face, to see whether he is doomed, whether he is reprieved, whether he is unconditionally pardoned, has something terrible about it. It is only to be met by an imperturbable mask of serenity, proof against anything and everything in a patient's aspect. The physician whose face reflects his patient's condition like a mirror may do well enough to examine people for a life-insurance office, but does not belong in the sick-room. (424–25)

Distinct from their patients', a doctor's eyes should represent blank slates to all who attempt to peer into them. The doctor who cannot render himself illegible the better to read his patients would be better off hanging up his stethoscope and assuming another role altogether.

This, actually, provides a rather apt description of what Holmes's narrator may be doing in the final chapter. The teary, relatively happy conclusion to Holmes's otherwise protorealist narrative suggests that at this moment the sentimentalist will out, especially once, with the death of *Elsie*, the clinical "requirement of embodiment"—which has governed the narrative up until this moment and which requires both the prominent display of the patient's body and the erasure of the observing I/eye's physicality—no longer applies (Elsie, after all, is beyond earthly observation and corporeal form).

It may also be that the doctor-narrator's final tears constitute signs that for Holmes clinical realism was ultimately not material enough. The genre's stipulated effacement of narratorial body might suit when the narrative eye is coolly gazing but not when moved to weep in response to what it sees. The materiality endemic to realism is, after all, a property associated with its characters at the expense of its narrators. It is sentimentalism that, by contrast, tends to foreground a palpable narratival presence (at the same time that it often attenuates its character's corporeality);[26] and it is a sentimental context that, ultimately, provides room enough to allow for the physical incarnation of Holmes's doctor-narrator.

One way to comprehend the professor's tears, then, is as the product of his narratorial rather than his medical role, although this hypothesis parses functions the novel strives mightily to conflate. But assuming for the moment that they can be disjoined, this subjective, affective closure may not, after all, muddle the authoritative, "objective" perceptions the rest of the narrative authenticates. For the doctor's tears would in this sense function strategically as an overtly fictional apparatus, an artifice imposed from without rather than a truth emerging from "within." Elsie's tears, by contrast, signal the emergence of a purportedly essential truth (her hitherto submerged femininity) and the end of a seemingly organic progression (from snake to woman). As such and despite a superficial parallelism, these consecutive weepy moments establish two genera of tears: the first an outpouring of an essential nature, the other a self-reflexive formal device. Ultimately, this distinction only further cements the association of the clinical gaze with masculine agency and increases the distance between the clinical gazer and the determined, feminine object being gazed upon.

At the same time (and here there is no need to separate medical and narrative functions as they nicely coalesce), if Elsie's final tears are curative—if they signify the emergence of an essential womanly nature despite her apparent snakiness—the doctor's final tears may be read as recuperative in a different sense—testifying to the physician's and his medicated narrative's essentially sympathetic bent despite his/its seemingly clinical exterior. Cast in such a light, the narrator's tears do not necessarily detract from the perceptive powers of the clinical gaze but rather work to confirm them, although here it is emotion and not detachment that signals its capacity (and perhaps its capacity alone) to discern Elsie's inherently pitiable nature. As such, this final tear could even be read as a realist device, especially when we recall that for Holmes, realism resided not so much in what is shown but in what is seen, and especially when we consider that what this teary-eyed moment makes visible is not only a woman's true nature but a physician's facility at unearthing it.

I make so much of this teary conclusion because it seems to me that it is at the site of what might otherwise appear an utterly conventional closure that the narrative's claims and conventions are strained to the breaking point. In particular, it is here, in this teary-eyed denouement, that the exigencies of narrative form work in the most pronounced fashion to mediate any direct translation of an author's preconceived notions about bodily forms. And yet, in the end, what we witness in this weepy moment turns out to be a bend more than a rupture: for ultimately, by articulating together sentimentality and corporeal subjectivity through the vehicle of the tear, realism and abstract(ed) objectivity through the vehicle of the gaze, *Elsie*'s ending furthers more than it stalls the project of desomaticization necessary to the efficacy of both the clinical gaze and clinical realism. At the same time, however, this tearful ending palpably documents the extent to which, at midcentury, seeing and weeping were not necessarily discretely dichotomized but could be made to coexist (if uneasily) in the selfsame literary and bodily forms.

# 2

## "Where Soul Is Termed Sentiment"

*Sentience and Transcendence in the Works of Louisa May Alcott, Harriot K. Hunt, and Margaret Fuller*

> To cover what we are
> From Science—and from Surgery—
> Too Telescopic Eyes
> To bear on us unshaded—
> For their sake—not for Ours—
> 'Twould start them—
> We—could tremble—
> But since we got a Bomb—
> And held it in our Bosom—
> Nay—Hold it—it is calm—
> 
> Emily Dickinson, #443

Is the heart a balm or a "bomb"? Might it comfort or explode? In this verse, Dickinson ranges the intrusive power of "telescopic," scientific sight against the potentially destructive if momentarily calm force of a woman's heart. In so doing, she voices a mounting concern at midcentury that microscopic vision and surgical incision might operate to uncover an essential identity ("what we are") perhaps better left concealed. Intriguingly, however, Dickinson's scenario posits the medical gazer ("For their sake") more than the gazed upon ("not for Ours") as the one who is most endangered by these procedures, "startled" when confronted by the palpable force of heartfelt emotions. Still, as the last line quoted hints, for every beat of the heart there is also a caesura, a "calm" that interrupts and interrogates its potency as antidote.

Dickinson was not alone in expressing faith in the heart's powers and uncertainty about them at one and the same time. Elsewhere, non-traditional healers, skeptical of "heroic" medical interventions yet more confident in the powers of self-help, frequently hailed the extension and release of heartfelt emotions as potential remedies for a range of ailments afflicting both the individual and social body.[1] Yet as anatomical knowledge increased within the increasingly authoritative field of medical science and the brain supplanted the heart as the physiological site of human emotions, those who clung to the heart as emotional source and potent cure only risked advertising their anachronistic status.[2]

This was not the only complication. As Barbara Ehrenreich and Deirdre English attest in their groundbreaking gendered overview of medical history, beginning in the 1850s "a steady stream of popular advice books, written by doctors, on the subject of female health" (108) began to flood the market, concurrent with the emergence of the female invalid as type and widespread cultural concern. Along with dress, diet, and custom, many of these medical treatises identified as a prime suspect for the onset of disease a woman's "extreme sensibility," her "violent passions" and "intense emotions" (Doane 42, 259; Dixon 119).[3] One challenge for healers, then, was to determine not just *how* a patient was feeling but *how much*.

At the time, bodily health was frequently seen as a matter of avoiding prolonged "excitement." For instance, while some degree of stimulation or "excitability" was considered essential to the normal functioning of organs, it was generally believed that "too much or too little stimulation, whether from internal or external sources, was harmful" (Verbrugge 31; see also 32–34). Likewise, Elizabeth Blackwell vehemently criticized "the state of nervous irritability which is induced in young girls" and identified an "excited sensibility" as the cause and not just the symptom of what she called "hysterical diathesis" (*Laws* 141–42). In perhaps the most famous non-medical advice book of the 1850s, *Letters to the People on Health and Happiness* (1855), Catharine Beecher bemoans women's inherent susceptibility to the diseases induced by "excitement." To corroborate her own personal observations, Beecher cites a female doctor who pinpoints "mere *nervous debility*" as a potential cause of "pelvic displacement" and its ensuing hysterical repercussions (qtd. in Cott, *Roots* 271). As these examples attest, an emotional outburst could be identified as suffering's cause and not only as its cure; the emotional stimulation that in certain circles was being promoted for its powers to keep the doctor away could, when taken to extreme, necessitate medical intervention.

In this regard, describing midcentury America as "a culture of sentiment" is accurate only insofar as this description indexes the intensity of the debate about (rather than simply an unchecked enthusiasm for) sentimentality and its purported benefits.[4] Even in the primary artifacts of this "culture"—sentimental novels themselves—this debate is not so much resolved as it is forestalled. By "sentimental" I mean to indicate works that chronicle, in highly wrought emotional terms, scenes of deep, tear-jerking anguish which in turn engender both physical and emotional release.[5] My interest in these works' sentimentalism lies mainly in examining, as symptomatic of larger cultural beliefs, the ways in which their cathartic scenes negotiate the conflict over whether fervent emotions alleviate or only exaggerate female frailty.[6] Is the suffering typically chronicled therein triggered by a heightened sentiment, or is it ultimately cured by it? Do the intense emotions these texts sanction signify recovery or the final stages of disease? Although these would seem to be antithetical possibilities, what interests me about these passionately sentimental fictional scenarios is that they frequently synthesize them: that is, emotional intensity may precipitate therein *both* rapturous transport *and* an untimely demise, virtually simultaneously.

In her introduction to *The Culture of Sentiment*, Shirley Samuels identifies a tension in sentimental representations that causes "the natural body" to be both emphasized and disowned. Traditionally, women's writing in the Victorian era has been interpreted as downplaying the material for the spiritual, and as substituting emotional for physical agency.[7] And indeed, many of these works enroll sentiment as a moral force enabling a heroine to exceed human limitations and in the process to elevate the world around her to a higher spiritual plane. Certain sentimental stories, however, also stage scenes that literalize this process: a character experiences sensations so acute—an exquisite complex of pain and joy—that the ensuant release can only, quite literally, be terminal.

In turn, such intense moments often enhance a reader's sympathetic engagement, enabling her to "lose her self" in her absorption with character and work. Intertwining reading and weeping, sentimental fiction succeeds, as Karen Sánchez-Eppler has proposed, when the latter interferes with the former.[8] The more a reader engages with a text, the more intense her physical sensations become. And yet, although her sobs and tears might call attention to her physicality, they also somewhat paradoxically enable her momentarily to transcend it. In other words, these fictional visions of bodily transcendence are offered to readers through a process—reading—that is itself, in its most absorbing, identificatory moments, a sort of out-of-body experience. Less idealistically, such affective moments of empathic identification might also be seen as licensing readerly self-indulgence and self-absorption.

More than merely conjoined for readers, emotional and physical sensations are also habitually linked *within* the stories themselves. And therein, physical sensation may serve as the source and not just the effect of emotional intensity: at crucial moments, rapturous release from fleshly constraints is premised upon and virtually guaranteed by a character's acute and ostentatious suffering. Indeed, spectacular, pain-filled experiences precede and enable some of the most beatific transports: think of Little Eva, Uncle Tom, or Beth March.

In less highly wrought women's writing, the sentimental entanglement of emotional intensity and physical frailty—where both together signify and enable a higher spirituality—is toned down a bit. In her introduction to the second edition of *Woman's Fiction*, Nina Baym outlines at least four different ways that the female characters who people the realm of "woman's fiction" may inhabit the flesh.[9] There is the "invalid's" disease-induced reduction of self to body; the "belle's" or fallen woman's exhibitionistic identification of body as self; there is also the "true woman," for whom embodiment is improperly understood as a "drooping, jointless" passivity (xli).[10] Finally, standing as foil to all three conventionally sentimental characterizations, is the protagonist herself, whose power stems in part from her ability to model a more viable form of bodily existence than and for these three "misguided" types (xli). While she may not refute women's status as "the weaker vessel," the heroine transforms that weakness into a sign not of more but of "less body," which is in turn "translated ... into a sign of more spirit" (xxxvi). Where the heroine is concerned, at least, embodiment could signify disembodiment, of identity as more or other than bodily. The widely held belief in women's physical weakness thus becomes in these works (as well as in the larger cultural imaginary) a means of symbolizing as widespread a sense of her intrinsic spirituality and emotional health.

Although this symbolism may also translate in works written according to more sentimental formulas, a critical difference remains: when emotions enter into the woman's fiction plot, the heroine's desire is not to indulge them but to bring them under better control. Woman's fictions also differ from more sentimental versions because this emotional restraint as well as the heroine's diminished, spiritualized physicality are represented therein as "acquired"; if the protagonist can learn them (and she has), then other women—both fictional and actual—can and even must (Baym, xxxviii).

But just how easy a lesson was this to learn? Even these woman's fictions fail to clarify precisely when female frailty (qua heroine) serves as the prerequisite of a desired ethereality and when it only (qua invalid) precipitates further, chronic imprisonment in the flesh. Indeed, the fictionality of these works is apparent in their implication that spiritual elevation can override physical weakness rather than merely compensate for it. If a woman's finer sensibilities and feeble constitution did indeed provide fictional testimony to her spirituality, it is important to remember that this idealization did not always jibe with women's lived experiences. In this chapter, I am interested in women for whom it did not jibe—those whose firsthand experience was with sickness that accentuated body, not soul. What other options were available when, much as she may have been attracted to the equation of physical weakness with physical diminishment, a woman simply could not take a heroine's route and ignore the palpable demands of her physical body?

In the subsequent sections, I examine as case studies three women writers—Louisa May Alcott, Dr. Harriot K. Hunt, and Margaret Fuller—for whom bodily suffering and spiritual transcendence were connected, but not necessarily along the lines laid out in established fictional formulas. While each of these women longed for an ethereality evocative of sentimental transport, each would also have been suspicious of its dependence on a precarious physicality or an excessive emotionalism. Indeed, these writers' experiences with illness would have led them, to varying degrees, to doubt whether abasement (emotional or physical) could ever lead to transcendence, having witnessed firsthand its more typical association with the last stages of disease.

By definition, invalidism points out the dangers of the emotionalism that sentimentalism by definition heralds. Could both deeply felt sentiments and chronic invalidism be combined in such a way that the sensibility that elevates, even heals, would not be confounded with or by the sentiments that debase? And when and where such combinations were explicitly rejected, were other formulas available which could promise transcendence or at least relief? Each of the writers I examine here sought, in and through the act of writing, to exchange an invalid's experience of physicality for an experience approximating one of Baym's protagonist's. Each woman coped with disease (whether her own or other women's), and each wrote in hopes of not simply minimizing or escaping suffering but alleviating it.[11] Yet each also remained skittish about representing and especially sentimentalizing this suffering in print. In the following sections, I explore the friction ensuing when a desire to portray women as exuberant "hearts" or radiant "souls" rubs up against conventional generic and gendered depictions of this exuberance as signaling both disease and embodiment. Could these writers' dreams of excess (exceeding mere embodied existence) be realized without the preliminary excesses of suffering or sentiment? Could their experiences as *more* rather than *less* body still enable transcendence? Specifically, could a sense of the self as *more* physical ever presage *more* spirituality, given the fictional equation of *less* with *more*? And finally, could this fictional equation have something to do with these writers' difficulties with narrative forms, not to mention readers' difficulties with the alternative forms these women to varying degrees adopted and assumed?

⁌

Although to do so is to forsake strict chronology, I want to begin with a brief discussion of Louisa May Alcott and her Civil War–related works. Proceeding in this order will allow me to sketch the conventions (and problems) of sentimental recipes for transcendence in a bit more detail before exploring alternative, less prescriptive formulas. Like Hunt and Fuller before her, Alcott believed suffering, healing, and writing to be intricately if uncomfortably bound together, but she was the only one of the three women examined here to utilize sentimental models without grave reservation.

Best known for her *Little Women* and its sequels, Alcott served for a brief time in the Civil War as a hospital nurse and returned to this traumatic experience at least three times in her written corpus: in her thinly fictionalized memoir, *Hospital Sketches* (1863), in her loosely autobiographical bestseller, *Little Women* (1868–69), and finally in her sentimental bildungsroman, *Work: A Story of Experience* (1873). Alcott's six weeks as a hospital nurse marked a crucial transition for the author. As she maintained, "I was never ill before this time, and never well afterward" (qtd. in Cheney 137). While in Georgetown nursing Union wounded amidst the unsanitary conditions of the Union Hotel Hospital, Alcott developed typhoid pneumonia. Most likely it was the mercury in the medication she received and not the pneumonia itself that was ultimately responsible for ravaging her hitherto rugged constitution. In a sense, though, the empathy endemic to nursing deserves some of the blame; Alcott's sentimental therapeutics encouraged a proximity between patient and healer that bordered on identity—a potentially dangerous one considering that, as in Alcott's case, sympathy brought patients and healers so closely together that the latter could easily be exposed to devastating disease.

Although Alcott would try numerous remedies—ranging from water to "mind" cures, from morphine to massage, from homeopathy to a nursing home—she was never again to regain her formerly robust health. At least initially, writing seemed to serve as yet another potential therapy. Indeed, nursing and writing shared, for Alcott, certain structural similarities. What Alcott claims of nursing could just as easily hold true for writing: "Our work begins afterward," she writes in her afterword to *Hospital Sketches*, "when the poor soul comes to himself, sick, faint and wandering" (96).[12] As interventions after the fact, both nursing and writing rejuvenate the spirit even when and where they can do little for the body's wounds. At the same time, however, writing also appeared to simulate, even induce illness; intense writing sessions frequently left Alcott "unfit" and "pale" (*Letters* 59) and made her "head ... dizzy" and "legs shaky" (*Journals* 104). As such descriptions indicate, writing's materiality is not just evident on the page; its impact is clearly discernible on the author's body as well.

During the time immediately following her illness, in the very days set aside for recuperation, Alcott wrote at nothing short of a fevered pitch. In these convalescent months, she converted her letters home from Georgetown into a series of "Hospital Sketches" for the *Boston Commonwealth* newspaper and contributed a postscript when they were published in book form later that year; she also wrote and saw published both *The Rose Family* and *On Picket Duty, and Other Tales*, composed and saw staged her dramatization of Dickens's novels, and completed what she believed to be her best and most serious novel, *Moods*. Although always prolific, Alcott only began receiving critical attention for the writing she produced subsequent to her hospital experiences. Her journal entries from this period dwell on her pleasure in being considered "a new star" and "a literary celebrity" and speculate on how to build upon the "commendation" she was earning for "Hospital Sketches" (*Journals* 119). So while it is true that Alcott was never again physically well after her days in the hospital, in literary terms she was never better.

As her writing career evolved, Alcott became increasingly convinced of the power of, as well as the profit in, semi-autobiographical, sentimental forms. Writing what she knew best, she soon learned that one thing sentimentalism was virtually guaranteed to accomplish was to sell books, an outcome that always interested her. For instance, Alcott attributes her decision to publish what the *Commonwealth*'s editors deemed her "witty & pathetic" hospital sketches to the fact that she "wanted money." When, to her "surprise & delight," her readers were almost unanimously touched by the sketches, Alcott reaped the rewards in both praise and dollars (*Journals* 118–19). Later, after the rejection of *A Long Fatal Love Chase* (1867: recently issued by Random House, 1995) and the success of *Little Women*, Alcott apparently decided that the profit lay in sentimental rather than more sensational tales, and like Jo in *Little Women*, she "corked up her inkstand" and never wrote the latter again.

This decision was not, however, without personal costs. Among other things, her chosen mode provided little room for sympathetic representations of prolonged pain, as sentimental works typically depict suffering only to celebrate its cessation, not to attest to its potentially chronic, interminable nature. Additionally, while the proper response to pain, according to these fictions, is weeping, this response is cathartic rather than remedial. Put simply, sentimentalism's formulaic prescriptions do not include therapeutic prescriptions: for all its emphasis on suffering and sensation, the genre rarely holds out much hope for a worldly cure. Furthermore, while sentimental stories acknowledge the painful dimensions of existence, these scenes are typically moralized so that the suffering of good characters represents a judgment on the society that inflicts such pain, and their beautiful deaths signify their willingness to become martyrs for our sins. Alternately, the ills of bad characters serve as righteous judgments upon them. Sentimental works thus afford little if any room for depicting pain amorally, nor do their narratives code it a failure when the suffering body fails to be healed. There is simply no space within them for discussions of the prolonged suffering of good people who fail to see pain as elevating or death as merciful release: in her delirium, Alcott imagined that she'd gone to heaven and found it "very busy & dismal & ordinary" (*Journals* 117).

As her personal papers reveal, Alcott did not experience physical weakness as a loosening but rather as an intensifying of bodily bounds. For example, in the journal entry following the one recording her thoughts about heaven, Alcott lists the following symptoms: "Such long long nights—such feeble, idle days, dozing, fretting about nothing, longing to eat & no mouth to do it with, mine being so sore & full of all manner of queer sensations it was nothing but a plague" (*Journals* 117). In Alcott's depiction of invalidism, physical "sensations" offer no inspiration but merely "plague" the sufferer.

In Alcott's more public struggle to maneuver within sentimental forms, an inverse relationship develops between the author's advancing illness and the increasingly fictionalized portraits of her literary personae. In this sense, projection—the capacity to empathetically identify with a body other than one's own—needs to be explored vis-à-vis Alcott's corpus as not simply a readerly but an authorial gesture. Over the course of Alcott's three imaginary returns to the scene of her illness, the body of the fictional invalid is increasingly alienated from the author's increasingly infirm one; indeed, it must be so for the fictional work itself to remain both sentimental and ultimately upbeat. Consequentially, the more Alcott tries to lend a sentimental cast to elements of her life story, the less the resulting narrative resembles autobiographical account. One way to read the author's sustained investment in sentimental formulas is as an index of her belief in, and her desire for, the physical release they alluringly proffered, even if this physical release could only be afforded to a body increasingly unrecognizable as Alcott's own.

But this is not to say that other options available to Alcott at the time would have proven any more satisfactory. The realist school formally ushered in by the Civil War, with its anti-sentimental, "objective" representations of suffering and hardship, militated against the possibility of miraculous cures, emotional transformations, out-of-body experiences, all fictions stranger than truth but in which many sufferers, Alcott included, nonetheless may have desperately wanted to believe. Indeed, sentimental representations of pain and suffering could have struck certain sufferers as even more mimetic than so-called realist depictions, for, as the writers I discuss demonstrate graphically, suffering is neither simple nor simply concrete. Alcott's attraction to sentimentalism, then, might indicate an attempt to attend to this complexity rather than simply a hope that her pain might be surmounted.

In her postscript to *Hospital Sketches*, Alcott maintains that the supporting letters she received after the work's serial publication reassured her that she had "not let sympathy and fancy run away with [her], as that lively team is apt to do when harnessed to the pen" (101). Sympathy may be powerful, but only when harnessed *by* and not *to* the writer's pen. Although in so concluding, the author seems to be embracing certain realist tenets and limits, her concern over fancy's unmanageability has a biographical component that complicates such a reading. One reason that Alcott might have been particularly concerned about fancy "running away" with her was that she perceived fancy to be a sign of infirmity—in her journals Alcott lists "strange fancies" (*Journals* 116) as one disorienting symptom of her illness. In fact, it could be argued that sentimental projection—with its illusion that one can inhabit another form, its illusory dissolution of bodily bounds—is nothing if not fanciful. Paradoxically, then, the projectional capacity that would seem to provide a temporary release from suffering could also be scanned as further evidence of disease.

This may explain the ambivalence with which such desomaticizing desires are treated in Alcott's three semi-autobiographical works. In *Hospital Sketches*, the protagonist assesses the desire behind nursing as the "fervent wish that I could take off my body and work in my soul" (67). Yet even while Alcott's persona expresses this desire—one also shared by the two other writers I address—she is the only one of the three to acknowledge its potentially fatal consequences: "sometimes, in their sympathy," her nurse protagonist concludes, "[nurses] forget that they are mortal, and run the risk of being made immortal, sooner than is agreeable to their partial friends" (*Hospital Sketches* 74). As this reminder makes clear, healing is never disjunct from corporeality; effective, *affective* healing requires not just the meeting of two souls or hearts but two bodies. Whether potent or ineffectual anodyne, the heart's beat, after all, is the one sure sign (the *sine qua non*) of corporeal existence. For Alcott most of all, the yearning to escape embodiment always remained, even in the most pain-ridden moments, only a half-hearted one.

Just prior to enlisting as a nurse, Alcott met Rebecca Harding Davis, who, by 1862, had earned the praise of such luminaries as Alcott's Concord neighbors Hawthorne and Emerson for her *Life in the Iron Mills*, first serialized the previous year in the *Atlantic Monthly*. The author seemed to make quite an impression on Alcott as well, who described Davis in her journal as a "A handsome, fresh, quiet woman, who says she never had any troubles, though she writes of woes. I told her I had had lots of troubles; so I write jolly tales; and we wondered why we each did so" (109). Alcott's emphasis on jollity does not mean that she did not share Davis's focus on woes. Rather, the difference—one that speaks to Davis's later classification as an early realist and Alcott's as one of the last sentimentalists—lies in Davis's refusal and Alcott's compulsion to "jolly" them up.

Such a compulsion would prove increasingly debilitating in the wake of Alcott's illness, however. It informs and complicates her post-nursing attempts to depict her *own* troubles in the light-hearted sentimental framework her readers clearly loved and continued to expect—an uneasy conjunction between woes and sentimentality illustrated by the pseudonym she chose for the narrator-nurse in *Hospital Sketches*: Tribulation

Periwinkle. This, Alcott's first acclaimed work, was also her first attempt to enliven her autobiography (*Journals* 119–21). But if *Hospital Sketches* was to become her prototype, it would prove a constraining model. For in these sketches, Alcott not only makes a virtue of "not complaining" (55) about pain—indeed, out of 102 pages, only one-and-a-half are devoted to her own illness; she also reserves her sentimentalized (as well as her graphic) portraits of suffering for the dead or near-dying alone. Perhaps because the wounds were still fresh and not yet debilitating, the female invalid's body could in this instance be virtually ignored. Alcott's reluctance to elaborate upon the nurse's pain hints at both a belief and desire that her illness would prove transitory and insignificant. At the same time, *Hospital Sketches* justifies the seeming inexplicability of severe suffering by nationalizing it and enlisting it in the Union's cause. Alcott's and her patients' maladies thus are afforded a clear and noble origin; their individual bodies serve as patriotic emblems of the divided, pain-ridden nation's. The bewildering pain the author personally suffers is thus both minimized and, paradoxically, lent greater significance via its juxtaposition with larger geopolitical wounds.[13]

Even though *Hospital Sketches* incorporates sentimental scenes of suffering and transport, it is such globalizing analogies that operate therapeutically therein, while the more introversive powers of sentiment are questioned, especially concerning their curative properties. The narrative suggests that tears can work to heal broken hearts even while acknowledging that they are relatively powerless to end war-inflicted injuries like the author's own. For example, in an incident Alcott describes in the postscript to her "sketches," her alter ego hugs, then cries with a woman who arrived at the hospital only to discover that her brother was dead. As the narrator concludes about this episode,

> I mention this successful experiment as a receipt proved and approved, for the use of any nurse who may find herself called upon to minister to these wounds of the heart. They will find it more efficacious than cups of tea, smelling-bottles, psalms, or sermons; for a friendly touch and a companiable cry, unite the consolations of all the rest for womankind; and, if genuine, will be found a sovereign cure for the first sharp pang so many suffer in these heavy times. (93)

While effective, sentimental tears can restore the bodies—more specifically, the "wounded hearts"—of mourners only; there is nothing they can do to heal the mourned. The "pangs" and "suffering" they "cure" are psychical, not physical.[14]

By 1868, when Alcott sat down to write *Little Women*, she did so with a mounting suspicion that her own bodily suffering was to be interminable. Her journal entries for the first five months of 1867 are devoted almost exclusively to cryptic descriptions of her illness, which she attributes to "too hard work" (157). Rather than work providing a momentary escape from or remedy for pain, it functions now primarily to aggravate her illness: "Got a little better at one time," Alcott writes, "but tried to work & down I went again worse than ever" (157). Somehow, though, she still manages to hold on to her optimism, avowing that "with love, health, and work I can be happy, for these three help one to do, to be, and to endure all things" (165).[15] For Alcott, love, health, and work remain intertwined; if she could only arrive at the right admixture, it is implied, the combination might still prove a potent cure.

In *Little Women*, Alcott's fictional persona Jo finds the means "to do, to be, and to endure all things" but only through an intriguing metonymy. In the novel, it is the father who becomes desperately ill at the Civil War front, his tomboyish daughter who does what is in her power to rescue him. In her essay on Alcott's Civil War fiction, Elizabeth Young calls attention to an important aspect of Alcott's fictional representations of suffering characters: many of these invalids are male.[16] In *Little Women*, we could read this aberrant casting as a projection of the author's resentment at having to fulfill the provider role culturally coded as male—a role that has cost her *her* health and one that her own father, Bronson, has willfully shirked. More positively and not necessarily contradictorily, we might also interpret it as an extension of the author's still-lingering faith in the power of sympathetic imagination as a means of transcending one's own physiology and compassionately inhabiting another's.

Alternately, Beth's debilitating illness, though admittedly based on biographical fact, could also be read as a way to explore within the safety-net fiction provides the seemingly inevitable outcome of the author's own disease. Significantly, Beth's death is framed not simply as the end of life but, more specifically, as the end of *pain*; her face in death is "full of painless peace" and her death itself is described as "the long sleep that pain would never mar again" (514). Taken together, *Little Women*'s two projective transubstantiations offer, among their imaginative possibilities, a chance for the author to represent her own plight sympathetically by displacing it onto the bodies of others. They also allow her to demonstrate the selflessness so valued in woman, nurse, and sentimentalist while eluding the suffering such selflessness often simultaneously incurs. Finally, while love might not cure illness it can, in fiction at least, still substitute for it, as, for example, when the loss of Alcott's hair is represented in the novel as a gift of love given to purchase another's health, not, as in Alcott's own case, merely a side-effect of disease.

In 1873, when Alcott returned to her semi-autobiographical novel *Work* and, one last time, to fictionalizing her nursing experiences, she was concerned not just with her own illness—she wrote "slowly" for "fear of a breakdown" (*Journals* 187)—but with those of her older sister and mother. By this point, Alcott would have been hard pressed to interpret physical frailty as somehow elevating. In *Work*, her fictional persona Christie, like Alcott herself, goes off to war as a nurse, but unlike the author, she does not return an invalid. Or rather, she does return stricken, although not by disease but by heart-sickness, by too much love. And, as we know from the anecdote about the bereaved sister in *Hospital Sketches*, this is precisely the type of sickness that can be cured.

In this final reworking of her Civil War experiences, Alcott does not demonstrate the possibilities so much as the dangers of sympathetic identification—the dangers of the disembodiment for which Alcott's nurse fleetingly yearned in *Hospital Sketches*. In *Work*, it is not a father-substitute but a completely fictional husband, David, who becomes dangerously ill at the front, his nurse-wife Christie who arrives too late to restore him to health, although not too late to shed tears for him. The loss of David signifies for his "soulmate" Christie the near fatal loss of her own life; in the moment he dies she becomes "as tranquil, colorless, and mute as if her soul had followed David" (317).[17] The message here seems to be that too much commiseration can jeopardize one's very existence. What restores Christie's health is not more tears nor, through a sympathetic identification with the sufferer, the further attenuation of her physical being so as to render her pure soul; indeed, this last option would only indicate pending and untimely death. Instead, the cure—i.e., Christie's spiritual elevation (achieved in *this* world)—emanates not from a position of physical weakness but from the palpable demands of a creative body. Christie is resuscitated—both health and body are restored—with the news that she is pregnant. In *Work*, the nurse's traumatic Civil War experiences result in a body that creates, not deteriorates, thus evoking Alcott's experience as writer more than as invalid.

Before he dies, David offers Christie a plan for her future: "don't mourn, dear heart, but work, and by that you will be comforted" (315). In so concluding, David sets up the parallel between work and solace that Alcott tried but ultimately failed to implement in her own life. While initially, Alcott's illness did set her creative juices flowing, in the end she came to see even this creativity as more destructive than restorative. As Alcott confided to her journal in 1872: "Twenty years ago I resolved to make the family independent if I could. At forty that is done. Debts all paid . . . and we have enough to be comfortable. It has cost me my health, perhaps; but as I still live, there is more for me to do, I suppose" (182–83). Alcott's ambivalence ("I suppose") about both the effects and the future of her work suggests that what is lost as a result of creativity and self-sacrifice is not so much the self but, less mercifully, its health and vitality. For Alcott, at least, the selflessness that her selected mode of writing both depicts and necessitates doesn't lead to a redemptive shedding of fleshly constraints; instead, it only further imprisons the author within a bruised and broken frame. By the end of her life, in the late 1880s, Alcott rarely picked up her pen except to jot down in her journal abbreviated, clinical descriptions of her symptoms and sufferings—"Dizzy," "felt poorly," "pain in chest," "Head sore," "stomach rather qualmish" are but a few representative samples (*Journals* 330–34). It is hard not to read these epigrammatic passages as poignant acknowledgment that in certain cases the heart could function neither as balm nor bomb, that pain's pulse proved too throbbing to be regulated, recorded, or stilled within sentimental forms.

⁖

While Alcott gradually resigned herself to the notion that physical suffering might prove more enervating than elevating, "irregular" doctor Harriot Hunt did not experience a similar change of heart. Although she attended patients suffering from symptoms as severe as Alcott's if not more so, Hunt's faith in emotional intensity and physical frailty as potential conduits to a deeper, higher spirituality never appeared to waver. While the difference between the two women's views might be attributed to the distance between sufferer's and healer's perspectives, Hunt also perseveres where Alcott founders because the doctor was more ready to divorce the bodily from the spiritual whereas Alcott assumed their inextricability from the start. In some respects, especially in her abiding belief in the transformative powers of heartfelt emotions, Hunt was even more of a sentimentalist than Alcott. One explanation for how she managed to avoid some of the traps that ensnared Alcott may lie in her use of the memoir form to depict matters of the heart. As I'll discuss shortly, Hunt's memoir, with its authorial "I" and rambling, unstructured format, allows her to manipulate traditionally sentimental conventions so that the emphasis falls on uplift rather than abasement.

Hunt launched her medical career during a period in America's medical history when established therapies were increasingly seen as futile if not harmful. While "heroic" techniques like frequent bloodletting and heavy dosing remained popular among "regular" medical practitioners at midcentury, a number of healers argued concomitantly for the scientific merits and benefits of more moderate remedies, including Thomsonian, hydropathic, and homeopathic therapies.[18] The late 1840s and early '50s also saw a groundswell of support for women's admittance into the medical establishment.[19] Female practitioners, it was believed, would bring to the bargain their inherently empathic natures, hence literalizing as trained physicians the conjunction between sympathy and science documented by Regina Morantz-Sanchez in her history of women and medicine. As Dr. Angenette A. Hunt insisted in 1851: "It is certain that the health of the world, depends on the women of the world and at least, some of the qualities needed in the medical profession—as gentleness, patience, quick perceptions, natural instinct which is often surer than science, deep sympathy . . . all these belong to the [female] sex in an eminent degree" (qtd. in Morantz-Sanchez 28).

Whatever its benefits, grounding a woman's contribution to the healing profession in her "deep sympathy" could prove a potentially risky move. Voicing one relatively common objection, "regular" physician John Ware opposed women's egress on the very grounds that others were using to justify it: chiding women for being unable to withhold their "natural tendency to sympathy," Ware warned that "the profession of medicine does not afford a field for the display and indulgence of those finer feelings" (qtd. in Morantz et al. 10).[20] His comments suggest that sympathy was being defined synchronously as both an enabling and disabling emotion: while for some it constituted an inherent disqualification, only further justifying women's confinement within the domestic sphere, others, including prominent Boston suffragist and doctor Harriot K. Hunt, considered it a "suspension bridge" (x) allowing middle-class women like herself to journey confidently from realms codified as private into more public, professional domains.

In 1856, Hunt threw down the gauntlet to her male colleagues when she asked: "Man, man alone has had the care of *us* [women] and I would ask *how our health stands now*. Does it do credit to *his* skill?" (414). Roughly a decade earlier, convinced that *her* skill was needed, Hunt had written to Oliver Wendell Holmes, then Dean of Medical Faculty at Harvard, seeking permission to attend lectures at the university. Although already practicing as an "irregular" healer, Hunt hungered for the advanced training and knowledge she believed the Harvard classroom would provide. Less than a month later, the president of the university dashed off a brief note in which he curtly responded that such a possibility would be "inexpedient"—a conclusion Hunt devoted the rest of her medical career to disproving.[21]

Hunt's career as healer began in 1835, provoked by her beloved sister Sarah's prolonged bout with what one attending physician diagnosed as "a disease of the heart." When regular doctors appeared incapable of offering any hope or help, Harriot and her ailing sibling began perusing medical books for answers; what they found there—and what they did not—led both eventually to make medicine their chosen field. As Harriot contends in her memoir, her sister's illness provided not only the impetus but the methodology for her practice: "The sympathy I had given to my sister, I now gave to every sufferer" (116). For Hunt, sympathy doesn't just precede "professional" experiences (88), it remains integral to her therapeutics. Yet while in Hunt's own life such "heart experiences" (88) led her to medicine as career, similar experiences were leading many of her future patients to turn to medicine as cure. In other words, the distress and empathy that made Hunt want to become a healer were the very emotions making many of her patients ill and in need of one.

This potential contradiction did not faze the doctor. Indeed, throughout her twenty-year medical career, Hunt remained convinced that tapping into a patient's "heart experiences" and releasing the pent-up feelings contained therein by extricating "heart histories" (50) was a profoundly curative process. In this, she predates our own therapeutic culture's investment in "getting in touch" with buried emotions. Hunt's consultations quickly taught her, however, that the lines between the sensible and the maudlin, self-help and self-absorption, could easily be crossed. In her 1856 memoir, *Glances and Glimpses; or, Fifty Years Social, Including Twenty Years Professional Life*, Hunt incorporates many of the elements integral to sentimental scenarios—she details moments of intense suffering, heightened emotion, and a yearning for transcendence. But through a strategy of narrative reticence (indicated by the memoir's title and fostered by the memoir form) Hunt ensures a physical diminishment that both refuses the reduction of female identity to flesh or feeling and allows for a healthy excess. In short, it is her manipulations of *narrative form* rather than her representations of *female form* that enable her to depict a physicality minimized enough to yield transcendence but still palpable enough to be healed.

Hunt's ultimate therapeutic goal was to enable her patients to surmount bodily constraints and unshackle their presently imprisoned spirits—a metamorphosis she sought for the profession as a whole. As she clarifies in her memoir, Hunt was attracted to "medical science" not for its "physics" but its "metaphysics" (127). For Hunt, "technicalities, abstractions, knowledge ever so profound, are but the exterior" of the medical profession: "the essence is in the spirit." Unfortunately, she continues, extant "medical science ... lacked ... a soul; it was a huge, unwieldy body—distorted, deformed, inconsistent, and complicated" (121). Hunt wished to transform the physical weakness of medicine's "body" so that all that remains legible is a lustrous, revitalized soul; what she sought, we might say, was to make the body of medicine a little less "heroic" and a little more like a heroine's.

In order to accomplish this transformation, she wanted her colleagues to rethink what it meant to be a doctor. According to Hunt, healing was not a matter of reading bodies but reading hearts, undertaken as a joint venture between doctor and patient—in Hunt's own practice (which she holds up as exemplary) doctor and patient functioned as "coworkers" (156). As Hunt constructs the invalid, she is neither passive nor submissive but is instead emotionally engaged in her own recovery. If her fellow practitioners took only one thing away from reading her autobiography, Hunt wanted it to be this: "let there be more oneness between you and your patients. . . . Let that little word WE be the talisman"(89), the reminder that physician and patient must cooperate in order for true healing to occur. Hunt envisioned the doctor-patient relationship as, ideally, an encounter between two souls speaking through two hearts—hearts filled with emotion, yes, but not so full that effective communication dissolves into tears. Were this dissolution to occur, the heart experiences that Hunt elevates as potential cure would resume their original status as symptom and source of disease.

The threat of this resumption may explain why Hunt makes a point of deploring women's education in "sentimentality" (394). In particular, Hunt frowns on those social circles "where," for women, "*soul* is termed *sentiment*" (394) precisely because in this formulation a woman's expansive spirit is reduced to the narrow compass of her (excessive) sensibilities, leaving her wallowing in rather than learning from and transcending such emotions. Even when its only expression was tears, the language of the heart was for Hunt never the body's but the soul's very speech. In Hunt's practice it is the heart or soul that both needs and finds a cure; the body's healing is but a side effect.[22] Indeed, Hunt explicitly dissociates the heart from the body, as when she deplores "the abomination of dosing the *body* when the *heart was sick*" (401).

Still, the heart's persistent biological traces posed problems for Hunt's therapeutics. As metaphor, the heart offers a means of transcending embodiment at the same time that, as referent, it highlights it. While undermining conventional notions of the autonomous self, the sympathetic identification that the heart both symbolizes and enables risks reinscribing selflessness as an essential feminine trait and identifying feminine forms as little more than acutely feeling entities. For a woman at midcentury to equate the feeling heart with the healing art was hence to walk a fine line between imprisoning herself further within biological definitions of the self and, via what she saw as the heart's spiritual, transformative powers, liberating herself from them once and for all.

How, then, does Hunt manage to negotiate this tightrope safely in a narrative literally obsessed with matters of the heart (within one representative passage consisting of four sentences, for example, none are devoid of mention of this vital organ: "my heart sickens" follows "heart-histories" follows "broken-hearted" follows "heartless deception" [50])? As I have already suggested, by choosing to relate both her own and her patient's "heart-histories" in memoir form, Hunt manages to stave off the biological reduction she so vehemently resisted and that the content of her narrative at times rather perilously approaches. Among other things, the retrospective mood of memoir drains her emotional subject matter of immediacy even as its controlling narrative voice allows the author to unfold and withhold whatever portion of these histories she deems wise. If ever there was an intrusive "I," Hunt's is it, intervening to steer readerly response, agitate for certain readings over others, and ward off readers' potentially introspective inclinations.

Hunt clearly feared that, conditioned by highly wrought fiction, her own lay readers would sympathize with her patients' heart-histories only if she sensationalized them. This would not have been hard for Hunt to do: a full accounting of the details of each of her patient's cases, she avows, might brand her narrative even more sensational than conventional romances, for "no romance ever read portrayed such harrowing scenes" (139). In *Glances and Glimpses,* Hunt refuses to graphically depict such scenes, perhaps fearing that if her readers were to become "harrowed"—a response familiar to readers of sentimental works—their concern might be transferred from her patients' to their own well-being.

When Hunt does, reluctantly, offer carefully excised fragments of heart-histories, her status as the book's sole author rather than (as in her medical practice) a collaborator allows her to exert control over any potentially debilitating side effects. Before introducing these fragments, Hunt argues that they ought to do more than encourage pity for the individual woman; indeed, she seizes on any potential sympathy for the individual as a small stepping stone on the path toward political outrage on all women's behalf. As Hunt affirms after referring to dozens of women trained to no profession and cast off by heartless husbands, "Such heart-histories appeal powerfully to our sympathies, while they rouse our indignation at the degradation and uselessness of our sex" (50). While, according to form, these sentimental tales accentuate the "degradation" of their heroines, Hunt intervenes at the level of reception to argue that their impact on the reader ought to be utilitarian, inaugurating sisterly outrage rather than introversion. So while Hunt frets that she does not "touch this subject with the pen of inspiration" (50), in one sense hers is an *inspired* strategy. For although Hunt links degradation and transcendence here in ways that call to mind sentimental representations of martyred suffering, in her carefully directed restaging, both sufferer *and* audience are afforded the desired elevation. What's more, this elevation is explicitly framed as this- rather than other-worldly; thanks to Hunt's intervention the subjective is transformed into a profoundly political and collective experience.

As the first reader of her patients' heart-histories, Hunt herself manages to avoid being "harrowed" by maintaining a distance between herself as trained reader and the overwrought patients she reads. While certainly neither detached nor objective, Hunt's sympathetic reading of a patient's "tell-tale heart" does not result in total identification, either. Indeed, she believes that the healing power of sympathy both arises from and is ultimately preserved by a professional distance—a distance measured by a doctor's specialized ability to elicit and interpret the heart-histories hitherto locked inside the invalid's soul. We see this when Hunt suggests that "As heart-histories have opened to me, in my medical life the eternal spring—the newness—the sacredness which invests these subjects in my mind, has given me great power over my patients" (109). This power is precisely that of sympathy, of "the consoler," a power that "will light the heart for ever" (109) and hence make it forever legible to a reader equipped to interpret it correctly (i.e., with an eye toward transformation rather than mere consolation).

As such, and in contradistinction to the reading process associated with sentimental fiction, Hunt's hermeneutics posits sympathetic engagement not as the end of reading but merely the beginning; it does not initiate introspection and withdrawal but inspection and dialogue. As Hunt defines it, reading the contents of another's heart—an activity culturally encoded as sentimental—yields a result which transcends mere sentiment. The ideal reader (modeled after Hunt herself) does not sob in an empathy underwritten by a knowledge of her inability to cure but, dry-eyed, competently wields the therapeutic powers such insightful readings afford her.

But just in case such a hermeneutics appeals more to trained specialists than to lay readers, Hunt achieves essentially the same goal by offering in the memoir only "glances and glimpses" of the lives she recounts, including her own. In so doing, she thwarts the abject immersion—either in sentimentalized other or in sentimental self—that can stem from a reader's projective, identificatory engagement. As Hunt asserts in her conclusion, "I have never asked any one to look at myself" (416)—an odd claim for a memoirist to make—and when readers do look, no matter how penetrating their tools, Hunt conceals more than she reveals. As memoir, *Glances and Glimpses* comes close on occasion to depicting the history of Hunt's own heart, but hers is a tale of sentiments that refuses the indulgences of self-absorption. For one thing, the legible body in and of Hunt's autobiographical text is not, she contends, equivalent to the self: there is more to her than we can see or read. Indeed, she belabors her essential elusiveness: "Even now I stand in *conscious hiddenness*. True, you see *some* of the things I have done—*some* of the trials, sorrows, and joys of a happy life. But these are no more ME than the physique my spirit wears" (416). Hunt thus suggests that the narrative form she adopts and manipulates—which would seem to be the exhibitionist genre *par excellence*—matches her convictions about bodily form: just as the self or "spirit" exceeds the flesh so, too, does it necessarily exceed the text.

By only affording glimpses, Hunt frustrates a reader's will and desire to know and challenges the assumption that life can ever be contained within a bounded entity. Whatever its claims to verisimilitude, a memoir is, after all, selective, constituted piecemeal across conspicuous silences and absences. *Glances and Glimpses* foregrounds this absent presence, this "ME" that transcends both text and physique. Indeed, her "peek-a-boo" representational strategy could be seen as the aesthetic expression of her desire to conjoin corporeal and incorporeal emphases in her own as well as the wider practice of medicine.

Just as Harriet Jacobs, some five years later, would reject the bildungsroman claims of both biography and sentimental fiction and offer not the "life of a slave girl" but "incidents" from it, by permitting only glimpses of her own more privileged life Hunt resists both sentimental subsumption and utterly alienating readers. Although the "glances and glimpses" Hunt records serve to pique a reader's curiosity, she offers no uninhibited views of a prostrate heroine for a reader to weep over. In some respects, this is because—although in part bildungsroman—Hunt's is never the story of a single life; just when it seems as if she is getting wrapped up in her own personal history, she digresses, diverting our attention to, among other topics, proper child-rearing (e.g., 20, 101–2), women's health and education (e.g., 49–54), and the wayward state of medicine (e.g., 121, 129–31).[23] In the end, Hunt's alternately digressive and restrained styles of representation combine to thwart readers' tendencies toward self-absorption as well as to obscure any evidence of a patient's chronic invalidism—thereby obviating two of the largest obstacles to any equation of heart histories with transport or cure.

Both in her introduction and conclusion, Hunt encodes an ideal reader and stipulates an ideal reading as at once engaged and detached. At one moment in her preface, Hunt seems to yearn for sentimentalism's intimate and engaged reader when she contends that no reader of her memoir can be "a *stranger*, when the inmost life is depicted, and a *womanly* desire to present truth in a simple garb is felt" (xi). Only a page later, however, she boasts that even readers who use "a microscope" will be frustrated in their quest to "comprehend and discover what is *hidden* from the naked eye" (xii). Although Hunt may sympathize with such a probing hermeneutics, she willfully obstructs its desired insights. When focused on Hunt's text, at least, the microscope does not possess the power to make sense out of "*dashes* of the brush *not* to be completed; *touches, not* finishing strokes upon the canvas" (xii). What Hunt offers us, then, is less a mimetic or scientific than an impressionistic portrait. It is a portrait, moreover, that requires and empowers a contemplative and creative rather than a probing, clinical or alternatively weeping, sentimental gaze.

In the end, Hunt employs a representational strategy for relating her own history similar to the one she uses to portray her patients' histories: she establishes authority by refusing a reader unfettered access to inner being. As Hunt avows, she has only shown "the *outside* of her life.... [I]t may be, *all* of you will see nothing, *know* nothing of my *interior* self" (416)—even as she proclaims her own expertise at discerning the hidden qualities of the subjects she reads. Since earlier Hunt cautioned her medical colleagues that it is not "externally" but only internally, "in the centre of their being" (375), that a person can be understood, Hunt as her own first, best reader seems to be qualifying all subsequent readings of her text, her self, her subject(s), as unavoidably superficial. Like Holmes, then, Hunt attempts to efface a doctor's body but not behind an impenetrable gaze. Her point, rather, is that even a fully legible body never totally reveals identity, as subjectivity will always overflow bodily confines. What is essential to Hunt (or, she suggests, to any woman) is not something that can be seen or read by opening one's eyes; the closest one can come to "glimpsing" the complexity of subjectivity is by opening a heart. Readers of her memoir, offered a carefully crafted "heart history" but denied a full, uninhibited exposé (and hence denied the basis of her own diagnostic authority), will of necessity have recourse to their eyes more than their hearts and thus receive only a partial glimpse of her (as) subject. As a result, Hunt establishes herself (even as she hides her self) as superlative reader, possessing knowledge and feelings that will always, inevitably, surpass any attempt to contain them.

☙

Hunt's attempts to generate an ideal reader or reading are motivated by a presumption that we can predict how we are perceived and foreclose alternatives—that we are our own authors with the final say over how our story is not only represented but received. In order to exert such control, reading as an historical act must be severed from the social codes that structure it. Hunt's idealism rests in her perhaps willful overlooking of the extent to which others still not only read but help to write our lives, more or less.

Perhaps no other midcentury American woman writer's career exemplifies this fact better than Margaret Fuller's. For all her erudition and achievements, Fuller's legacy has in large part been shaped—at least until the relatively recent resurgence of critical interest—by how certain influential others perceived her. And very few of these readers engaged empathetically with the unconventional text that was Margaret Fuller. Although Fuller differs from Alcott and Hunt because her search for transcendence is through (and not just over) pain and because this search explicitly eschews conventional frameworks, sentimental or otherwise, ironically, despite or perhaps because of this eschewal, Fuller's friends and foes alike retroactively imposed these conventional frames in their posthumous readings of her life and works.

In her lifetime, it is true, few of Fuller's critics could discover anything conventionally sentimental or even womanly about her. Perhaps best known is Nathaniel Hawthorne's dismissal of Fuller as a "humbug," lacking "the charm of womanhood" (J. Hawthorne 260); Hawthorne's aversion for Fuller was apparently so great at times that he once wryly thanked "providence" when he managed to escape being in her formidable presence (Woodson 107).[24] His son Julian insisted to all who would listen that Fuller was his father's model for the overbearing bluestocking Zenobia in *The Blithedale Romance* (1852), whose watery death both mirrors and (if so, tastelessly) mocks Fuller's tragic end (J. Hawthorne 392).[25]

Hawthorne's difficulties with Fuller may have stemmed not just from his distaste for the woman herself but for her published writings, which are marked by a conspicuous abstraction, both at the thematic and formal levels. At least one critic felt that the problem with Fuller's public appearance (whether in prose or in person) was that it was so vexingly hard to pin down, so disturbingly unwomanly. Charles F. Briggs's critique of *Woman in the Nineteenth Century* (1845) for the *Broadway Journal* identifies "the great defect of Miss Fuller's book [a]s a want of distinctness" (11).[26] He goes on to point out, in a thinly veiled insult, that "Miss Fuller names Mrs. Siddons as an instance of what a woman may effect in public; but Mrs. Siddons came before the public only as a woman, representing always a woman, either as a wife, a mother, or a betrothed wife" (14). The implication seems clear enough: since Fuller was none of these three (yet), she was no woman. Briggs was by no means alone in attacking the apparently indeterminate gender of Fuller and her prose; nor was he the only critic who expected a woman writer to reveal her gender identity in every word and glimpse.[27]

Fuller detested such expectations. Although Edgar Allan Poe did not so intend it, we could read his infamous quip that there are three types of people, "men, women and Margaret Fuller" (qtd. in Chevigny 19), as a backhanded compliment, pointing not to Fuller's "freakishness" but to her urgent desire to transcend—to posit an alternative to—fixed, traditional categories and forms. Hence Fuller criticizes Madame de Staël for not being able to "forget the woman in the thought" (*Woman* 82). Railing against this collapsing of "woman" and "thought" as well as against the equating of "woman" and "body," Fuller endeavored throughout her life to divorce them by experimenting with more complex abstractions, perhaps nowhere more explicitly than in *Woman in the Nineteenth Century*.

Fuller's dissatisfaction with existing forms—both bodily and rhetorical—is clearly expressed in a meditation recorded in a note she wrote to a friend: "For all the tides of life that flow within me, I am dumb and ineffectual, when it comes to casting my thought into a form. No old one suits me. If I could invent one, it seems to me the pleasure of creation would make it possible for me to write" ("To [?]" [n.d.]). The form Fuller invents in *Woman* draws on existing modes even as it refuses allegiance to any single mode. A medley of essay, exegesis, history, jeremiad, lecture, poetry, philosophy, and sermon, *Woman* as a formal construct remains notoriously difficult to pin down; fluidity and abstraction define both its mode and motif.[28] Although Fuller had already primed her fictional skills when she sat down to write *Woman*, in it she forsakes not only fiction but narrative.[29] Perhaps most closely approximating the "conversations" conducted by Fuller in her living room, *Woman* tends to efface the bodies integral to the act of conversing, leaving in their place only an absract(ed) voice.

Remarkably for a book with its title, *Woman in the Nineteenth Century* is a work in which gender no longer seems to *matter* (that is, to be materialized), either at the level of content or of form. "Exaltadas" (152), after all, is the term Fuller chooses to personify radiant, spiritual femininity; in her ideal incarnation, Fuller's true woman, like her domesticated sister, is both spiritually exalted and physically attenuated. Unlike her sibling, however, Fuller's ideal woman is not actually *woman*, man's binary opposite, but *soul*, man's essential equal. Fuller's utopian vision of a "perfect," "Olympian" democracy is composed of men and women who are "each ... a purified intelligence, an enfranchised soul—no less!" (51).[30] Throughout her account of women in the nineteenth century, the emotional state singled out as climactic entails none of the martyred suffering we find in sentimental narratives; what Fuller emphasizes almost exclusively is a spiritualized rapture and transcendence resembling that which typically ensues from martyrdom but lacking this explicit prerequisite.

Yet for all Fuller's idealism, it would be inaccurate to portray her account of nineteenth-century women as consistently abstract or exalted. In the interim between the publication of "The Great Lawsuit" in 1843 and the release of the revised, expanded *Woman* in 1845, Fuller read about and even interviewed jailed prostitutes, an experience that fueled her intolerance of both sexual and racial inequities (many of the prostitutes were African-Americans). Stirred by these encounters, Fuller incorporated into the completed manuscript of *Woman* graphic discussions of sexual matters and clarion calls for the reform of sexual and racial relations.[31] Not only does she cite in *Woman* her prison interviews with prostitutes, she urges readers ignorant of such suffering to consider these "unfortunates" the "fairest" of "souls," largely because their sorrows have "brought some of them to feel the need of better life, nearer truth and good" (146). By their very presence, these passages—combined with the ones in which, for instance, Fuller challenges the double standard that celebrates women's frailty while expecting "negresses to endure field work" (25) or begs still pure maidens to embrace the man "in whom brute nature is entirely subject to the impulses of his better self" (122)—confirm *Woman*'s hybridity, its interspersing *and interlinking* of the debased and the ethereal, the concrete and the abstract, or, to use the author's own idiom, society and the soul.

Upon finishing the manuscript in 1844, Fuller confided to William Henry Channing that she "put a good deal of my true life in it" (Hudspeth 3: 241.) Where, in the range between *Woman*'s more refined and its more defined portraits of its titular subject, does Fuller's personal understanding of self line up? Is the jubilant spirit of the piece solely attributable to Transcendental beliefs, or does it evoke as well Fuller's own "true life" experience?[32] At first glance, there appears to be a radical disjunction between Fuller's public celebration of woman's potential as ecstatic soul and the suffering, gendered existence she often privately lamented. It seems likely that if Fuller identified with any of her representations, it would have been with the downtrodden rather than the ideal woman. Indeed, Fuller's personal history of suffering might seem a prime candidate for sentimentalization. Yet while others proved more than willing to lend it this cast, Fuller herself firmly resisted any such interpretation. Unlike Alcott, Fuller managed to forge a connection between pain and transcendence that withstood even the weakening force of chronic illness. Unlike Hunt, she made this connection in such a way that it neither invoked tears nor in any way called attention to itself as in some unique or essential sense feminine.

Having to identify her self as feminine at all was a task Fuller often performed reluctantly. In her private writings she frequently depicts her gender identity in terms of physical circumscription; she contends, for example, that even though she "loves best to be a woman," "womanhood is at present too straitly-bounded to give me scope" (Hudspeth 6: 143). Here, Fuller ranges a restrictive "womanhood" against a "me" that requires more room. One explanation for Fuller's view of gender as constraint can be found in her relatively unflinching acceptance of the binaries that associate men with mind and women with heart. No doubt because she associated a woman's heart with a kind of immanence that brooked neither escape nor desire for it, Fuller considered possessing such a heart more an encumbrance than a virtue. As she said of herself, "A man's ambition with a woman's heart, is an evil lot" (*Memoirs* 1: 229). For Fuller, the heart as synecdoche for womanhood doesn't enshrine woman as domestic angel or spiritual vessel but instead impedes her transcendence and ensures a stifling domestication. She feared this repressive outcome not just for herself but for other women as well. In her reading notes on George Sand, for example, she writes, "I am astonished at her insight into the life of thought. She must know it through some man.... [W]hen it comes to interrogating God, the universe, the soul, and, above all, trying to live above their own hearts, [women] dart down to their own nests like so many larks" (qtd. in *Memoirs* 1: 247). Fuller thus suggests that women who have the ability to "live above their own hearts" may find a voice unmuffled by physicality and thereby become souls. What the sufferer needs to express is not, à la Hunt, the heart's language, but the insights that emerge once women get beyond or (more accurately) above the immediacy of their own pressing emotional needs.

The difficulty of this assignment was apparent even to Fuller, who was herself not immune to the "nesting" impulse: "I have been always wishing to call myself into the arms of some other nature," Fuller once confessed. "This was womanish, I own. I am not yet a man" (qtd. in Russell 29–30). Her desire to surrender to another's embrace is a recognizably "womanish," sentimental one; the desire underwriting this passage is to transcend such desires altogether, to move beyond conventionally feminine sentiments and constraints—and, in the process, to move beyond the corporeal needs and desires that prompt all such longings for surrender or solace.

For Fuller, it was the potential contingency of any gendered construction—its restrictiveness in her own time notwithstanding—that made this movement a possibility. She was capable of imagining a time when the construction of gender would not be so constricting: hence her emphasis on temporality ("womanhood is *at present* ... ," "I am *not yet* ..."). What she ultimately institutes in her gendered definitions is a continuum that positions physically circumscribed womanhood at one end and radiant "Exaltadas" (or, along a different scale, manly independence) at the other—implying that it might be possible to move between the poles in some unspecified future.[33] What makes this continuum especially interesting is that Fuller celebrates it without necessarily dismissing the fundamental importance of nature. At one point in *Woman*, Fuller juxtaposes the fluidity of gender identities against a more fixed, physiological understanding of form: "male and female represent the two sides of the great radical dualism. But, in fact, they are perpetually passing into one another. Fluid hardens to solid, solid rushes to fluid" (103). Fuller then goes on to jeer "at the attempts of physiologists to bind great original laws by the forms which flow from them. They make a rule; they say from observation, what can and cannot be. In vain! Nature provides exceptions to every rule" (103). In Fuller's schema, "Nature" provides not the rules but the exceptions to them, which is to say that she considers the nature of Nature both more plastic and more indeterminate than many physiologists were willing to allow. In *Woman*, Fuller explicitly distinguishes a woman's gender from her nature at a time when the two were fast becoming synonymous, arguing that "what woman needs is not as a *woman* to act or rule, but as a *nature* to grow, as an *intellect* to discern, as a *soul* to live freely and unimpeded" (*Woman* 27, emphasis added). The valorized terms here—nature, intellect, and soul—are not equal but sequential stages of *bildung* in which the soul, luminous and unbounded, is the highest. While Fuller's belief that women—no matter how "incarcerated"—qualify as "souls" (*Woman* 105) reverberates with sentimental equations of spirituality and femininity, she ultimately refutes such equations by insisting that no conventionally feminine prerequisites exist. Indeed, the sooner a woman can rid herself of feminine attributes, the quicker will her qualifications as a soul emerge.

As her gendered dissociations indicate, Fuller was convinced that the complexities of human nature could not be reduced to a single essence, least of all to a gendered essence. As she proclaims in *Woman*, "it is no more the order of nature that [femininity] should be incarnated pure in any form, than that the masculine energy should exist unmingled with it in any form" (103). In Fuller's view, it is only after nature has been fully divested of the gendered properties erroneously assigned to it that the fluid gender identities she values as "natural" will be capable of realization. Rather than merely embracing androgyny, Fuller explicitly differentiates both a "woman's nature" and a "woman's heart"—which she considered limiting—from the liberating, elevating soul, unconstrained by the dross of gender. In particular, she attempts to retain nature as identificatory category and experiential base for women as for men even as she bemoans conventional, naturalized definitions of gendered existence.

While *Woman*'s emphasis on soul ("all soul is the same" [103], she claims, "there is but one law for souls" [26]) may be attributed to Transcendentalism, the fact that it is a woman making the argument pushes the Concord school into territories where no beard nor bard had gone before.[34] Indeed, Fuller stakes out new territory by mapping a continuum from mute body to articulate soul, in contrast to Emerson's metaphysics in which the body is defined as the "not me."[35] In Fuller's view, transcendence was never simply a metaphysical concept; it also retained palpable if vestigial physical dimensions. By conjoining the physical and metaphysical, Fuller not only claims Transcendentalism for fellow sufferers but radicalizes it by recognizing that selves are corporeal in ways that are unequally open to transcendence but that cannot be reduced to mere encumbrance.

Fuller's willingness to retain and celebrate a nature irreducible to existing constructions of femininity can be attributed to her firsthand experience of physical suffering. While Alcott sought release or at least distraction from pain, and while Hunt sought to alleviate it once and for all, Fuller was willing (if not always eager) to subject herself to its lessons even when there was little hope for relief. By exploring Fuller's particular take on the links between pain and transcendence, we can flesh out some of the formal and thematic insubstantialities that distinguish her prose, aspects which have hitherto either been shrugged off as idiosyncratic flaws, futile utopian longings, or derivations of male-dominated intellectual traditions.

"The secret of all things is pain" (*Woman and Kindred* 359), Fuller once wrote, and although this secret is ostensibly kept in the prose published in her lifetime—"The Great Lawsuit" and its expanded version, *Woman*, are devoid of the graphic descriptions of personal suffering that recur throughout Fuller's more private musings—this does not mean that pain is irrelevant to its rhetoric and revelations. For it was often her most painful experiences that equipped Fuller with the kinds of euphoric, spiritual, and universalizing insights celebrated throughout *Woman*. Indeed, pain helped to teach Fuller some of her most important lessons about the essential contingency of all corporeal experiences. For Fuller, pain was never without purpose. It almost always enabled its apparent opposite: a greater rapture, a heightened spirituality. Pain also provided Fuller with both means and rationale for repudiating conventional sentimentality as well as conventionally gendered roles and expectations.

Severe migraine headaches often made Fuller's physical existence excruciating. Fuller traced what she would refer to as "that frenzied headache" (*Woman and Kindred* 361) in part to her unusual upbringing: Timothy Fuller rigorously schooled his eldest daughter in the classical tradition, subjecting her to nightly study drills that she later blamed for the "premature development of the brain, . . . which at the time prevented the harmonious development of my bodily powers and checked my growth, while, later, they induced continual headache, weakness, and nervous affections, of all kinds . . . [wasting] my constitution" (*Memoirs* 1: 15).[36] Subscribing to the doctrine of stimulation and depletion—which holds that the organs are so "sympathetic" that too much expenditure of energy in one would inevitably lead to atrophy in another—Fuller here links the development of her mental powers and physical suffering, as she does in many passages throughout her writings.[37]

For Fuller, this etiology has a gendered dimension: she suspects that her female form is responsible for her inability to pursue without ill effect the strenuous mental activities she identifies with the male mind—and hence for her migraines. In Fuller's tortuous reasoning, her "womanliness" induces the migraine headaches that advance her intellectual growth by providing insight into life's meaning, even as her gendered identity only seems to thwart such discoveries. Thus in a fanciful letter to Beethoven, in which she proclaims her soul to be "as deep as" the composer's "and of a kindred frame," she asks why her genius has not been inspired by errors and suffering as Beethoven's was. Tentatively answering her own question, Fuller writes, "Is it because, as a woman, I am bound by a physical law, which prevents the soul from manifesting itself?" (November 1843, qtd. in Chevigny 61). While confessing here to a fear that her gender might impede the manifestation of her soul, Fuller does not seem concerned that pain might have a similar effect. In fact, she is far more likely to identify physical suffering as an essential discipline. Her recognition that Christ's spirituality was not only enhanced but confirmed by his martyrdom, for example, leads her to speculate about whether she herself "might be educated through suffering to the same purity" (qtd. in Higginson 97.).

This is not to say that Fuller chose to wallow masochistically in her pain. She eagerly sought alleviation but increasingly came to believe that her only hope for a cure lay within herself. As she confides in a short piece written after a month-long headache, "I know well there is no healing for me except in the depths of my own self, my spirit" (qtd. in Higginson 97). Indeed, Fuller appears willing to prolong this treatment, as if convinced that an internal examination—no matter how painful—may provide insights that could outweigh even the gift of health. In his section of *The Memoirs*, Emerson maintains that Fuller "was all her lifetime the victim of disease and pain. She read and wrote in bed, and believed that she could understand anything better when she was ill. Pain acted like a girdle, to give tension to her powers" (*Memoirs* 1: 229).[38] According to Emerson, by both constraining and intensifying her mental powers, pain's grip gives Fuller's writing and studies both form and context.[39] Pain thus both accentuates the bounds of corporeal subjectivity and enables their surmounting—in short, pain teaches the lessons of transcendence through immanence. This is a paradox beautifully illustrated by Fuller's habit of writing in bed, an awkward process that would have unavoidably foregrounded the oscillation between corporeality and transcendence. At its most intense, though, pain seems to have functioned for Fuller less as a "girdle" than as a laser capable of burning through external encumbrances, enabling at last the emergence of the soul's voice and will.

While Fuller's gender identity caused her a great deal of discomfort, this discomfort was not coterminous with that induced by migraine. Ultimately, Fuller associates her headaches with a potential surmounting of bodily limits, enabling a loftier transcendence and a deeper insight free of gender's persistent distortions and obfuscations. In November 1840, for example, after "a long attack of nervous headache," Fuller claims in a letter to Channing, "I feel now such an entire separation from pain and illness, such a calm consciousness of another life while suffering most in the body, that pain has no effect except to steal some of my time" (Hudspeth 2: 184). Here Fuller's "I" asserts a separation from her body at the very moment when the body's dominance must have seemed most acute. Anyone who has ever suffered severe pain is aware of this paradox: while constantly reminding us of our physical limits and limitations, extreme pain simultaneously produces an eerie sense of disembodiment, of suspension just outside or above the body's frame. In Fuller's case, what might seem the most deeply embedded moments of physical existence are precisely those that enable her keenest insights into the "other life" of the soul.

At the same time that Fuller's headaches prompt such spiritual insights, they also seem to provide opportunities to shed the trappings of femininity. One degendering side effect of Fuller's chronic migraines appears to have been the loosening of the supposedly necessary connection between woman's writing and sentimentality, enabling her temporarily to explore alternative forms. In *Woman*, Fuller makes her distaste for "sentimentalism" self-evident (117, 118).[40] Elsewhere, in a letter to Channing after a particularly crippling attack, Fuller suggests that pain provides her with both method and excuse for eluding conventional sentimental formats:

> I am still quite unwell, and all my pursuits and propensities have a tendency to make my head worse. It is but a bad head,—as bad as if I were a great man! I am not entitled to so bad a head by anything I have done; but I flatter myself it is very interesting to suffer so much, and a fair excuse for not writing pretty letters, and saying to my friends the good things I think about them. (Hudspeth 2: 184)

Taking a swipe at the double standard, Fuller jests that what in a woman signifies disease in a man is taken as a sign of greatness. More positively, pain not only draws attention to herself but, importantly, excuses her from having to write "pretty letters" full of flattering comments. In other words, her experience of pain exempts her—if only fleetingly—from predictably gendered roles and modes. So if it is true that Fuller preferred to write not "like a woman, of love and hope and disappointment, but like a man, of the world of intellect and action" (qtd. in Higginson 188), then her migraines helped to provide an opportunity to do so. As Fuller confesses to Channing in a letter of March 1840, "when I write, it is into another world, not a better one perhaps, but one with very dissimilar habits of thought to this where I am domesticated" (Hudspeth 2: 125–26). Interestingly, writing and pain yield comparable effects for Fuller, both seeming to liberate her momentarily from gendered confines even as they illuminate them.

In this sense, migraine headaches, an affliction that would seem designed to keep a woman securely in her place, operate instead to facilitate her escape from it. Thus, in the aftermath of "a week of more suffering than I have had for a long time"—seven days full of obstacles "which the hand that would be drawing beautiful lines must be always busy in brushing away"—Fuller realizes that "at such times the soul rises up. . . . casts aside his shrouds and bands, rosy and fresh from the long trance, undismayed, not seeing how to get out, yet sure there is a way" (qtd. in *Memoirs* 2: 135). Only moments after making this connection, Fuller records her famous epiphany concerning her emerging "sovereign" subjectivity: "The Woman in me kneels and weeps in tender rapture; the Man in me rushes forth, but only to be baffled. Yet the time will come, when, from the union of this tragic king and queen, shall be born a radiant sovereign self" (qtd. in *Memoirs* 2: 136). In this instance, what pain inaugurates is not simply transcendence but a specifically transgendered vision of it; indeed, Fuller implies that the "way out" resides in precisely such forms. Moreover, while her "radiant" epiphany might seem idealized and metaphoric, what inspires it is materiality and metonymy—or, to use Fuller's exact words, "a week of suffering" and the act of "brushing away." At such moments, pain seems an essential precondition for Fuller's transcendent visions.

For Fuller, then, it is not physical womanhood so much as physical weakness (the two are not, for her, equivalences) that best demonstrates the nexus between materiality and spirituality. Similarly, it is illness, not womanliness, that provides the keenest glimpse into spiritual existence. In short, what Fuller repudiates is not the body or pain but gender; to be precise, she displaces gender from physical to spiritual nature, thereby allowing woman the chance to fulfill at last her (always pending, "not yet" achieved) promise of being "electrical in movement, intuitive in function, spiritual in tendency" (*Woman* 102). The body thus emerges not as the physiological site of gender but as the physical source of metaphysical insights into the intersections between nature and soul, suffering and transcendence.

To the extent that she succeeds in making the body, even the suffering body, both literate and articulate, Fuller counters Elaine Scarry's claim in her *The Body in Pain* that of all bodily experiences, from hunger to fear, love to hate, pain lacks an external referent and hence resists objectification in language. According to Scarry, pain destroys language and voice and thereby robs the self of power and author-ity. Scarry claims, in fact, that "resistance to language" is an *essential* characteristic of pain: "Intense pain is ... language-destroying: as the content of one's world disintegrates, so the content of one's language disintegrates; as the self disintegrates, so that which would express and project the self is robbed of its source and subject" (35). Yet in Fuller's case, pain is not opposed to language or transcendence but can be a powerful catalyst for each. Reversing and inverting Scarry's formula, Fuller suggests that *acceptance* of pain is *essential* to language—that experiencing the depths and heights of pain can yield, even or especially during its most intense moments, some of the sufferer's most articulate descriptions of liberation or elevation.

As with the other writers I've addressed in this chapter, then, Fuller does not seek to ignore or diminish the body; she certainly does not reduce it to its sensations. Her aim is to make the body, even in its most excruciating moments, a viable, inspirational ground for speech. In this regard, Fuller's private experiences as suffering body no longer seem disjunct from *Woman*'s more radiant portraits. Reading *Woman* alongside her more private musings, we can understand both text and context better if we recognize them as mutually informing, particularly since Fuller's own uplifting response to physical suffering doubtless fortified her belief, firmly conveyed in *Woman*, that transcendence is possible even for those most physically encumbered. More to the point, there are a number of fundamental similarities between private and published accounts. In both, Fuller works to dissolve, or at least render porous, the opposition between the body and soul, retaining the former as vehicle for the latter. Formally, Fuller's conviction that body and soul are intertwined is expressed through the manuscript's weaving together of stories of prostitutes and mythical women, of vivid descriptions of forced sex and paeans to women's "flowing," "breathing," "singing" soul (103). This downbeat-upbeat pattern not only harmonizes classic oppositions but, ultimately, strategically bolsters Fuller's insistence on the possibility and necessity of transcendence for even the most circumscribed of women; in Fuller's opus, the deeper the basenote, the greater the need to syncopate the beat.

Additional parallels might also be adduced, including that between Fuller's personal insights into the contingent, oscillating nature of embodied subjectivity and the fluctuations that define *Woman*'s voice, rhythm, and style. The lessons its author learned from her intermittently painful existence qualify as one potential "true life" source for *Woman*'s celebration of flux at both the syntactic and the semantic levels. While Fuller's belief in the socially constructed and potentially changeable nature of gender might seem a more obvious basis, we should remember that during her lifetime Fuller could only wish that gender would prove contingent, while her migraines repeatedly taught her how transient and potentially uplifting physical circumscription of a different sort could be.

In this respect, Orestes Brownson's metaphor of illness, used in his review of *Woman* to convey the formal "uneasiness" he finds in Fuller's prose—"She is feverish," he concludes, "and turns from one side of the bed to the other, but finds no relief" (19–20)—can be taken quite literally. As Emerson reflects in the *Memoirs*, Fuller was often "in jubilant spirits in the morning, and ended the day with nervous headache, whose spasms ... produced total prostration" (1: 227). Both men's descriptions are not only apt but revealing: Fuller's "feverishness," her alternating between "jubilation" and "prostration," is characteristic not only of her "true life" but of *Woman*'s very cadence and substance.

Emerson's description of Fuller's reaction to pain as "total prostration" is also revealing in a different sense—one well suited to my argument here, as it evokes the kind of suffering upon which sentimental metamorphoses hinge. As I have discussed, within a sentimental iconography femininity is typically personified by a physically frail and emotionally overwrought figure, a potential casting of her own pain-filled subjectivity that Fuller throughout her career sought to elude. Yet although Fuller clearly disdained highly wrought writing, from a certain perspective her own contingent experience of pain evokes sentimentalism's imbrication of physical weakness and spiritual elevation. After all, for Fuller, the experience of pain did reveal how intricately connected (rather than merely opposed) the material and spiritual realms actually were—a connection also illuminated within sentimental formulas. Fuller's personal history could be interpreted, then, as bearing out the lessons of sentimental scenarios: physical frailty can indeed lead to transcendence and even bliss. And yet, to view this trajectory as somehow sentimental is to ignore the extent to which Fuller herself vehemently resisted sentimentalizing her personal history. If Fuller's published prose does in fact celebrate a kind of spiritual elevation that, as in sentimentalism, is intricately linked to suffering, we ought not to forget that Fuller thoroughly excises any possible suffering subtext. What she foregrounds and even isolates in works like *Woman* is the transcendental afterglow that lingers in pain's wake.

Given Fuller's resistance to what she saw as a debasing sentimentality, it is all the more disturbing that attempts to account for her life and work posthumously not only restore this suffering subtext but explicitly sentimentalize it. Despite Fuller's insistence on transcendence and contingency in her lifetime, contemporaries who reflected on Fuller's life after her death tended to accentuate her gendered, suffering existence, dwelling, as Higginson did, on the fact that Fuller was a "martyr to ill-health" (89), or even exulting, as Hawthorne did, that she proved "a very woman, after all" (Cowley 659). One explanation for the bias of these postmortems lies in the fact that the editors of the *Memoirs* decidedly skewed them toward embodiment despite their subject's ardent emphasis on transcendence. The *Memoirs'* editors, Emerson, Channing, and James Freeman Clarke, notoriously blacked out and excised passages from Fuller's papers in order to highlight her prolonged suffering and essential womanliness, after all. "Of" her but not "by" her, the *Memoirs* have proven instrumental in the process not just of representing Margaret Fuller but of re-membering her. They have restored, through editorial comments and offhand remarks, a circumscribed, sentimental materiality that Fuller spent her brief life struggling to defy. Among other things, this bias indicates the compilers' impulse to opt for the simplest frame available whereas Fuller's own inclination was to opt whenever possible for complexity. It also documents the tenacity of conventions casting any potential links between degradation and transcendence, however radical in intent, as inherently sentimental.

This certainly holds true for Arthur Fuller's efforts to paint a more "womanly" portrait of his sister in the 1855 edition of *Woman*; his preface pays "tribute to her domestic virtues and fidelity to all home duties" (v) at the expense of her intellectual abilities. Even Horace Greeley, Fuller's usually supportive boss at the *Tribune*, remarked after her death that "great and noble as [Fuller] was, a good husband and two or three bouncing babies would have emancipated her from a great deal of cant and nonsense" (qtd. in Douglas *Feminization* 280). Even before she died, critics were wont to make much of Fuller's physical and gendered identity despite her contrary intentions. For instance, in his 1846 essay "Sarah Margaret Fuller" for *Godey's*, Poe concludes a disparaging survey of his subject's ideas by conjuring up for the reader her "personal" physical presence (Poe 39). By traveling from concept to corporeality, Poe essentially reverses the teleology Fuller sought to instantiate.

Henry James is one of the few authors whose comments on Fuller after her death attempt to deal with her as a more or less abstract entity. Intriguingly, in James's formulation it is not Fuller's actual and imposing presence—"Margaret's mountainous me," as Emerson put it—that looms large, but a ghost-like apparition. James confides his anxious and often condescending musings about the "Margaret-ghost" who haunts him and other writers in "The Last of the Valerii" (1874), in his biography of *Hawthorne* (1879), and most conspicuously in his biographical study of *William Wetmore Story and His Friends* (1903). In the last of these, James identifies "the unquestionably haunting Margaret-ghost" and ponders "the wonderment of *why* she may, to any such degree, be felt as haunting" (qtd. in Rowe 39). An answer to James's question may lie in Fuller's having assumed, after death, the disembodied, spiritual identity she so ardently wished to personify during life.

As each of these critical reassessments suggest, Fuller's attempts to defy simplistic understandings of form would prove not only radical with respect to the culture of sentiment and the emergent ideology of biological determinism. They would also prove utopian in light of both Fuller's own often troublesome relationship to the flesh and others' attempts to simplify and domesticate that relationship. All three of the women I've discussed here sought in their respective writings not just to defy the reductive equation of identity and physicality but to reconfigure the physical so as to unveil its hidden potential and complexity. Each adopted (or adapted) forms of writing in hopes of extending spiritual release even to the weak of flesh and spirit, and they each did so without necessarily explicitly acknowledging this preliminary weakness.

As Fuller's example, makes clear, however, others could quite easily step in to foreground what an author herself omitted. Fuller famously concludes in *Woman* that "It is not woman, but the law of right, the law of growth, that speaks in us, and demands the perfection of each being in its kind" (177). Yet, the sentimentalized, somaticized re-presentation of Fuller after her death demonstrates that such questions as "what speaks in us?" and "when?" may ultimately be less important than "who's listening?" and "how are those who speak being heard?"—questions that Alcott, always savvy about her market and audience, and Hunt, convinced of the inadequacies of isolated suffering as a ground for subjectivity, insisted upon asking as well as answering beforehand. To the extent that my analysis offers provisional answers to these questions on Fuller's behalf, it is my hope that what now remains audible is not simply a naked cry of pain but also the conjoined, ecstatic sigh that signals pain's surcease.

# 3

## Irregular Yet Balanced

*Elizabeth Stuart Phelps's and William Dean Howells's Woman Doctor Novels*

In what sense might we conclude that a body, corporeal or textual, is closed or finite? And can such a conclusion itself ever be considered conclusive? Although these questions might seem tediously postmodern, this chapter proves that they have been preoccupying diverse thinkers for well over a century.

In the fall of 1872, Doctor Edward H. Clarke of Harvard University was invited to address the New England Women's Club in Boston. There he delivered a jeremiad-cum-lecture on the potentially pernicious influence of education upon women's sexual development. His thesis stirred up so much interest (and ire) that approximately a year later he published an expanded version of the speech as the controversial *Sex in Education* (1873). During a time when women's colleges and co-educational institutions were both multiplying and gaining credibility, Clarke's treatise struck a dire note of caution, providing an answer to "the woman question" that few "new women" wanted to hear but that—if only because of its rapid dissemination as formidable scientific "truth"—still fewer could afford to ignore.

In *Sex in Education*, Clarke proposes that the solution to the woman "problem" could be derived from "physiology, not from ethics or metaphysics" (12). While conceding that both sexes share the same nutritive and nervous systems, and that bourgeois women's fashion and diet contribute to disease, Clarke pinpoints biology and co-education as primary culprits and calls for gender-distinct educational systems based on gender-distinct reproductive systems. Schools that treat male and female students exactly alike ignore to their peril "the periodical movements which characterize and influence woman's structure for more than half her terrestrial life, and which, in their ebb and flow, sway every fibre and thrill every nerve of her body a dozen times a year" (26–27). Neglecting such functions might make the female student an exceptional scholar but an aberrant woman, her ovaries and breasts shriveled and deformed, her children, if she was capable of bearing any, sickly and neurotic.

The theory undergirding Clarke's treatise is that of the body as a closed energy system. It is Clarke's fundamental premise that "the system never does two things well at the same time" (40). Therefore, should a woman expend too much energy in rigorous study during her reproductive years, "the results are monstrous brains and puny bodies; abnormally weak digestion; flowing thought and constipated bowels; lofty aspirations and neuralgic sensations" (41).[1] The demands Nature makes upon girls should always outweigh those made by her studies; reversing these priorities will, Clarke warns, inevitably result in debilitating physiological consequences.

In so concluding, Clarke borrows from English social theorist Herbert Spencer, who popularized in such works as *First Principles* (1864) and the two-volume *Principles of Biology* (1866–67) his theory of the body as a finite system, where expenditures in one area are necessarily offset by economizing in another. As a "vital aggregate" the body will always "counter-balance" any "extra dissipation of force" through a process Spencer identifies as "equilibration" (*First Principles* 483–517). According to Spencer, an organism always strives for "consensus": the continuous redistribution of energy therein means that mental and bodily processes are always "quantitatively correlated to certain energies expended in their production, and to certain other energies which they initiate." These correlations exemplify what Spencer called the principle of "the persistence of force," by which he meant that "each manifestation of force can be interpreted only as the effect of some antecedent force" (*First* 221; see also *Principles of Biology* vol. 1, esp. 167–200). In Spencer's account of bodily processes, energy is never expended in a vacuum; it is always but a link in a chain extending backwards and forwards indefinitely. Nor, according to Spencer, is this process of expenditure generic; rather, it is modified according to specifically gendered physiological requirements. Spencer believed that women have lagged behind men developmentally because the greater portion of a woman's allotted energy is (and ought to be) devoted to reproductive processes, leaving less energy for mental and physical stimulation ("Development Hypothesis," 1–7). In Spencer's view, healthy physical, mental, and emotional balance for a woman necessarily entailed just such an evolutionary imbalance.

Although Spencer and his ideas would attain a remarkable popularity in America, Clarke's application of the British philosopher's naturalized economic model provoked a decidedly mixed response.[2] In the wake of *Sex in Education* came numerous rebuttals in editorial and book-length form, including two books published in 1874: Eliza Bisbee Duffey's popular *No Sex in Education*, and a collection of essays edited by Julia Ward Howe under the title *Sex and Education* (its titular displacement of Clarke's prepositional "in" with the conjunction "and" is indicative of the volume's larger deontologizing project). To discredit Clarke's central arguments, Howe compiled an anthology of refuting testimony from several colleges and universities along with contributions from such notables as Thomas Wentworth Higginson, Mrs. Horace Mann, and Elizabeth Stuart Phelps.[3] Among the refuters, Higginson, a former Harvard classmate of Clarke's, insists that the doctor could only have concluded as decisively as he does by overgeneralizing from a few specific cases. We cannot truly know whether co-education was a physiological success or failure, Higginson counters, until the "comparative physiology of American women in different localities" (37), "of different races" (38), and "of different social positions" (39) are taken into account. And even were such a comprehensive study to substantiate Clarke's hypotheses, this should not in all fairness preclude an acknowledgment of the "*physiological benefits of education for women*"—benefits Higginson faults Clarke for taking "absolutely no account of" (41).

Higginson's call for greater balance is echoed by Elizabeth Stuart Phelps in her contribution to the volume. Yet for Phelps, the imbalance lies not simply (à la Higginson) in Clarke's theory, nor (à la Clarke) in female bodies. What Phelps takes issue with up front is the medium in which Clarke's theories are couched. That is, her critique extends beyond Clarke's theory of the body as closed energy system to his text presented as such; her own essay, she suggests, provides a much-needed counterpoint to a study she finds neither balanced nor finite. Her opening statement demonstrates that Phelps's initial objections arise over issues of form: "the only really serious thing about Dr. Clarke's book is the confusion of the author's ideas as to the precise defining line between a work adapted to popular instruction and a medical treatise" (126). Phelps contends that although Clarke's book was written for and widely disseminated among a lay audience, his tone conjures up a professor offering conclusive facts before his medical students—as if he were "a theorist who does not desire to be answered" (126). Whatever his intentions, however, according to Phelps the doctor's tract cries out for a balancing response, for an "essay ... written to mate it," whether that reply comes from a fellow physician best suited to address Clarke's clinical points or a woman best suited to reply to Clarke's representation of womanhood (127). Even as she naturalizes expertise as an inherent property of one's professional or gender role, Phelps highlights the inconclusiveness of Clarke's seemingly definitive essay by claiming that "the physician is not the person whose judgment upon a matter involving the welfare of women can possibly be final. His testimony ... is but a link in a chain" (127–28).[4] While Clarke suggests that his treatise represents the last word on the subject of sex in education, Phelps's polemic belabors the fact that he has only started a dialogue, not stopped one.

According to Phelps, indeterminacy is not just a property of Clarke's text but the bodies Clarke erroneously represents as finite. In her rejoinder, Phelps contends that the meaning of womanhood will always exceed any single framework, especially where that frame is reductively physiological: "a question so intricate and shifting as that which involves the exact position of woman in the economy of a cursed world is not to be settled by the proximate principles of the human frame, with the proportions of the gray and white matter in the brain, or with the transitional character of the tissues and the exquisite machinery of the viscera" (128). As we are more than biology, we are more than those who study biology say we are; in order to acquire a fuller picture of womanhood, one must consult not only the doctor and the woman herself but the psychologist, the theologian, the political economist, and so on (128). There is in Phelps's understanding of subjectivity what Mikhail Bakhtin insists holds true of all individuals:

an individual cannot be completely incarnated into the flesh of existing sociohistorical categories. There is no mere form that would be able to incarnate once and forever all of his human possibilities and needs, no form in which he could exhaust himself down to the last word . . . .no form that he could fill to the very brim, and yet at the same time not splash over the brim. There always remains an unrealized surplus of humanness. (37)

Bakhtin's playful use of "form" here—connoting as it does both corporeality and textuality—testifies not only to the complex relations between ideologies of bodily and textual forms but to the persistence of a surplus which will always overflow any perceived limit—a sense intimated in Phelps's conclusion as well.

Phelps's rebuttal does not end by identifying and insisting upon this necessary surplus, however. Directly refuting Clarke's theorems, Phelps maintains that the mind and body stand in a relation not of *compensatory* but of *commensurate* force. Reversing Clarke's conclusions point by point and sounding a theme the mother whose name she adopted had also expounded, Phelps argues that women are not sickened by studying but enfeebled the moment they stop doing so: the nineteenth-century girl is "made an invalid by the plunge from the 'healing influences' of systematic brain exertion to the broken, jagged life which awaits a girl whose 'education is completed.' Made an invalid by exchanging the wholesome pursuit of sufficient and worthy aims for the unrelieved routine of a dependent domestic life, from which all aim has departed" (135). Phelps's critique of biologized notions of equilibrium does not discard balance as the ideal state but instead redefines its constitutive elements. According to Phelps, the *lack* of energy flowing to one area—i.e., the brain—triggers a similar depletion in the rest of a woman's body, resulting in the enervation characteristic of invalidism. Phelps thus frames the conservation of mental energy as *draining* energy from other vital processes rather than *dynamizing* them. Rather than concentrating the majority of one's available energy in a single organ in order to ensure its vital functioning and the organism's overall health, Phelps advocates proportioning that energy to create a healthy, commensurate balance among the body's various systems—a balance achieved not via the reconciliation of negative and positive energy sources but by stabilizing equally positive supplies. Phelps concludes this in an essay where she also, somewhat contradictorily, points out that the essence of womanhood is never a function of biology alone, that there will always be something extra or even excessive that strictly biological explanations cannot account for.

In the end, Phelps strategically appropriates this surplus to benefit not just women's bodies but women's texts, with her own setting the example. Just as a woman, to be healthy, should maintain a dynamic equilibrium while remaining aware that such physiological balance by no means incarnates or ensures health and happiness, so, too, does Phelps's rebutting essay seek to balance out Clarke's while ultimately tilting the balance in her favor with its insistence on an identity that surpasses biological frameworks. For Phelps, compensation is a goal worth pursuing only *between* rather than *within* forms, and it is a goal best achieved by refusing and refuting the conclusiveness of seemingly delimited, seemingly proportionate entities.

Several years after her critique of Clarke was published, Phelps returns—in correspondence with her editor at *Atlantic Monthly*, William Dean Howells—to the question of balance, this time tackling the desired symmetry between art and life. Ironically, despite her already noted objections to Spencerian theories when applied to corporeal forms, Phelps's mimetic concerns owe a debt to the British philosopher—as we see when Phelps praises Spencer in an 1881 letter to Howells. This letter, whose ostensible purpose was to discuss the pending serialization of her novel *Doctor Zay* (1882), closes with a reminder of Spencer's contention in *First Principles* that realism stands at the endpoint of literary evolution. Paraphrasing Spencer's evolutionary views from memory, Phelps writes, "'Even the modern novel' he said, 'begins to show a tendency to diverge from the "plots" which rarely occur in actual life.'" Phelps cites this tendency approvingly immediately following her criticism of Howells's most recent novel, *Doctor Breen's Practice* (1881), for not being "a fair example of professional women" ("To Howells" 1881). Even as Phelps's critique explicitly links mimetic representation to "fair" (i.e., not simply just but balanced) portrayals, it also suggests that she believed her own pending doctor-novel would compensate by providing a verisimilitude that the story by the "Dean" of American literary realism had forsaken.

In particular ways, *Doctor Zay* continues Phelps's dialogue with

Clarke but expands this conversation to include Howells himself. Responding to Clarke, Phelps had argued that the best person to invalidate the doctor's spurious claims would be a woman physician, whose gender and professional identity single her out as the ideal respondent to Clarke's claims (130). In *Doctor Zay*, Phelps gives this female doctor a voice to countermand the testimony offered not only in Clarke's but in Howells's medical narratives, each of which, albeit with varying degrees of urgency, ultimately concludes that a woman had best conserve her energy for marriage.

Recently, feminist narratologists have demonstrated that many women writers distrusted such conventional conclusions and preferred more open-ended understandings of formal structures.[5] For example, Rachel Blau DuPlessis claims that the writers she studies intervene at the level of both sentence and sequence to disrupt the heterosexual imperative that determines the outcome of so many narratives of women's lives. As a result, these authors—themselves often marginal to hegemonic social scripts—render ambivalent what others might conceive of as a "happily ever after," frequently substituting different, more communal understandings of happiness in convention's stead (4–6).

DuPlessis's theory, however, pertains almost exclusively to twentieth-century narratives; Phelps's novels, on the other hand, appeared at a time when happy, heterosexual endings were generally *de rigueur*—when, in the end, and by conjoined ideological and narratalogical imperatives, the female *Bildung* plot no longer diverged from but more often than not was collapsed into the romance plot (typically, it was either this collapse or the only other viable outcome, death). At least initially, Phelps's project as a novelist seemed to include resisting such closural pressures and adhering to her own moral-political agenda. For example, her belief that marriage might signal not a "happy ending" but the end of happiness is evinced in *The Silent Partner* (1871), where Phelps's heroine refuses to marry in order to remain true to her ideals, and in *The Story of Avis* (1877), where marriage is presented as posing disastrous consequences to the aspiring woman artist.[6] How, then, to explain the fact that the story of her independent heroine Doctor Zay concludes with Zay's surrender—and that is precisely the word for it—to an eager suitor?

One explanation would be that this promised marriage represents the surest way—within both the culture and the format in which Phelps was working—for the author to lend an air of normalcy to her "irregular" female homeopath; fusing as it does the professional plot with the marriage plot, it would seem to prove that the heroine is capable of achieving the "rewards" of both at once. All the same, this conclusion bears an eerie resemblance to the ones prescribed by Clarke and inscribed in Howells's novel. Indeed, the very forces that bring *Doctor Zay* to a close parallel those Phelps found so objectionable when she criticized Clarke's and Howells's unfair and unrealistic portraits. Not only does the love match with which the narrative ends suggest that Zay (originally portrayed as inherently equilibrious) does require some outside stabilizing force; it conjoins marriage and closure and thereby seemingly acquiesces to the naturalized, heterosexual prescriptions for women's health offered by the likes of Clarke and Spencer and, in fictional form, by writers including Howells. Rather than providing counterbalance to what Phelps perceived to be the distortions of these earlier narratives, in the end *Doctor Zay* seems merely to be reprising them.

But is this actually what happens at the end? At first glance, the novel's ending may seem to replicate the ideologies of balance and closure Phelps elsewhere protests. Alternately, however—and, I think, more accurately—the ending could be seen as signaling the onset of imbalance and indefinition. For the very feat—marriage—which for Clarke and Howells represents a "symmetrical" resolution instigates in Phelps's novel a form of dissymmetry which defies correction even as it renders any conclusion inconclusive. Given that it is at the point of closure that theories of finite economic systems are both tested and contested, *Doctor Zay*'s ending may be understood as representing an attempt to reconcile the author's simultaneous and potentially contradictory commitments to commensurability and surplus—and, failing this, as indicating an ultimate faith in the latter as a more vital necessity than the former. What *Doctor Zay*'s denouement seeks to instantiate, in short, is a realistic but not necessarily unhappy (or unhealthy) ending that effectively retains the "happy surplus" guaranteed even the most apparently bounded frame. The novelist's efforts to satisfy both goals at once amounts to what we might call a real balancing act, one that I will argue is accomplished on behalf of *Doctor Zay*'s form at the expense of Dr. Zay's form. But first, in the following sections, I want to take a moment to trace the pressures conventional mimetic and closural mandates place upon given forms, generic and individual, textual and corporeal, and to explicate by historicizing how theories of equilibrium and disequilibrium contribute to the designation of certain plots, certain endings as more healthy or realistic than other more "happy" or less proportionate ones.

∽

In addition to expounding the principles of life, Herbert Spencer ventured on several occasions to outline those underlying literature, envisioning both life and literature organically. As Phelps reminded Howells, in *First Principles* Spencer contends that literature has (or, at least, should have) evolved in dialectical relationship with life from a rudimentary, unrealistic brand of storytelling toward more advanced compositions reflecting all of life's intricacy and coherence. Unlike the "unnatural" stories of "primitive times," lacking both "natural connexion" and "natural sequence," "a good modern work of imagination" depicts events which as products of a complex individual in a complex historical moment "cannot at will be changed in their order or kind, without injuring or destroying the general effect." As human nature is in Spencer's mind relatively fixed from the beginning, to be true to life no miraculous fictional metamorphoses can or should occur. In contrast to those "crude" works whose characters are incoherent and static—unmodified by interaction with other characters or involvement in events—"mature" works allow change to occur slowly, in the vortex of "complex moral relations" and as a result of characters "acting and re-acting upon one another's natures" (326–27). Synergy in the art form, like that in the human form, is achieved only through such interactions and reactions. In Spencer's lexicon, evolved literary forms are those whose representations reflect an "increasing density of matter" compensated by "a loss of relative motion" (327)—in other words, they trade unlimited agency for a deeper materialism. Given that this same trade-off is integral to literary realism, it is little wonder that Spencer praised this mode as evolution's apotheosis or that the realists and "new realists" would find in Spencer substantiation of their own increasingly deterministic understandings of human nature.

For Spencer, literary balance reflects not only a culture's maturity but an author's. In a lesser-known earlier essay entitled "The Philosophy of Style" (1852), Spencer represents literary works as relatively vital aggregates depending on a writer's use of Anglo-Saxon words, his organic sense of style, and his "natural aptitude" ("Philosophy" 1). Indeed, Spencer suggests that "the habitual mode of utterance depends on the habitual balance of the nature" (41) of the author, and hence that the complexity and balance of a writer's representations reflect the complexity and balance of the writer himself. One can only imagine the creative pressure such views placed on authors influenced by Spencer's theories—as both Howells and Phelps were, to varying degrees.

Spencer was not alone in tying the health of an author's composition to the capacity to create complex and symmetrical literary works. Roughly two years before writing his own novel featuring a female doctor, *The Bostonians* (1886), Henry James famously described in "The Art of Fiction" (1884) what to his mind was the erroneous equation between "good" novels and "happy" endings. Some people, James suggests, think that a novel's quality "depends on a 'happy ending,' on a distribution at the last of prizes, pensions, husbands, wives, babies, millions, appended paragraphs, and cheerful remarks.... The 'ending' of a novel is, for many persons, like that of a good dinner, a course of dessert and ices, and the artist in fiction is regarded as a sort of *meddlesome doctor* who forbids agreeable aftertastes" (168–69, emphasis added). As opposed to those who spoon out saccharine prose, James's doctor-like "artist" knows that such syrup is toxic and, for a reader's own good, offers instead a taste of his own more subtle medicine. In the process, James deftly links realism and health at the same time that he characterizes conventional "happily ever afters" as not only implausible but potentially noxious.

For realism, narrative closure typically produces as many problems as it resolves. Stories must end, even realist ones, but these endings connote a finality rarely sensed in the reality the realists sought to depict as accurately and transparently as possible. It is in the final pages of realist fictions that the struggle for mimesis often appears most intense and most doomed. Indeed, two frequently interwoven aims of American literary realism—verisimilitude and proportion—often work at cross-purposes when it comes time for the narratives to close.[7] In theory if not always in fact, James solves (or sidesteps) such conundrums by proposing formal symmetry as compensation for a reality he suggests is inherently unstable and ragged. This helps to explain why James's ridicule of certain types of endings does not extend to the concept of closure itself. In fact, his distinction between art and life rests on just such a conceit: "Really, universally, relations stop nowhere, and the exquisite problem of the artist is eternally but to draw, by a geometry of his own, the circle within which they shall *happily appear* to do so" ("Preface" 5, emphasis added). James's skilled artist lends a finitude to the "one bright book of life" that is inherently lacking in life itself. But this finitude is the product of great art(ifice), not of a narrative's inherent content. For James, the "happiness" of an "exquisite" story is determined by highly crafted formal balance, not implausible thematic imbalance.

Whether addressing formal or thematic elements, narratologists tend to join James in focusing on the ending as the site at which narrative equilibrium is most typically gauged.[8] According to Frank Kermode, we engage with art as well as life because we want to make sense of and in them, and it is often at the end of each that this sense is both sought and conferred. Explicitly psychologizing such needs, Peter Brooks analogizes narrative closure and death as well as the compulsion toward either. Brooks argues that "the sense of a beginning ... must in some important way be determined by the sense of an ending. We might say that we are able to read present moments—in literature and, by extension, in life—as endowed with narrative meaning only because we read them in anticipation of the structuring power of those endings that will retrospectively give them the order and significance of plot" (*Reading* 94). In essence, Brooks proposes that were it not for an ending, for the fact that both narratives and lives do end, both literature and life would lack meaning and structure. These critics make manifest what is latent in James's argument, which is that closure is never merely an inherent formal necessity but always also a sign of historical pressure.

What unites these variant narratological approaches is the notion of compensation. Compensatory theories of narrative suggest that its forward-driving energies are dedicated to offsetting the tensions and imbalances that inaugurate a story. As D. A. Miller has argued, the "narratable" forces that motivate an author to pick up a pen include "instances of disequilibrium, suspense, and general insufficiency" (ix). A story's relative conclusiveness thus represents an attempt to compensate for the inconclusiveness of life. Such narratological theories share with Spencer's or Clarke's corporeal ones an organic conception of form, wherein equilibrium is the ultimate goal if not always the actual outcome. Turning now from narrative theory toward narrative itself, it seems clear that both Howells's and Phelps's respective woman doctor novels are motivated by a desire for equilibrium. Where they differ is over how they define imbalance and balance, and how they seek to trade the former for the latter.

⁓

In an epoch still reeling in the aftermath of the Civil War and from the onslaught of rapid industrial and technological advances, William Dean Howells looked to realism as a means of healing these and other rifts in the social fabric. He also saw it as means of offsetting the overly "passionate" plots and endings he associated with "romanticistic" novels. Howells's theory of realism defines its essential texts as providing fictional ballasts in an apparently unstable and destabilizing real world. As Amy Kaplan has persuasively argued, "realism is not to reflect passively a solid reality; it is to face the paradoxical imperative to use fiction to combat the fictionality of everyday life; unable to anchor itself in a stable referent, it must restore or construct a new sense of the real" (20). As do Clarke and James, Howells starts from the perception of an instability, diagnoses this state as unhealthy, then tries to correct it through a theory of formal compensation.

For Howells as for many other realists, it wasn't simply the social body but the individual one that could appear incoherent. The instability in Howells's personal life around the time the author commenced his "Realism War" must have lent an urgency to his drive to create stable forms. In the early 1880s, his wife Elinor was beginning her slow slide into invalidism and his cherished daughter Winnie developed the mysterious illness that culminated in her untimely death at the end of the decade. Never a well man himself, Howells suffered from what was to prove one in a series of nervous breakdowns around the time that he was completing *Doctor Breen's Practice* and composing *A Modern Instance* (late Fall, 1881).[9] In the aftermath of a subsequent breakdown while writing *The Rise of Silas Lapham* (1884), Howells described these bouts as making him feel like "the bottom dropped out" (qtd. in Cady, *Road* 244). For both the realist and the genre he embraced, maintaining a grip on reality entailed maintaining a sense of a stable ground.

For Howells, realism mattered because it conferred a stability ostensibly lacking in real life. Yet ironically, to depict life as possessing this stability was to risk swerving from mimetic representation into idealism. At one point, Howells acknowledged the impossibility of his mandate that art be true to life even as he nonetheless strove for this verisimilitude: "As a matter of fact," Howells asserts, "we see nothing whole, neither life nor art. We are so made, in soul and in sense, that we can deal only with parts, with points, with degrees; and the endeavor to compass any entirety must involve a discomfort and a danger very threatening to our intellectual integrity" (*My Literary Passions* 202). It's not that life or art lacks wholeness, necessarily, but that our inevitably partial perspective prevents us from accessing this whole and may even imperil the writer who makes the attempt. What the artist may not be able to perceive he could, however, create, although not without accompanying "discomfort."

Regardless, Howells continued to insist that a realistic literary work ought to be crafted with symmetry foremost in mind. Hence his proposal in "Novel Writing and Reading" that "the business of the novelist is ... to arrange a perspective for you with everything in its proper relation and proportion to everything else" (*Selected Literary Criticism* [*SLC*] 231). Such a conclusion supports Kaplan's contention that Howellsian realism is primarily about balance, about the effort to "frame a plenitude of details within a coherent form" (46). Howells's depiction of a novelist's "business" also lends credence to Leo Bersani's claim that realism is "a form which provides this society with a reassuring myth about itself. The realistic novel gives us an image of social fragmentation contained within the order of significant form—and it thereby suggests that the chaotic fragments are somehow socially viable and morally redeemable" (60–61). Yet Bersani's further contention that the realist's investment in his project stems from the writer's "reassuring belief in psychological unity and intelligibility" and his "blindness" to "the psychic discontinuities and incoherence from which all our fragmented experience ultimately derives" (61–62) does not pertain to Howells, who was fully aware of psychic and social instability. In Howells's case, it is not his blindness to but his cognizance of disorder that lent his investment in proportion such intensity.

Howells's emphasis on proportionality also resonates with Spencer's ideas about the compensatory nature of literary forms. Biographical evidence suggests that Howells had at least one ear open to the British philosopher's views.[10] His neighbor, John Fiske, was an ardent Spencerian and often spoke to Howells of his enthusiasm. Even though Edwin H. Cady stipulates that Howells's Swedenborgian roots undercut his zeal for Spencer (*Road* 149–51), the influence of Spencer's evolutionary theories remains undeniable (Van Wyck Brooks 61). As Donald Pizer insists in *Literary Realism and Naturalism*, Howells was clearly persuaded by evolutionary critics and eagerly applied scientific theories to literature. Howells certainly shared with Spencer (and with Hippolyte Taine) the belief that truthfulness, sincerity, and vigor represent literary maturity while a naive idealism epitomizes an immature stage. The road to realism constitutes the road to progress, not only in terms of formal and technical improvements but for the way its dedication to the truth reflects the evolved state of its readers and writers. Howells's evolutionary thinking is pronounced in such essays as "What Should Girls Read?," where he maintains that "[l]iterature is the biography of the race ... it forms the consciousness of civilization, and marks the far way which the enlightened man has come from being a savage" (*SLC* 235). A society thus evolving, according to Howells, "require[s] of a novelist whom they respect unquestionable proof of his seriousness, if he proposes to deal with certain phases of life; they require a sort of scientific decorum. He can no longer expect to be received on the grounds of entertainment only; he assumes a higher function, something like that of a physician or a priest, and they expect him to be bound by laws as sacred as those of such professions" ("Propriety in Fiction" *SLC* 120–21). Like his friend James, Howells compares the realist artist to a physician and deems each's practice scientific, venerable, and, as a result, valuable. Like James as well, Howells divorces art from popular entertainment. And like Spencer, he suggests that realism as an elevated art form is alone capable of reflecting life's complexity and scale.

Recently, Michael Davitt Bell has argued that Howells's translation of art as science foregrounds his resistance to art as style. Bell traces this resistance to Howells's repugnance, from boyhood onward, for literary craft as both effeminate and effeminizing. As did Henry James during

Howells's lifetime, Bell bemoans this aversion; but Bell takes James's critique of Howells's apparent antipathy for style a step further by arguing that "the apparent *problem* of Howellsian realism—its persistent denigration of the 'literary'—is in fact one of its principal tenets" (21). In order to seem the more "natural" and "real," Bell contends, Howellsian realism by definition lacks a theory of fictional representation; defiantly, it refuses to take account of the novel as form. While Bell's argument is not without merit, it seems to me to overstate the case. In particular, it overlooks Howells's recurring insistence on the need for formal proportion, compensation, and coherence—what Harold Kolb, one of the few critics to acknowledge and explore the formal dimensions of American literary realism, describes as the realists' commitment to "the concept of organic form, the appropriateness of technique to subject" (58). Perhaps Bell concludes as he does because his argument is derived solely from Howells's literary criticism. But there is no simple or direct correspondence between discourse on the novel and novelistic discourse. While a theory of form may not be deducible from Howells's critical essays on realism, it may, as we'll see, be induced from his realist works.

⁓

Whether Howells liked it or not, realism did not evolve from and effectively replace idealism but co-existed alongside of it, with both veins struggling synchronously to survive. In fact, as Cady points out, readers began to criticize Howells's novels precisely when, in the late 1870s and early '80s, they began to diverge from their formerly vestigially sentimental cast. As example Cady cites one critic from this period who chastised Howells for his recent inclusion of "Holmes-inspired" representations with "all those physiological, psychological vagaries playing round simple characters in an everyday story" (qtd. in *Road* 195). Howells countered this criticism by contending that overidealized portraits were ultimately more rank: "and as far as morality goes I believe that when an artist tries to create an ideal he mixes some truth up with a vast deal of sentimentality and produces something. ... extremely noxious as well as nauseous" (qtd. in Cady, *Road* 233). It is idealism, not realism, that Howells finds potentially revolting, for its sentimental admixture not only pollutes but overrides the all-important truth. Nonetheless, Howells's definition of truthful fiction is not without its own traces of idealism, although what is idealized is the means by which closure is achieved rather than the narrative's content or message. Put another way, the idealism in Howells's theories of realism lies in his equation of the medium and the message, his insistence that the realist artist not only must but could create proportionate literary forms even though the glimpses of reality afforded us were often fragmentary, disproportionate, and potentially discomforting.

At the same time that the most ardent advocate of American literary realism could not utterly renounce idealism, proponents of idealism were arguing that their works "outrealed" the realists. Among those leading the "Idealism War" in its struggle for survival was Elizabeth Stuart Phelps. In her memoir *Chapters from a Life*, Phelps once again self-identifies (as she did in her letter to Howells discussing *Doctor Zay*) as an artist devoted to depicting "actual life," but she presents a distinctly different understanding of actuality than does Howells. For Phelps, it entails the conscientious truth to "an ideal of life rather than to life itself"—in fact, she considers such ameliorative representations not just her artistic but her Christian duty (250).

The dialogue between Phelps and Howells over what constitutes reality was inaugurated at least two decades earlier, in their correspondence over *Atlantic Monthly* contributions. Beginning as far back as 1874, Phelps resisted Howells's definitions of both realistic and great art, not to mention his collapsing of the two.[11] Responding to a letter in which Howells described some of Phelps's recently submitted poems as obscure, Phelps maintained that he and she held different understandings of clarity. Because Howells's misgivings caused her to doubt her own judgment, she had shown the proofs to an "uncritical," "unliterary" friend, and found her vindication in the fact that "He returned it with tears, without a word" ("To Howells" 1874). In Phelps's account the critical gaze's judgment is overridden by the tear-filled verdict. Yet while for Phelps tears signify an artwork's success, in *The Rise of Silas Lapham* Howells famously translates tears (idle tears) as "slop, silly slop"—i.e., as signs of a flawed sentimentality. Weeping functions in Howells's corpus not as a sign that the truth has been mined or expressed but as an obstacle thwarting its very telling.

Like Howells, Phelps conceives of the writer's role as telling the truth about the world and measures artistry by assessing the degree of truthfulness found in a given work. The difference lies in how each author defines "truth." Mentioning Howells specifically by name in *Chapters* as a member of the opposing "school," Phelps challenges his peremptory dismissal of such works as Stowe's *Uncle Tom's Cabin*, which Howells considered "marred by ... intense ethicism" (260).[12] Although she aligns herself with Stowe, Phelps acknowledges an overlap between Howells's realist aims and her own attempts to portray "life exactly as it is": "Now there is something obviously very familiar about this simple proposition; and, turning to trace the recognition down, one is amused to perceive that here is almost the precise language of the school [realism] to which one [Phelps] does not belong. Truth, like climate, is common property; and I venture to suggest that the issue between the two contending schools of literary art to-day is not so much *one of fact as of form*" (259, emphasis added). As Phelps puts it in her memoir, it is not what they represent—the truth of life—that separates Howellsian realism from her own more idealistic version, but how they represent it and where they locate it. Phelps herself situates this truth squarely in the moral realm; it is the duty of the artist in Phelps's schema to compose an ethical structure that makes "moral responsibility" (263) its central focus and governing precept.

Phelps's particular, idealistic twist on Spencerian evolutionary ideas is conspicuous in her contention that the struggle facing the nation is one which pits moral, not physical, adversaries against each other: "The last thirty years in America have pulsated with moral struggle. No phase of society has escaped it. It has ranged from social experiment to religious catechism, and to national upheaval. I suggest that even moral reforms, even civic renovations, might have their proper position in the artistic representation of a given age or stage in life" (265). Life entails a struggle over fitness, Phelps concedes, but this fitness is moral rather than physiological, and hence the novel that plots the moral struggle is inherently the most mimetic. As Phelps puts it, "since art implies the truthful and conscientious study of life as it is, we contend that to be a radically defective view of art which would preclude from it the ruling constituents of life. Moral character is to human life what air is to the natural world;—

it is elemental" (261). Defining morality as the "first principle" of life, Phelps insists that its "persistent force" ought to permeate and propel any realistic depiction of that life.

Rather than positing realism as a counterforce to idealism, Phelps establishes a commensurate relationship between the two schools. A work is balanced when the two are equally present, indeed when the two are recognized as indistinguishable. Her problem with realists like Howells is that they relegate moral impulses, if anywhere, to literary structure and seem to have no problem with morally ambiguous content. Responding directly to Howells's criticism of her "school," Phelps avows, "It is for us to remind you, since it seems to us that you overlook the fact, that in any highly formed or fully formed creative power, *the 'ethical' as well as the 'aesthetical sense' is developed*" (262, emphasis added). Though "specialism"—by which Phelps means the pursuit of one "sense" to the exclusion of the other—may, "as in science," have its place, "it is not symmetry" (263), which Phelps identifies as the one true prerequisite of the "highly-formed" work. While for Howells formal proportion compensates for a potential disorienting dissymmetry evident in both narrative theme and socio-historical context, for Phelps no such compensation is necessary, as each of these components is, ideally, equally symmetrical, just as all, ideally, cooperate to constitute a measured, viable whole.

This debate about the nature of reality and the function of form is staged nowhere more dramatically than in the two authors' corresponding doctor-novels, conceived of independently and virtually simultaneously. For all Phelps's championship of commensurability, *Doctor Zay* is—especially since she had yet to finish drafting it when she read Howells's attempt—overtly positioned as a compensatory form, rectifying what Howells's portrait lacked in fairness and balance. A host of problems ensue: for one thing, the novel seeks to counterbalance the formal ideologies of not only Howells but also Clarke—and though the two overlap they are not synonymous, hence making Phelps's task all the more complicated. Additionally, *Doctor Zay*'s ostensible compensatory positioning inadvertently sets the novel against itself. After all, the success of her rebuttal of Clarke's and Howells's views depends on a theory of compensation that her own novel intrinsically rejects in favor of the more aesthetically and ethically viable principle of commensurability. Finally, the author's idealization of symmetry as formal imperative does not always jibe with her simultaneous insistence on surplus or excess. As these problems indicate, any attempt to assess Phelps's dialogue with her two interlocutors cannot focus on the content of the dialogue alone but must also take into account the formal principles and practices that inform it.

⇝

In the autumn preceding the serialization of *Doctor Breen's Practice* in the *Atlantic*, Henry James wrote to "applaud" Howells's decision to write a story featuring a "lady-doctor," proclaiming this topic "rich in actuality" (*Selected Letters* II, 258 n. 2). This description seems an odd one, as female practitioners were by no means common: in 1880, women represented only approximately six percent of practicing physicians. In fact, more often than not they were perceived as both uncommon and "irregular" by regular doctors as well as by many laypersons.[13] It was only in 1876 that the first female delegate was admitted to the American Medical Association. In 1871, the encroaching threat of women's membership in that organization caused its then-president, Alfred Stillé, to devote his inaugural address to the subject of women who attempt to "ape" men, which he concluded by suggesting that "if . . . woman is unfitted by nature to become a physician, we should, when we oppose her pretensions, be acquitted of any malicious or even unkindly spirit" (qtd. in Fishbein 83). The "unnaturalness" Stillé perceived in a woman's doctoring might help to explain James's applause, as a story featuring such a character would seem to provide in bountiful supply the disequilibrium necessary for narrative to commence. James's sense of the subject's "richness," then, could derive from the opportunities it provided for crafting symmetry out of dissymmetry rather than from a sense of its representativeness.

Howells's and Phelps's female doctors would have been perceived as all the more "irregular" (and, perhaps, all the more "rich") given their status as homeopaths, a form of medicine which members of the "regular" profession repudiated outright.[14] Around the time that the two novels appeared in print, homeopaths of either sex were the subject of both scrutiny and controversy. From the moment of its founding, the AMA established in its code of ethics a clause forbidding consultation with anyone "whose practice is based upon an exclusive dogma, to the rejection of accumulated experience of the profession" (*Transactions* 18–19). Since homeopaths essentially fit this description, they were to be excluded not only from the AMA but also from professional contact with any of its members. By the 1870s, there were several factious attempts to bar homeopaths from local medical societies and faculties, including one campaign in Boston in which Oliver Wendell Holmes played a significant role (Kaufmann 80–86).[15] These attacks notwithstanding, at least until the turn of the century homeopathy remained a force to be reckoned with. At midcentury, even while regular practitioners were having difficulty organizing themselves, homeopaths had already established the nation's first medical organization, the American Institute of Homeopathy. Typically well educated and upper-class, these alternative healers were most frequently patronized by similarly upper-class patients who shuddered before the "heroic" heavy dosing and bloodletting of regular practitioners. As such, homeopaths often wielded a clout that their allopathic counterparts could only envy.

Samuel Hahnemann, the founder of homeopathy, spurned regular medicine because of what he perceived as its obsession with an "imaginary and supposed material cause of disease" (Rothstein 152). Regular physicians, according to Hahnemann and his disciples, were far too physiologically minded; a chief difference between homeopaths and allopaths lay in the former's belief that "disease [was] fundamentally a matter of spirit; what occurred inside the body did not follow physical laws" (Starr 96). Homeopathy's idealism rendered it potentially incompatible not only with the more materialist practices of regular medicine but with realist literature as well. But this was not the only potential incompatibility. Homeopathy's governing doctrine of *Similia similibus*, or like is cured by like, directly defies the compensation endemic to prevailing theories of forms as closed energy systems. Rejecting ideologies of formal balance that mandated an equilibrium between opposing forces, homeopaths sought to treat a perceived imbalance by providing more of the same.

Among the things that Howells and Phelps shared in common in the early 1880s were frail health and a homeopathic bent. In fact, both Phelps and Howells suffered breakdowns around the time they wrote their respective doctor-novels. Phelps's symptoms at this time included physical frailty, sensitive nerves, insomnia, brain fever, and partial blindness (Coultrap-

McQuin 175). To relieve these symptoms, Phelps unwaveringly relied on homeopathic remedies. As Phelps would later claim in *Chapters from a Life*, "I believe in the homeopathic system of therapeutics. I am often told by skeptical friends that I hold this belief on a par with the Christian religion; and am not altogether inclined to deny the sardonic impeachment" (252). Howells's trust in homeopathy, on the other hand, was primarily a function of his wife's preference. The tentativeness of this trust is evidenced by his switch, when his daughter Winnie's health seemed increasingly threatened, to an allopath (S. Weir Mitchell) despite Elinor's protests.[16]

While Howells was writing *Doctor Breen's Practice*, however, both he and his family were still under a homeopath's care (Bardes and Gossett 137)[17]—which makes Howells's less-than-flattering portrait of Grace Breen, homeopath, initially puzzling. It is not homeopathy that Howells represents as causing his protagonist's oddness, however, but her reasons for choosing this career. The fact that Grace has loved and lost lies behind both her choice of profession and her apparent instability. In fact, the two outcomes are equated, as seen in the following passage depicting the effects of this failed romance upon Breen: "when she returned to the knowledge of the world she showed no mark of the blow except what was thought a strange eccentricity in a girl such as she had been" (12). The onset of this "eccentricity" is coterminous with Breen's decision to pursue medicine as a career and occurs just prior to the narrative's commencement. Despite the fact that she finds aspects of her newly chosen profession "insuperably repugnant," the lovelorn Breen declares her intention to dedicate her life to her career—to sacrifice herself and all other goals in order to devote herself exclusively to her practice and her patients. For Breen, homeopathy compensates for the role love once played. The fact that, ultimately, it does not satisfactorily do so suggests that this bargain is inherently disproportionate, swapping as it does an "unnatural" (professional) for a "natural" (sexual) role.

Rather neatly, this initial exchange of the role of beloved for the role of doctor creates a disequilibrium that drives the narrative forward. Almost as neatly, it is offset at the end when she trades the role of doctor for the role of wife. The two roles—in Howells's novel, at least—cannot be simultaneously undertaken; one must come at the expense of the other. Breen took up medicine because of a failed romance and ultimately leaves it because of a newfound one, a resolution that nicely dispels the disequilibrium that launched Dr. Breen's practice, both novel and career. Once thoughts of love again fill her head, "she could only have claimed in self-defense that she was no longer aiming at a professional behaviour; that she was in fact abandoning herself to a recovered sense of girlhood and all its sweetest irresponsibilities" (238).

Almost from the very beginning, Grace devotes far more energy to fending off potential suitors than she does to fulfilling her professional obligations. In fact, Dr. Breen is never really given the chance to pursue her "practice," which consists of only one patient, an old school chum and pending divorcée, Louise Maynard, who is only consulting Dr. Breen because she happens to be stopping at the same inn (and is permitting Breen to pay for her room and board). Further tilting the scales, the moment that Mrs. Maynard's life appears endangered, Dr. Breen relinquishes both patient and profession, freeing up the rest of the narrative's and her own energy for the development of the courtship plot. And yet, as we shall see, the marriage with which *Doctor Breen's Practice* concludes affords the plot and structure a sense of proportion that is not necessarily available to the protagonist herself.[18]

From the story's outset, Breen's gender identity is portrayed as hindering both her professional persona and the authority the latter requires: as the doctor herself admits, "A woman is reminded of her insufficiency to herself every hour of the day. And it's always a man that comes to her help" (43). For Grace, this insufficiency registers both professionally and personally; the town's regular physician, Dr. Mulbridge, is called in to save Mrs. Maynard's life when Breen proves incapable; likewise, a young industrialist and friend of the Maynards, Walter Libby, ultimately rescues Breen from her profession by marrying her. Intriguingly, Dr. Mulbridge had also offered marriage, accompanied by a promise that he would allow Breen to continue working—this despite the fact that her status as homeopath and his as allopath might entail his dismissal from both state and national medical societies. In fact, when Grace first consults with Mulbridge about her ailing patient, he initially refuses to work with her precisely because of this threat. Acknowledging the danger, Grace abdicates to Mulbridge completely, promising to overlook her training and credentials and aid him solely in the role of nurse.

Grace is further humbled once she realizes, watching Mulbridge by her now-former patient's bedside, that he was "all physician, ... chosen by [his profession] as if he had been born a physician. He was incredibly gentle and soft in all his movements, and perfectly kind, without being at any moment unprofitably sympathetic" (107). As Mulbridge combines all the traits requisite for doctoring within his one person, it is hardly surprising that Breen finds herself both superfluous and insufficient—witness her concession when she rejects his marriage proposal: "I judge your fitness by my own deficiency" (219). His sense of self and balance may also explain why she rejects his proposal, for if marriage serves, as Howells suggests that it does, to round out a person, this man requires no rounding out: unlike Breen, Mulbridge is sufficient unto himself. Furthermore, a marriage between Breen and Mulbridge would effectively reward a woman for successfully pursuing two goals at once and thus defy the compensatory logic the novel ultimately upholds.

While it would be easy to dismiss Howells's rejection of this potentially progressive and equitable match (and his endorsing of the eventual, more traditional one between Breen and Libby) as confirmation of the author's relatively conservative views about gender roles and marriage, Howells's beliefs about narrative energy and formal symmetry complicate any such overly simplistic reading. Indeed, the conventional endings of novels like Howells's deserve consideration not as unmediated transcriptions of gender ideologies but as influenced by a panoply of motivations, among them ideologies of narrative form and closure as well as the pressures of audience and reception. In *Doctor Breen's Practice*, the fact that both the protagonist's career and the story itself ends with a marriage may have had less to do with the author than with readers: as Howells himself acknowledged about his characters, "it is the readers and not the writers of novels who decide their fate" ("Novel" *SLC* 224).

In the early 1880s, Howells did make several attempts to abandon what he and James deemed "the everlasting young man and young woman" ("Novel" 226). In fact, in the two novels written prior to *Doctor Breen's Practice*, Howells tried to script an alternative ending for his characters.[19] When he failed to end *Chance Acquaintance* with the expected promise of matrimony, readers voiced their disappointment. In response, his publishers insisted and Howells eventually agreed that his next novel,

*A Foregone Conclusion*, could not end where he wanted it to—in a crushing, climactic scene of love betrayed. The story instead stages a reconciliation promising betrothal, an ending Howells must have viewed as compromised (see Cady, *Road* 190–91). Such pressures and his resistance to them may also help to explain why *A Modern Instance* (1882)—the novel Howells began while in the process of completing *Doctor Breen's Practice*—ingeniously starts with the marriage he was typically compelled to end with, only to record its unraveling.

Although *Doctor Breen's Practice* does conclude with a coupling, it rather masterfully satisfies conventional closural demands while simultaneously avoiding the idealism so often associated with narrative endings, particularly romantic ones. While in serial, the story evoked a good deal of anxiety over whom the protagonist would eventually marry. William B. Mead exemplifies this concern in a letter he wrote to his cousin, Elinor Mead Howells, beseeching her to reveal the contents of the last chapters of her husband's novel; these chapters are the ones in which Breen would reject Mulbridge and opt for Libby instead. Elinor refused to reveal the secret (Elinor Howells 238). When Breen's choice was finally disclosed, those readers who expected the coupling of the "eternal young man and woman" were simultaneously appeased and disappointed. As a reviewer for the *New York Times* noted,

> when she calls back the correct young man and marries him lest she should fall into the clutches of Dr. Mulbridge, there can be few who will not wish events had another turning. . . . interest will necessarily concentrate on the heroine and hero, and of neither can the report be completely satisfactory. Miss Breen is thrown away upon a stick of a man who can drive a horse and sail a boat. One turns with sympathy to the somewhat coarse, slovenly physician who proposes to continue the heroine's experiment if she will marry him, although on a somewhat different plan. Her marriage to a well-to-do young manufacturer deprives her of all the sympathy the reader has had for her as a person attempting a problem, or struggling with fate; she is utterly obliterated the moment she decides to marry him. ("Literary Notes" 10)

This critic's dissatisfaction with the union of Libby and Breen is expressed within the novel itself by characters who, according to the narrator, regard Grace "as sacrificed in her marriage" (271). In addition, the story ends with the narrator's acknowledgment that, since the new Mrs.

Libby excels in caring for the children of her husband's factory employees, "the conditions under which she now exercises her skill certainly amount to begging the whole question of woman's fitness for the career she had chosen" (271). In other words, the narrator equivocally concludes that the new Mrs. Libby, if given the proper chance, might have proven a more than adequate doctor, leaving unsettled a point seemingly settled from the very first page. Thus the novel bends the conventional happy ending so as to lend it a realistic ambivalence rather than, according to custom, a romantic gloss. This ambiguity reflects life's uncertainty even while the proportionate structure of the narrative works to compensate for it. *Doctor Breen's Practice* thereby achieves formal balance while resisting idealism. Or, rather, it transposes idealism from content to form.

⌒

In writing a story about a woman doctor, Howells may have thought he was exhausting the topic, but if so, he thought wrong. Just prior to his novel's serialization, he was surprised to learn of Phelps's intention to write a novel in the same vein, and then of another young woman's similar intentions. To convince the latter that he had not plagiarized her idea, Howells paid the would-be author a visit, bringing with him the handwritten manuscript of *Doctor Breen's Practice*; she gracefully refused even to look at it and abandoned her intention of writing her own book (Cady, *Road* 207). Though Howells encouraged Phelps to go forward with her version and even promised to publish it in the *Atlantic*, he penned an "open letter" as a preface to *Doctor Zay* ensuring readers of *Doctor Breen's* originality and distancing his own work from Phelps's. In this letter, Howells refers to the "mixture of amusement and anxiety" with which he first heard Phelps's plans to write a book so similar to his own, then modestly assures the author that no one "would suppose you to have borrowed any feature of your plot from so poor a contriver of such things as I am" ("To E. Phelps" 1).

Phelps's impulses upon learning of Howells's novel ran counter to her editor's. As she had done with Clarke's *Sex in Education*, Phelps eradicates any distance between the two texts and instead immediately sets up a dialogue between them. Even before her novel was completed, Phelps positioned it as a sort of "response" to Howells's "call." In the same letter to Howells in which Phelps commends Spencer's evolutionary views, Phelps elaborates on her views of Howells's "unfair" representation of his woman doctor:

> Let me be quite honest and say to the author what I would say of him:—I don't feel that Dr. Breen is a fair example of professional women; indeed, I know she is not for I know the class thoroughly from long personal observation under unusual opportunities—but I think you make it clear to any fine eye that it was the failure of an individual, not of a cause.
>
> It is all the better for *my* doctor who will contrast as gloriously in that respect, as Alas! she will suffer in comparison with your work in others. I shall have a little curiosity, if you take the trouble to read my story, to know how you like it! ("To Howells" 1881 1).[20]

In this letter Phelps sets up two key expectations for her own doctor novel: first, that it would be both more realistic and more equitable than Howells's (hers serving, in fact, to balance out Howells's imbalanced one), and second, that her doctor's success will not just be as "an individual" but for "the cause." This was not Phelps's expectation alone. After *Doctor Zay*'s publication, a reviewer for *Lippincott*'s also contrasted Howells's "eccentric" portrait with Phelps's more political one: "The subject of female doctors has been treated by Mr. Howells, who allows a young and pretty woman to practice medicine just as he allows her the indulgence of any pretty whim or caprice, and by Miss Phelps, who shows the coming of the Golden Age together with the days and works of female doctors" (qtd. in Bardes and Gossett 140).[21] *Doctor Zay* is thus situated as both a reply to its predecessor and a call to arms, a revision of the past and a vision for the future.

Phelps's simultaneous revisionary and visionary impulses are most apparent in her attempt to conclude *Doctor Zay*'s story without undermining the heroine's considerable accomplishments. As Timothy Morris and Michael Sartisky have each suggested, both Doctor Zay and *Doctor Zay* resist marriage and/as closure. Sartisky even notes that the novel's ambivalence toward marriage stems from the conflict between the author's feminist politics and the sentimental formula in which she couches them. He skirts analysis of this conflict, though, when he quixotically asserts that Dr. Zay, although momentarily vanquished by her engagement, will somehow eventually (outside the narrative's confines) "win the race" against her future husband (307–8). Appealing as it may be, there is little textual evidence for such a reading. In addition, Phelps did not identify as a sentimentalist but as an ethical realist. She may make use of sentimentality in her novel, but she would not have been wedded to sentimental outcomes, especially where they might strike her as politically or morally offensive.

Morris connects the narrative's resistance to closure to its author's simultaneous conservative and radical impulses; hence his claim that "*Doctor Zay* is radical with respect to gender roles, conservative with respect to sexuality" (142). These two views, Morris maintains, conjoin in an ending where the doctor gets to keep her job but the woman gets to marry her love. I want to suggest that the conservatism may not lie in Phelps or even the themes her narrative explores so much as in the formal concepts and conventions which filter and at least partially contain her narrative's radical elements. Ironically, Phelps's desire to counterbalance both Clarke's and Howells's formal precepts contribute to an ending that, at least upon preliminary reading, undermines more than it affirms the principle of commensurability that she elsewhere ardently advocates.

Up to a point, Phelps's narrative mirrors Howells's in numerous ways. Both stories begin with a female doctor taking on a new and difficult patient and consulting with a powerful and respected male colleague in the process. Each woman also rejects this colleague's marriage proposal in favor of a man who does not share her profession. In Phelps's version, however, the chosen suitor is also her patient—a significant difference between the two plots. In addition, by making the patient male, Phelps calls into question the association of femininity and frailty. Having this patient fall in love with the doctor—and, ultimately, vice-versa—works to prove the doctor's fitness as both woman and physician simultaneously; in fact, the woman and the physician are not represented as discrete and opposing roles in *Doctor Zay* (as they were in *Doctor Breen's Practice*) but as commensurate, complementary duties. To the extent that Phelps's story was written expressly to refute Howells's, it explicitly demonstrates as Howells's novel does not that a woman can manage both a career and a marriage at once.

At the same time, Phelps believed that marriage was not the be-all but more often the end-all of a woman's existence. Long single herself, Phelps expressed reservations concerning marriage that are evident in her response to Clarke, where she strenuously protests his disparaging "flings at women who, either from subjective preference or objective pressure, are debarred from marriage and maternity" (138). In *Doctor Zay*, it is the protagonist's "subjective preference" to remain single; but "objective" pressures—including pathologizing views of female irregulars, the author's awareness of the normalizing power of narrative conventions, readers' expectations of a conventional ending, and the author's dedication to her own brand of formal symmetry—all combine to make marriage too persistent a force to resist.

One of the narrative's most intriguing devices involves telling Doctor Zay's story from Waldo Yorke's perspective (see also Morris). Doing so enables a reader potentially resistant to the idea of a female homeopath (and especially one who tends to a male patient, a rarity in fact as well as fiction) to occupy the structural position of the also initially resistant Yorke: "He knew nothing of the natural history of doctresses. He had thought of them chiefly as a species of higher nurse,—poor women, who wore unbecoming clothes"(63). His total conversion, then, could be seen as a model for skeptical readers. This transformation of Yorke-as-opponent into Yorke-as-fan, however, takes up the first half of the plot only. The second half charts Dr. Zay's voyage from resistant lover to capitulating one.

It makes sense to attribute the first conversion story—central to the "new woman" or professional plot—to Phelps's aforementioned "ethical sense," the second—the courtship plot—to the author's "aesthetical sense," and to see the two as an attempt to establish a commensurable balance of the narrative energies. Quite explicitly, Yorke's metamorphosis jibes with Phelps's political sensibilities, her dedication to fairness and feminism. Zay's wooing, on the other hand, seems more a function of Phelps's authorial duties—her ultimate obeisance to the conventions of literary form—and her dialogue with both Clarke and Howells. In bringing the two parts together in one narrative, Phelps avoids the "specialism" (concentrating either on "ethical" or "aesthetical" issues instead of both at once) she abhors in Howellsian depictions and aims for the "symmetry" she so values in art. Yet ultimately, while at the level of narrative form the two parts may thus combine aesthetics and ethics in equal proportion, at the level of theme this combination causes more problems than it solves. Within the story itself, the closing portion only seems to undermine the point and upset the balance celebrated in the first part. The narrative closes with more questions than answers about whether a woman can be both beloved and employed at one and the same time. It leaves us wondering whether a woman's attempts to combine the two contribute to health (as commensurate theories would allow) or only deplete energies to the point of exhaustion (as compensatory theories hold).

Contra Howells's and Clarke's portraits, Phelps's novel initially emphatically denies that a woman who devotes herself to her profession thereby depletes her stores of femininity. From the very first, all who look at Dr. Zay are forced to conclude that, as a Mr. Butterwell succinctly puts it, "*There's woman clear through that girl's brains*" (101). What are elsewhere represented as mutually exclusive forces are in *Doctor Zay* presented as mutually conducive: the more Zay develops and uses her mental powers, the more truly womanly she becomes. As an increasingly smitten Yorke notices, "She had the decisive step which only women of business acquire to whom each moment represents dollars, responsibilities, or projects. Yet he liked to see that she had not lost the grace of movement due to her eminently womanly form. She had preserved the curves of femineity" (97). In fact, debunking more conventional, clinical views, Phelps represents professionalism as, precisely, the source of her protagonist's radiant "femineity": "She was the eidolon of glorious health. Every free motion of her happy head and body was superb. She seemed to radiate health, as if she had too much for her own use, and to spare for half the pining world. She had the mysterious odic force of the healer" (98). Her role as healer not only intensifies (it by no means exhausts) Zay's luminous health; it also enhances her physical attractions, rendering her irresistible to her future mate:

She leaned against her own physical strength, as another woman might lean upon a man's.... She had the repose of her full mental activity. She had her dangerous and sacred feminine nerve under magnificent training. It was her servant, not her tyrant; her wealth, not her poverty; the source of her power, not the exponent of her weakness... The young man acknowledged from the bottom of his heart that she was a *balanced* and beautiful creature. (111, emphasis added)

With this acknowledgment, Phelps signifies on medicalized narratives of female imbalance and invalidism in the same moment that Yorke signifies both his acceptance of Zay's profession and his love for her. Indeed, for Yorke, accepting the doctor and loving the woman are identical impulses—at least at this point in time. With this acknowledgment, moreover, Yorke's transformation is completed—his doubts assuaged, Phelps's ethical point made, her cause vindicated.

Yorke's capitulation represents the novel's first attempt at closure, and, indeed, it does bring to a close the story's professional plot. But any sense of resolution proves short-lived, especially as the courtship plot is only beginning to unfold (Dr. Zay has yet to experience the passion Yorke feels for her). Yorke's conversion occurs halfway through the novel; the sense that there is an equal and opposite storyline yet to come is reinforced by his reflection, only a few pages later and at the exact midpoint of the narrative, that "It seemed to him that he was taking her [Zay] up in new and unknown conditions, like the second volume of a novel. He turned the leaves with a dull uneasiness. Something in him urged, 'Throw the book down!' He searched his soul for power to arise and do so. He found there only a great compulsion ... which he knew would bind him down to read on to the end" (126). Here, Yorke's identification with or as a reader is made explicit. Yet the "compulsion" he experiences as Doctor Zay's reader might more accurately describe the narrative energy from this point on, as it presses forward toward a seemingly inevitable conclusion it also simultaneously resists.

There are several reasons for this resistance. Since Dr. Zay is represented from the first as self-sufficient, the marriage implied by the ending seems to instigate an imbalance where none existed before—an imbalance that risks lending grist to arguments about gendered equilibrium Phelps found reprehensible. While Zay intimates that she will maintain her career after her wedding, statements from Yorke suggest otherwise. When, for example, Zay asks if "it is *me* you want,—a strong-minded doctor?" Yorke instantly replies, "A sweet-hearted woman!" (254), a substitution (not a synonym) that does not bode well for Zay's plans. More explicitly, Yorke's insistence that he will not "give up" his "brave lonely girl" to her "diphtheria and smallpox" and that he will never "leave this accursed State of Maine again without" Zay (254) suggests that the doctor's romantic acquiescence signifies the end of her practice. If so, the story's conclusion doesn't simply fail in its mission to compensate for those proposed by Clarke and Howells. It also appears rather eerily to emulate those proposals, inscribing a form of compensation the two men championed and that Phelps, her narrative, and its eponymous heroine originally, vehemently defied.

But there is another way to interpret the doctor's acquiescence and the seeming sacrifices it entails. Zay's consent may not, after all, shore up compensatory theories of organic forms but instead serve to critique them, given that such a conclusion is represented as less than happy and far from equilibrious. In his study of the marriage plot, Joseph Allen Boone catalogs both traditional and counter-traditional novels, counting as "counter-traditional" texts that either work within the tradition only to critique its conventions or those that posit fictional trajectories outside marital confines. While Boone identifies the former's revisionist project as "following the course of wedlock beyond its expected close and into the uncertain textual realm of marital stalemate and impasse" (19), *Doctor Zay* may still be considered a counter-traditional text; its lack of an ambiguous coda notwithstanding, the narrative could be seen as transferring the "unease" thematically associated with married life into the "narrational 'unease'" of its "decentered, multivocal, and ultimately open-ended" structure (Boone 20). Indeed, although its "revolt" against the "*thematic* limitations imposed by the novel's love ideology" may in the end be compromised, *Doctor Zay*'s rebellion against "the *structural* confines of conventional plotting" (19) is, I believe, less easily put to rest.

For one thing, *Doctor Zay*'s seemingly compensatory ending initiates a disequilibrium that contests the value and resolution of compensatory theories of closure. At the same time, it serves, by negation, to exemplify and reinforce commensurable theories (indeed, the heroine's disequilibrium is not only *not* offset at the formal level but could even be said to be matched by a corresponding formal dissymmetry). Finally, the indecisiveness with which the novel ends could be taken as indicative of the author's belief that no conclusion could be considered finite or final. In other words, the irresoluteness of *Doctor Zay*'s closure may not signify Phelps's reluctant acquiescence to formal pressures so much as her belief that even the most apparently conclusive forms or commonplace conventions might, in the end, prove indeterminate.

Twice, the story seems to end with Zay rejecting her patient and rededicating herself to her profession; the first time, she sends Yorke back to his native Boston, seemingly for good. Although there is a sense of finality hovering over this banishment, the story is far from over. Yorke returns one more time, and in the interim Zay has somehow, inexplicably, come to love him (contra James's assumptions, implausibility here works to ensure an outcome we cannot call "happy").[22] Zay informs Yorke of her love not by telling him that she has lost her heart; instead, she rather desolately confides "I have lost my self-possession.... I have lost—myself" (231). Although in a final attempt to resist such self-effacement Zay once again tries to send Yorke away, her feeble efforts prove futile. Most inauspicious is the fact that Dr. Zay's ultimate acquiescence to Yorke's persistent proposals occurs in virtual silence, as she glides into her former patient's arms with just a whisper. In fact, her final words, the final words of the narrative, raise a question that could be directed not just to Yorke but, intriguingly, to the story itself: "'Is *that* all?' she whispered" (258).

Much of the tension in *Doctor Zay* arises from the friction produced when competing concepts of what comprises individual and narrative equilibrium rub up against each other. Marriage, epitomizing conventional formal closure (equilibrium) and even what would have been considered at the time both ethical and historically realistic closure (verisimilitude), is in *Doctor Zay* represented as generating the female character's disequilibrium. Significantly, in Phelps's novel this disequilibrium commences at the narrative's end, not, as is conventional, its beginning—more tension is stirred up there than is quelled or than was ever aroused from the first. In *Narrative and Its Discontents*, D. A. Miller differentiates between the "narratable" tensions that give rise to a narrative and the "nonnarratable," the "state of quiescence assumed by a novel before the beginning and supposedly recovered by it at its end" (ix). Miller's "supposedly" underscores the fact that closure rarely offers the conclusiveness implied by the term, that there is always something artificial and ideologically fraught in any narrative ending. A narrative does not progress from quiescence through turbulence back to quiescence again; in fact, once agitated, the energy that impels a plot is never fully expended.

Still, Miller's "nonnarratable" intimates that closure depletes narratable tensions sufficiently so that no more needs to be said. The very term "nonnarratable" connotes an inarticulateness that fits nicely with the whisper with which Phelps's novel concludes, although not necessarily with that which is presumed to follow it. Regarding Miller's theory, Alison Booth has argued that he "appears to overlook the fact that the nonnarratable is distinctly gendered, guided by what is 'unspeakable'—for example, a *female* story of ambition" (8). Yet what is noteworthy about Phelps's conclusion is that what is "nonnarratable" or "unspeakable"— what is presumed to follow narrative closure—is not a tale of female ambition but of defeated acquiescence. In other words, reversing customary expectations concerning both gender and genre, the narratable in *Doctor Zay* is precisely that which the societal script codes as unspeakable—a woman's desires, dreams, ambitions—while the nonnarratable represents the all-too-conventional. The whisper with which Zay surrenders to Yorke's embrace may signal the onset of a nonnarratable (and stultifying) quiescence, but even if so, it simultaneously interrogates—"is that all?"— whether the equilibrium a novel's last words typically initiate will necessarily ensue.

Recently, feminist narratologists have suggested that a focus on a novel's conventional ending as the repository of meaning risks slighting the tensions, incongruities, contradictions, and possibilities that are stirred up prior to their relative containment in the end.[23] Although this is an important corrective, I would argue that *Doctor Zay*'s closure (or, more precisely, its interrogation thereof) is itself highly significant. As we have seen, closure for realists constitutes the problematic site where mimeticism breaks down; yet, in Phelps's own brand of "realist" narrative, closure represents its most mimetic moment, to the extent that its irresolution mirrors life's ragged inconclusivity and effectively represents Phelps's points about its fundamental uncontainability. While other critics have diverted attention from *Doctor Zay*'s ambiguous conclusion to the protagonist's triumph in earlier portions of the plot, I would suggest that the novel's tentative close is itself climactic, constituting the site of the narrative's tensions and contradictions rather than their container. For it is there, in closing, that form meets history, that the drive toward narrative symmetry meets a resistance to the essentialism that affixes meaning securely, solely, or finally within finite forms.

# 4

## Form Follows Function?

*Charlotte Perkins Gilman, Re-presentation, and the Literature of Estrangement*

> But in the ever-growing human impulse to create, the power and will to make, to do, *to express one's new spirit in new forms,*—here she [woman] has been utterly debarred.
>
> Charlotte Perkins Gilman, *Women and Economics* (emphasis added)

When S. Weir Mitchell introduced a chapter of his 1886 novel *Roland Blake* with the epigraph "the man who has not known sick women has not known women" (113), he had yet to encounter perhaps his most famous patient, Charlotte Perkins Stetson [Gilman].[1] It is unlikely that Mitchell would have amended this supposition when, a few years later, he treated Gilman for a form of nervous breakdown. Although the neurologist's analysis of nervous prostration originated from his treatment of traumatized Civil War soldiers and veterans, and although he himself periodically suffered from a similar condition (*Doctor and Patient* 58, 60, 63–64), Mitchell nevertheless believed that "the mass of women are by physiological nature more liable to be nervous than are men" (*Lectures* 137). Anna Burr, friend and biographer of Mitchell who describes herself as otherwise "ebullient in praise of Dr. Weir," summarizes the doctor's perspective:

For years, his knowledge of women had come largely from seeing her [sic] as a patient and this fact naturally colored his attitude toward her and her problems. Inevitably, he came to associate her with weakness, till the association crystalized into a cliché. The ideal he had for her was earlier than early Victorian and far earlier than early American. . . . The truth was his standard was extremely conventional; his ideal was the well-sheltered woman and this view at his age was unlikely to change. (373)

In our own day, Mitchell's name is usually cited only to criticize his pathologizing views of women. In all fairness, however, it should be acknowledged that he was neither the originator of these views nor even their most ardent proponent. As early as 1869, for example, a Dr. Dirix spoke for many of his colleagues when he proposed that the diseases from which his female patients suffered were "in reality, not diseases at all, but merely the sympathetic reactions or the symptoms of one disease, namely, a disease of the womb" (qtd. in Ehrenreich and English 122). For the most part, Mitchell shared Dirix's assumption, shoring up etymological links between hysteria and the womb by arguing in *Fat and Blood* that "some local uterine trouble starts the mischief" in hysterical cases and concluding that "if the case did not begin with uterine troubles they soon appear" (38–39). If hysteria has a logic, these two doctors concur, it is that depth governs surface, internal organ dictates external gestures.

Mitchell's etiology of the disease was actually more complicated than this schema suggests, however.[2] As he observed in an 1888 lecture on the treatment of nervous diseases, hysteria was the most vexing of all, precisely because it manifested itself in "infinite numbers of forms and [an] infinite variety of masquerade" (*Lectures* 217). Testifying to this multiformity, Mitchell tentatively identified a class of hysterics whose symptoms register somewhere between the "charlatans" who fake illness as a mask for selfish behavior and those who genuinely suffer from "womb troubles" (*Lectures* 224).[3] This third type, by Mitchell's own admission more difficult to categorize or dismiss, suffered from what he once evocatively called "dreamed pains"—which, Mitchell sympathetically urges, "are, to her, real enough" (*Doctor and Patient* 133). In thus giving credence to both dreams and psychical reality, Mitchell anticipates the work of his contemporaries, Freud and Breuer, in this field.[4]

Clearly, for all the emphasis on hysteria as a disease of the womb, it was never perceived as an exclusively organic ailment. In part, this is because doctors often could detect no discernible trace of pathology in nineteenth-century hysterics who were nonetheless exhibiting ostensible symptoms of disease.[5] This absent cause led many physicians to dismiss the hysteric as "morally delinquent" and her illness, in the parlance of the time, as "ideational" (Smith-Rosenberg, "Hysterical" 205). Walter Benn Michaels phrases the conundrum nicely, suggesting that "what was most fascinating about hysteria was precisely the way it resisted the familiar reduction, since it seemed to be *in* the body (it produced real physical symptoms) without being *of* the body (the symptoms were unaccompanied by real organic damage)" (*Gold Standard* 23). We might call this modification of the uterine hypothesis the "illogic" of hysteria, in which symptoms defy clinical etiologies, resisting interiorization and intractably remaining, despite intimations of buried depths, a matter of pure surface. The clinical term for this hysterical simulation is "mimosis"—the variation in spelling connoting its pathological deviation from a more normative and "healthy" *mimetic* repetition.

The implication that mimesis proper requires a clearly articulated biological origin suggests a resonance between what I have called "hysteria's logic" and realist logic. In addition to referentiality, literary versions of naturalism share much in common with their clinical counterparts, including a faith in the processes of determinism and (d)evolution. In particular, both modes acknowledge an ineluctable "biological necessity"; to acquiesce to either's mimetic mandates is to circumscribe agency by and within ontology. So, if mimesis constitutes the norm, do representations that lack or reject organic bases—and instead foreground surface as both what matters and what is the matter—set themselves up to be read as not just anti-mimetic but "mimotic"? And might this be the outcome even where this lack or rejection signifies a "healthy" resistance to naturalizing narratives claiming to represent a preexisting organic reality that is actually constituted through the process of repetition?[6] This chapter seeks to answer these questions by examining the role representation plays in both Charlotte Perkins Gilman's uncanny short story, "The Yellow Wallpaper" (1892), and her utopian novel, *Herland* (1915). Within these works, does representation function primarily to reiterate or—when imitation proves simulation—does it instead overtly interrogate the construction of not just bodily but literary forms as organic?

Before exploring Gilman's representational strategies in detail, however, I want first to sketch out the author's beliefs about form, human as well as literary. As I will discuss, Gilman strenuously resisted psychological constructions of selfhood, yet she was not entirely averse to surface-depth models of subjectivity, even when these posited some form of physiological origin or base. For example, in an article entitled "Mind-Stretching" published in *The Century Magazine* in 1925, Gilman reluctantly concedes the existence of the unconscious mind, comparing it to a "mysterious cellar" which contains all sorts of "unpleasant" things (218). Ideally, Gilman argues, we should do our best to reserve our mental processes not for "cold storage" but for "mind-stretching": that is to say, this cellar should be cleaned out in order to best utilize the "vast, clear, luminous spaces of the human mind" (219) for future expansion rather than excavation into the repressed past.

Whatever her misgivings about the mind's powers, as a confirmed maternalist Gilman more readily acknowledged the womb's undergirding role, albeit as a source of women's health rather than disease. Indeed, it would not have been Mitchell's biologizing views of women *in se* that Gilman disputed but, more accurately, his pathologizing ones. In an article entitled "Motherhood and the Modern Woman," for instance, Gilman asks, "What is a woman?" then immediately answers, "The female of *genus homo*, one capable of being a mother" (384). The slippage here that conflates gender identity and biological capacity informs Gilman's habitual glorification of "the maternal instinct, which goes so deep" ("Human Nature" 1).[7] For Gilman as for Mitchell, the womb lies at the core of a woman's identity, but in Gilman's model this "deep" basis is fundamentally healthy and (re)productive rather than potentially pathological or pathologizing.

At times, Gilman comes across as a more enthusiastic convert to naturalistic understandings of subjectivity than Mitchell may ever have been—but, again, with the important caveat that hers was a progressive rather than regressive determinism.[8] Consider, for example, Gilman's eager embrace of Darwinian evolutionary theory as explanatory force. Viewing human life—both individual and collective—as an organic entity, Gilman regarded all of its forms, for so long as they were duly governed by natural laws, to be not only constantly evolving but also clearly improving. And since biology dictates that "all the tendencies of a living organism are progressive in their development" (*Women and Economics* 59), all that does not lend itself to the organism's development must be intrinsically alien to it. Positioning herself as a sociobiologist (61), Gilman insists in her preface to *Women and Economics* that "some of the worst evils under which we suffer, evils long supposed to be inherent and ineradicable in our natures, are but the result of certain arbitrary conditions of our own adoption, and ... by removing these conditions, we may remove the evils resultant" (xxxix). If nature was left to its own devices, she avows, both male and female would continue to flourish over time.

However, while natural selection makes us human, sexual selection makes us gendered beings, and it is here, as Gilman entitles a chapter in *His Religion and Hers* (1923), that we see "the natural beginning of an unnatural relation" (195). Due to "the prolongation of infancy," due to the fact that humanity is a collective noun and individual interests are often subjugated for the good of the group, an inequity, a sort of temporal lag, gradually developed in the evolution of females versus males. Although this discrepancy pertains across all species, Gilman contends that it is among humans alone that this service to the child unnaturally evolved into service to the adult male as well, a practice soon naturalized as custom (see *His Religion and Hers* 195–217). The result, as she famously concluded some twenty-five years earlier in *Women and Economics* (1898), was that humans became "the only animal species in which the sex-relation is also an economic relation" (5).

How is it that the "natural" could be transformed into the "unnatural"? Gilman found her answer in those environmental forces that redirect, even inhibit what she considered inherent evolutionary tendencies. In a lecture from the 1890s entitled "Our Excessive Femininity," Gilman contends that "function precedes organ rather than organ function" (3), and ultimately concludes that "the thing is the product of its circumstances" (4). According to Gilman, disease does not originate within the body but ought to be viewed instead as the result of its interactions, its use. Moreover, what pertains at the individual level holds true as well for the social aggregate. Despite our best efforts and natural impulses to progress, interactions with extrinsic factors including climate, habitat, nourishment, and other people both "form and limit" our chances of improvement (4). The word "limit" is key to Gilman's brand of determinism: if it is "natural" for humans to evolve, then environmental circumstances typically operate as devoluationary, degenerative forces. For Gilman, the "natural" is not reduced to or replaced by the social: it is retained as a relatively plastic category that, for all its naturalness, is still capable of being altered through its functions and dysfunctions. We might call Gilman's a "laissez-faire" evolutionism.[9] Her model also maps determinism's directional flow as traveling from outside-in and not simply from inside-out.

I suppose Gilman's attraction to evolutionary and deterministic theories could be attributed to the hum and buzz of the age; she was by no means the only literary persona in the *fin-de-siècle* period to espouse Darwinian views. Yet Gilman's naturalizing precepts are quite distinct from those expounded by such figures as Herbert Spencer or Frank Norris. Indeed, even while acknowledging a debt to Spencer, Gilman did not adopt his Social Darwinistic tenets in the generally unequivocal, fervent fashion of her male counterparts. Among other differences, Spencer denounced attempts to improve the lots of the less fortunate as misguided at best, whereas Gilman (whose defining organism was always the social and not the individual body) believed it was our obligation as part of a collectivity to intervene (see also Magner 121).[10] Essentially, Spencer and Gilman read Darwin through divergent moral frameworks and from different epistemological standpoints. As a result, they disagreed over evolutionism's mechanics: where Spencer saw combat, struggle, and self, Gilman envisioned growth, change, and selflessness. It is little wonder, then, that evolutionary views function in Gilman's lexicon not to reflect Hobbesian understandings of life but to instruct her readers about the inherent unnaturalness of such "nasty" and "brutish" versions of it. Resisting naturalism's requisite moral ambiguity, Gilman manipulated orthodox naturalistic doctrines so that they might serve to teach, even preach, a manifest lesson in progressionism.

With varying degrees of intensity, not just her nonfictional but her fictional writings aim to inculcate this lesson. Contemplating current literature in 1911, Gilman found herself disgruntled with conventional modes, both "masculine" and "feminine." Denouncing romances for their deceitful "happily ever after" (*Man-Made World* 102), she reserves just as much scorn for popular adventure stories, with their overemphasis on struggle and individualism (94–95). In particular, Gilman deplores the fact that these seemingly opposing fictions—one foregrounding desire, the other, conflict—essentially unite around their common celebration of aggressive pursuit. Objecting to fictions that strike only "one dominant note," Gilman defines "great literature" as that which relinquishes its focus on the androcentric past, transcends sex, and encompasses all of human life (100).[11]

This latter qualification evokes the mimetic impulses behind literary realism and naturalism. Yet Gilman elaborates on these schools by disdaining verisimilitude as a goal sufficient unto itself, especially when it entails imitation of subjective or intrasubjective life alone. Truthful fictions, she proposes, should "teach us life easily, swiftly, truly; teach not by preaching but by *truly re-presenting*; and we should grow up becoming acquainted with a far wider range of life in books than could ever be ours in person. Then meeting life in reality we should be wise—and not be disappointed" (*Man-Made World* 101, emphasis added). Although Gilman believed that the truth could be captured and conveyed within literary forms, she held a very distinct conception of what that truth might be and how it ought to be expressed. Where other theorists typically range didacticism against mimesis, Gilman aligned the two by widening the mimetic mirror so as to reflect not only life's broad expanse but the important lesson that life is broader than either conventional literary representations or our own discrete individual experiences would have us believe.[12]

This alignment may explain why Gilman found Howellsian realism personally distasteful—why she derided the "Dean's" clinical understanding of truth as "that of the elaborate medical chart, the scientific photograph." His stories, she complained to a friend, "awake no other emotion in the class portrayed than a pleasant surprise at their own reproduction. Like a child with a looking glass" (qtd. in Hill 176). In Gilman's view, fiction should be reflective, but of the entire social body rather than the individual one. Rather than viewing mimetic representation as meritorious in its own right, Gilman considered improvement—specifically, "social service"—to be the inherent purpose of both literary and physical organisms. Hence her distrust of the "modern artist," who, she feared, was exclusively "engaged in exhibiting to us his own interior—which is not always beautiful" ("Summary of Purpose" 290). The difference between Gilman's mimetic theory and more conventional variants lies in her rejection not of organicism in and of itself but of the kind whose sole, myopic goal is "interior exhibitionism."

Gilman sought throughout her career to defamiliarize naturalism's "familiar reduction" (Michaels, *Gold Standard* 23) of agency to ontology, not because she disagreed with it, necessarily, but because naturalistic representations tended to depict this ontology, especially where women were concerned, as inherently pathological and immobile. Throughout her career, Gilman sought to wrench such rigid models from their seemingly irrevocable constraints and get them moving again along their proper evolutionary track; in at least two instances—specifically, in her uncanny "The Yellow Wallpaper" and her utopian *Herland*—she adapted the literature of estrangement to perform this defamiliarizing work. In order to call attention in "The Yellow Wallpaper" to the way external factors could warp natural processes so that they come to resemble unnatural or pathological ones, Gilman utilizes a surface-depth model, but one that defamiliarizes "hysteria's logic" by reversing the directional flow of its determinism. What results is a story whose emphasis on the manifest and interrogation of organic determinism so closely approximates mimosis that confusion has arisen over whether it is documenting hysteria's *illogic* or defying its *logic*. By contrast, the utopian *Herland* combines externalism and organicism in such a harmonious, salubrious, and natural relationship that there can be no question of hysterical or uncanny representation.

It is not just the content but the form of the two stories that accounts for the difference. In Gilman's ideal organicized aesthetics, generic form and narrative content would collaborate holistically toward one motivating, illuminating end. Yet while such a collaboration might pertain in theory, in practice—in particular, in the very mechanics of her best-known fictional composition, "The Yellow Wallpaper"—narrative mode functions less to enhance (as organic property) than to inhibit, even distort (like one of those environmental "enemies" Gilman identifies) the story's presumable lessons and truths. Published a quarter of a century later, *Herland* rehearses many of the earlier story's central issues, but does so in a format that, while no less estranging, is far less uncanny. Understood as a more truthful re-presentation than (or even of) "The Yellow Wallpaper," *Herland* deserves examination not simply as a formal and naturalized representation of utopia but as illuminating testimony concerning Gilman's utopian and naturalizing re-presentations of form.

Is "The Yellow Wallpaper" a naturalist work? I, for one, have frequently taught it as such, introducing it as a narrative that, imbibing the deterministic spirit of the age, casts its protagonist as a woman ensnared by circumstances—a woman who, to borrow from Dreiser's description of Sister Carrie, is finally more written than she writes (although she writes copiously, frenetically).[13] Certainly, the story's ending, where the once articulate, upper-class narrator is reduced to an atavistic creature crawling about the room on all fours, remains one of the creepier fictional representations of devolution. Yet when the author's distinctive deterministic views are taken into consideration, the story's putative naturalism rests not in any mimetic portrayal of "woman's nature" but instead in its depiction of what might be called, twisting Gilman's own epigraph, "the natural *result* of an unnatural relation."

What produces this result has remained a subject of some dispute. Classic feminist interpretations of the tale—beginning with Elaine Hedges's "Afterword" in the 1973 Feminist Press reissue—read it allegorically, with the protagonist as Everywoman driven mad by a wallpaper symbolic of patriarchy's script, which as it envelops the heroine both represents and causes her subjectification.[14] Psychoanalytic literary critics typically invert this pattern, suggesting that the heroine projects her madness outward, writing her hysteria large upon her surroundings.[15] Also divergent are interpretations of the story's "maddening" (both literally and critically speaking) conclusion. While some have read it as a defeat, others attempt to mitigate the tale's severity and wrest a degree of agency for the protagonist by suggesting that the conclusion instead represents a triumph—the only sane, imaginative response to an insane world.[16]

The sheer amount of scholarly attention devoted to this chilling first-person account of a nervous breakdown has prompted one critic to call "The Yellow Wallpaper" the "most famous narrative of hysteria" (Herndl 68). There is biographical basis for this dubious distinction: before writing her now-famous tale, Gilman suffered from what would today be called post-partum depression (which Mitchell's rest cure only aggravated), was actually diagnosed with "uterine displacement" prior to delivery, and, at the time of her pregnancy, described herself as "so hysterical" (*Diaries* I, 296, 318).¹⁷ It is possible to read the tale as mimetically representing this unsettling period in Gilman's biography. But even in this early narrative, Gilman combines mimesis and didacticism, crafting a story that reflects her own experience even as it—at least implicitly—preaches against Mitchell's views. As Gilman contends in her autobiography, the "real purpose of the story was to reach Dr. S. Weir Mitchell, and convince him of the error of his ways" (*Living* 121).¹⁸

It is easy to see how "The Yellow Wallpaper's" content rebuts Mitchell's diagnostics—especially his refusal to entertain the possibility that the hysteric's disease and her symptoms originate elsewhere than in the subjective, submerged, or somatic. And yet, the story's structural foregrounding of hidden depths functions better to reinforce than to unravel hysteria's logic and to submerge rather than clarify its potential lessons. In other words, as both Mary Jacobus and Diane Price Herndl have provocatively suggested, Gilman's tale is not simply *about* hysteria but might be seen as itself hysterical, which is to say that its form as well as its content can be read symptomatically. "The Yellow Wallpaper's" digressive, distracted narrative voice, its frenzied pacing, its omissions and accents can be diagnosed as formal, "hysterical" symptoms of that which the narrative and narrator never overtly, thematically articulate. Indeed, the story's intimation of hidden depths but refusal to identify, precisely, the nature of that which lies hidden there only facilitates such classifications.

Within psychoanalytic theory, hysteria and narrative (spoken, but also written) are positioned in inverse relationship: as Steven Marcus attests, the most compelling index of psychic health for Freud was a patient's ability to compose a coherent narrative, as opposed to the fragmentary and incoherent digressions hysterics typically offer (70–71). And yet, as Marcus also notes, incoherence is not solely symptomatic of hysteria. Narrative circumlocution and involution, an unreliable narrator, a "fragmentary technique" that "allows the material to emerge piecemeal"—all these elements also distinguish Freud's most controversial (in Marcus's eyes "modernist") case history: "Fragment of an Analysis of a Case of Hysteria," familiarly known as "Dora's case" (64–66). They also define the form of "The Yellow Wallpaper." Viable readings of Gilman's story, in other words, could situate it as told from either analysand's or analyst's perspectives, allowing it to be interpreted simultaneously yet contradictorily as an attempt, on the one hand, to provide a first-person account of hysteria and, on the other, to bear witness to the disease at some remove and authoritatively document its etiology.

Regardless of which scenario a reader accepts, the narrator's affliction is never clearly attributed to an organic source. Bearing in mind Gilman's belief that the origin of disease lies outside rather than within the organism, is it possible that the story gestures toward an alternative, external cause? While it is clear that there are a number of specified and unspecified causes for the speaker's illness, there is provocative textual and contextual evidence to suggest that the house's pathogenic role has been slighted. Throughout her career, Gilman espoused a sort of domestic determinism, a theory emanating from her belief that environmental forces tend to impede natural progress. A brief detour through Gilman's anti-domestic ideology will help us to gloss, upon return, the determining force of "The Yellow Wallpaper's" own haunted house.

In the year following "The Yellow Wallpaper's" publication, the city of Chicago hosted the Centennial Exhibition, an event Gilman had hoped to attend (Hill 213). A decade later, she waxed rhapsodic about the fair in her *The Home: Its Work and Influence* (1903). In the exhibition's wake, Gilman proclaims in *The Home*, "a wave of beauty spread into thousands of homes." At the same time, however, she insists that the distance between the "White City" exhibited during the exposition and the sadly more permanent "Black City" (Chicago) still on display by the lake augured the pressing need for yet "another extra-domestic uplifting" (152). The term "extra-domestic" is revealing: not even an honorary member of the cult of domesticity, Gilman routinely situated the home as the root of all ills—of, in particular, debilitating gender differences.

As Gilman testifies in *The Home*, ammunition for such an argument was on visible display at the World's Fair in the form of two statues commissioned by a Dr. Sargent. The shape of each statue, one male and the other female, was based on the mean average of a collection of college students' measurements. Acknowledging visible differences between the aesthetic properties of these representative figures, Gilman attributes the female statue's evident inferiority to women's confinement within the home: "the figure of the man is far and away more beautiful than that of the woman," she writes. "We are softer and whiter *for our long housing*; but not more truly beautiful" (210–11, emphasis added). Gender differences, Gilman infers, are the result not so much of biology as of domesticity. Her point is clarified in a 1903 article that appeared in *Success* magazine: "The effect of the home *and nothing else* upon women," Gilman avows, "has been precisely what it would have been on men—cramping, dwarfing, blinding, choking, keeping down the higher human instincts" ("The Home as an Environment for Women" 411). If the situation were reversed and men were secluded in the house and women set free upon the world, men would develop "women's brains" and women "men's": "We have called the broader, sounder, better balanced, more fully exercised brain 'a man's brain,' and the narrower, more emotional and personal one 'a woman's brain'; whereas the difference is merely that between the world and the house" (*Home* 274). Gilman's analogy nicely conveys her conviction that, for most women domesticity, not anatomy, is destiny.[19]

According to Gilman, a house not only molds bodily identity but is, at times, analogous to physical and mental states. For example, she frequently refers to herself in architectural terms in courtship letters written to her cousin (soon to be husband) Houghton Gilman. One such missive is signed "your dilapidated cousin" (June 22, 1897), another declares that she was "a wreck on that side of me: the inside" (October 15, 1897), yet another finds her "shaken to the very foundation" (July 29, 1898), while a more upbeat note concludes that she was "settling more and more" (September 1, 1898).[20] Just as Gilman in these confidential notes employs domestic descriptives to depict her own "wobbly" self, they also serve her well in her published prose as tropes for what she saw as a bourgeois woman's cramped and stunted lot. For instance, believing that, especially in men's eyes, "the woman and the home [had become] one and indivisible" (*Home* 22), Gilman takes this supposed symbiosis and renders its stultifying effects symbolically. Thus in her poem "In Duty Bound," she likens the traditional housewife trapped in the home to the soul imprisoned in that housewife's body:[21]

>A house with roof so darkly low
>The heavy rafters shut the sunlight out;
>One cannot stand erect without a blow;
>Until the soul inside
>Cries for a grave—more wide. (*Living* 77)

Just as the woman cannot move within such a home, the soul cannot move within such a domesticated, feminine body: both confines are unhealthy because both are confining, claustrophobic. Elsewhere, Gilman represents the existing home not as the hallowed site of reproduction and nurturing but as what she calls "a little ganglion of aborted economic processes" ("Curious Views" n.p.). While still organicized, the latter characterization graphically dissociates the home from robust fertility. And robust fertility, after all, is what Gilman posits as a woman's birthright.

Gilman scholars typically connect the author's critique of traditional domestic structures to her unhappy childhood, to the fact of her father's abandonment and her mother's distressingly distanced method of child rearing.[22] Domesticity's negative connotations apparently were intensified for Gilman in the wake of her marriage to Walter Stetson, during which, she later confided, she "was well while away and sick while at home" (*Living* 95). This association of disease with domesticity may help to explain why "domestic" remains a better description of Gilman's thematics than of her aesthetics. Rejecting the formula perfected in earlier decades by, among others, her great-aunt Harriet Beecher Stowe, Gilman did not write domestic fictions so much as she exposed the fictions concerning domesticity—an exposé that assumes its eeriest form in her chilling "The Yellow Wallpaper." Indeed, we might read the story as an early, fictional attempt to articulate the domestic determinism she expounds repeatedly in her later expository prose. The fact that, in 1892, her deterministic theories were still emergent and provisional may help to explain the story's own inarticulateness concerning the etiology of the dis-ease it so visibly enacts.

In that now famous moment in 1887 when Gilman sought Mitchell out for treatment, she was informed by him that his "rest cure" depended, in Gilman's telling paraphrase, upon the patient's leading "as domestic a life as possible" (*Living* 96). As Gilman reveals in her autobiography, "I went home, followed those directions rigidly for months, and came perilously near to losing my mind" (96). Gilman's transcription of Mitchell's words is significant because it pinpoints the pivotal role of "domesticity" in inducing her mental collapse. If it is true that she wrote the story to convince Mitchell of "the error of his ways" (*Living* 121), then, given that Mitchell's "ways" were frequently guided by his belief that woman was and should be both the "source and center of the home" (*Wear and Tear* 55), we can read "The Yellow Wallpaper" at its most conscious level as a fictional attempt to demonstrate the errors inherent in such a view.

But the story also documents the pernicious truths of its reverse—that is, of the possibility that the home may, unnaturally, be the source of the woman. Put another way, rather than viewing woman as "homemaker," it is more accurate in this instance to posit the home as "woman maker." The very first "character" we meet in the story is, after all, the house, variously described as an "ancestral hall," "a colonial mansion," "a hereditary estate," "the most beautiful place" (3–4). In many respects, the house is more fleshed out than any of its inhabitants: we get more detailed description of it than of anything or anybody else—even its furniture and furnishings seem animated (7–8). This anthropomorphism may simply signify that the narrator, starved for creative activity, is projecting her own personality onto the inanimate objects surrounding her. Yet Gilman's already outlined "domestic determinism" prompts a counter-reading, one in which the house's "personality" might be seen as literally contouring the impressionable protagonist's rather than the reverse.

Rather than presuming the narrator's identity to be fully formed from the start, "The Yellow Wallpaper" could even be read as a bildungsroman run amok; for the protagonist learns a form of reproduction that—displacing yet uncannily evoking her "natural" role as mother (a role the narrator has yielded to a nanny)—consists in replicating herself not so much *in* the wallpaper but *as* wallpaper. Ultimately, this blurring of the boundaries between self and house constitutes the inevitable if "unnatural" result of a domestic determinism which transforms re-presentation from truthful depiction of life into a sort of "mimotic" *mise en abîme*, in which Gilman is reconfigured as the narrator who is reconfigured as the wallpaper-woman whose very appearance, despite appearances, affirms that "there is no there there"—no underlying organicism, after all. This reading lends new meaning to the fact that the protagonist remains unnamed until the final page of the story. It is only after the house has effectively solipsized her that she is named ("Jane") and that an identity is revealed, or, more accurately, conferred.[23] Although numerous readers have assumed that the narrator's final accusatory "Jane" is merely a typographical or authorial error meant to indicate (and indict) "Jennie," John's sister, it is equally plausible that the hitherto unnamed narrator is identifying the self she must utterly alienate in order to recognize.

It is in the story's early pages, when we first meet the still nameless "I" who tells the tale, that she appears the most lucid, the most "sane." And it is there that she performs her own diagnosis of what ails her, insisting that "there is something strange about the house—I can feel it" (4). Her objections to the fact that the house stood for so long "untenanted" are by no means unwarranted, nor is her concern over its secluded location—"it is quite alone, standing well back from the road, quite three miles from the village" (4). Throughout the story, the narrator's idea of a cure necessitates removal not just from the room that torments her but from the house itself, as shown when she begs John to take her away (11) and even when she at one point "seriously" contemplates "burning the house" (15). We see this desire expressed as well through the protagonist's persistent, yearning glances from her attic window at the outlying gardens and enticing lane, areas soon declared off-limits by her doctor-husband. The bars on the windows, the bolted-down bed, the gate at the stairs, the rings on the walls, all suggest that this home has served as a place of incarceration, perhaps a madhouse: it thus makes sense given Gilman's domestic determinism that someone enclosed therein would go mad. One reason such a reading has only attracted cursory attention may be that it seems so obvious, so superficial. The fact that it is also compelling should prompt us to reassess the purported shallowness of the superficial, the inconsequentiality of the obvious.

"The Yellow Wallpaper" was composed before Gilman was exposed to Freudian theories and is explicitly positioned against Mitchell's views, not Freud's. All the same, Breuer and Freud were conducting their studies on hysteria a continent away around the same time that Gilman published "The Yellow Wallpaper," and it is interesting to juxtapose the hysterical case studies written by each. While initially, Breuer's work with "Anna O." (between 1880 and 1882) had convinced Freud that the "infallible" root of every case of hysteria was "the realm of sexual experience" (Breuer and Freud 193), in the wake of "Dora's case" (1901) he would substantially and controversially recast this experience as phantasy instead of reality-based. Although Freud is often and rightly praised for acknowledging the complex psychic causes of hysteria, his reassessment nonetheless signals a retreat from the socio-cultural and objective to the psychical and the subjective—a retreat that precisely reverses the direction of Gilman's proposed route to mental and emotional well-being.

Two decades after "The Yellow Wallpaper" was published, Gilman began to take a decided interest in Freud. Although Ann J. Lane contends that Gilman read hardly any Freudian works (*To Herland* 332), there can be no doubt that even the largely second-hand version of what she would call Freud's "perverted sex-philosophy" (*His Religion and Hers* 164) incensed her. Gilman blamed the Viennese doctor—whom she once dismissed as a "sex-olator" for his persistent emphasis on the formative role of sexuality ("This 'Life Force'" 5)—for "the lowering of standards in sex relations" and for promoting "as 'natural' a degree of indulgence utterly without parallel in nature" (*Living* 323). Distancing herself from such notions, Gilman avowed that "the real life force which has filled the world with all its varying forms is a far wider deeper thing than sex" ("This 'Life Force'" 2), meaning by "sex" both sexuality and gendered distinctions. Her antagonism would ultimately provide Gilman with material for several lectures on "The Falsity of Freud" and "The Freudian Fallacy"; his theories would prove so agitating to her that on a list of "great issues of today," included among her private papers, Gilman ranked "Our Absurd Sexolatry—Exit Sigmund Freud" third, directly beneath "Socialism" and "Races, Nations, and Our World" ("Great Issues" n.p.).

But this alleged hypersexuality was not the only thing bothering Gilman about psychological constructions of the self. In an article devoted to debunking "What the 'Threat of Man' Really Means," Gilman ridicules the notion of a "beast" lurking within man, hiding behind his gentlemanly veneer (1). This contempt for the concept of submerged, contradictory meanings also surfaces in the careful notes Gilman took, both hand- and typewritten, summarizing and condensing Freud's "A General Introduction to Psychoanalysis." Gilman pays especial attention, indicated by marginal notations and exclamation points, to Freud's theory of the intentionality of "tongue slips, pen slips," and "forgetting" ("Extracts" n.p.). What Gilman objects to, her marginalia suggests, is the very idea that such actions conceal an unconscious, suppressed content, that we cannot simply take someone at her word.

Even before she was to become Freud's outspoken adversary, Gilman offers us a horrifying narrative wherein it is precisely this search for an elusive, latent subtext or "sub-pattern" ("The Yellow Wallpaper" 9) that, rather than clarifying mental processes, causes the mind to break down. Numerous critics have discovered untold layers of meaning not only in the yellow wallpaper but in the story of the same name—layers as complex and convoluted as those detected by Gilman's fictional protagonist. But this hermeneutic parallelism should tell us something, given that it correlates Gilman's reader and her readers—links, that is, an increasingly deranged interpreter to her increasingly sophisticated critics.[24] In fact, it is precisely the practice of analytical inspection, the supposition that there is more here than meets the eye, that typifies the narrator's evolving (devolving?) investment in the wallpaper—she detects in it "a kind of sub-pattern in a different shade, a particularly irritating one" behind which "a strange, provoking, formless sort of figure" (8) can be discerned. This "formless figure" could be viewed as a projection of the heroine herself or even, as Elizabeth Ammons argues, as a surrogate for Gilman's distanced mother (43). But in a very specific sense, it is not so much *what* is latent in the paper as it is the *assumption of latency*—the positing of underlying form where there is only "formlessness"—by which the story indicates mental disorder. More, it is the desire, and its eventual "liberating," if surreal, accomplishment, to make this perceived latency manifest—to trade a rational, salutary focus on manifest causes for a more disorienting focus on subtle, lurking intricacies—that signals (both à la Freud's therapeutics and contra Freud's theories) the narrator's descent into insanity.

Forced to avert her gaze from the external world, the narrator begins her study of the back pattern of the wallpaper, eventually coming to feel quite proprietorial about its hidden meaning—catching Jennie studying the pattern, she confesses in her journal that "I am determined that nobody shall find it out but myself!" (14). Focused as she now is solely on the hitherto indiscernible subtext, the protagonist cursorily dismisses what was initially posited as curative—for example, Jennie's attempts to get her out of the room—as "too patent!" (17). She even goes so far as to secure herself to the pattern by a rope, proclaiming that "you don't get *me* out in the road there!" (18). That which, in a less introversive moment, was considered therapeutic now appears both suspect and punitive, while what once seemed punitive and suspect now appears therapeutic—an inversive logic simulating the one undergirding John's treatment (what his "little girl" thinks is good for her is really bad and vice-versa) and Mitchell's rest cure (prescribing domesticity for a woman who complains of being "sick while at home"). She has also shifted focus from the over- to the underlying. What the narrator has done in the end is to embrace the very hermeneutics adopted by her analysts. And it is when she does so that we begin to suspect that she is—to use an appropriately architectural term—unhinged.

Thus far, I have proposed two potential readings of Gilman's story, one that foregrounds the role of domestic determinism and another that suggests the disorienting dangers of latency or, better, the presumption thereof. Although both debunk hypotheses of lurking, organic sources and stress instead the significance, the healthiness of what we might call a hermeneutics of the overt, these readings have ironically come to occupy a covert position over the course of "The Yellow Wallpaper's" critical history, uncannily replicating the front pattern's overshadowing by the back one so that it is the manifest that becomes latent and vice-versa. How might we explain this submersion other than by simply (and too simplistically) dismissing it as evidence of a sustained critical misreading?

It is my belief that this overshadowing has been prompted in significant ways by the story's own inarticulateness, which is in turn tied to the sublimation endemic to the story's uncanny format. In an important essay for my analysis, Mary Jacobus maintains that Gilman's story is one "that has forgotten its 'real purpose' (conversion)" (278). Jacobus calls for readings that move beyond thematic analysis and attend to the tale's "literariness, the way in which it knows more than it knows (and more than the author intended)" (281). She goes on to practice what she preaches by connecting hysteria—that overdetermined "physiological" disease—and the uncanny—that remotely corporeal literary form—through the "creepiness" associated with each. The two come together when the narrator starts creeping around the room, the creepiest moment in the story (see Jacobus 283ff). In Jacobus's reading, what the story represses at the level of content—the female body and its desires—resurfaces at the level of (uncanny) form. My point is that the reverse also happens, in that what the story thematically *foregrounds* as causal—the home's stifling claustrophobia—is *repressed* by its distractingly uncanny (*unheimlich* or unhomelike) generic properties.

While Jacobus maintains that the uncanny by definition cannot be overtly thematized—it makes "itself felt as a 'how' not a 'what'—not as an entity, but rather as a phenomenon" (282), in his provocative study, "The Uncanny," Freud intimates that his titular subject is both a "how" and a "what," that there is an entity behind this phenomenon.[25] Probing beneath the extant definition of the "the uncanny" as that which is "novel and unfamiliar"(221), Freud finds that uncanny feelings are provoked by a compulsive return to something familiar which has been repressed, frightening precisely because it "leads back to what is known of old and long familiar" (220). For Freud, the explicitly frightening is never the uncanny—the source of fright comes not from without so much as from within, not from some external source so much as from the deepest recesses of the human psyche and anatomy, from "an urge inherent in organic life to restore an earlier state of things" (Freud, *Beyond the Pleasure Principle*, qtd. in Hertz 119). Eventually, after a careful archaeology, Freud arrives back at the "entrance to the former *Heim* [home] of all human beings," the womb ("The Uncanny" 245). Although not the sole source of uncanny sensations, "womb-phantasies" (248)—phantasies "of intrauterine existence"(244)—are perceived by Freud to lie at the root of such uncanny fears as being buried alive. To the extent that it evokes the womb as both organic site and psychic phantasy, we might say that the uncanny's uncanniness arises from its entertaining both mimetic and mimotic modes of re-presentation at one and the same time. Or, to put it more simply, what makes an uncanny experience so creepy is the niggling doubt it arouses but does not assuage about the presence of a biological source for that experience. For Gilman to use this form, then, is to risk undermining her story's thematic denigration of what I am calling "hysteria's logic" by not divesting it fully and formally of traces of "hysteria's illogic."

In her non-fictional prose, Gilman does at times associate home and womb in ways that approximate Freud's understanding of the uncanny. Her treatise *The Home*, for example, initially defines its titular subject as "a place wherein young are born and reared, a common shelter for the reproductive group" (15) and soon details how the home appears at once "'tabu,'... 'the forbidden'—a place shut and darkened—wholly private" (49) and "the very temple of the flesh" (272): descriptions which might also apply—without too much of a stretch, I believe—to the womb itself. And yet, in Gilman's *The Home* there is nothing remotely "natural" about a confining domesticity. Indeed, the work is explicitly dedicated to historicizing and politicizing the reasons why the existing home might appear uncanny or unhomelike, to uprooting such "deep-bedded" conceptions, and, finally, to lifting the "mystery and shadow" surrounding this "darkened room" (4), this "the deepest, oldest, darkest, slowest place in all man's mind" (35). As would Freud, Gilman locates something eerily "homelike" in the mind's recesses. Yet the home embedded therein has in Gilman's rendition an external, historic source, not an interior, organic one. For Gilman, that which frightens is *not* hidden from sight, subjective, or even imaginary but all-too-real and tediously familiar. What is not so much repressed as it is so quotidian as to be invisible is precisely how haunting, unnatural, and claustrophobic the conventional home actually is or can be. While for Freud, the recognition of unhomelikeness paralyzes with fright, for Gilman this recognition is meant to mobilize rather than transfix.

Even though "The Yellow Wallpaper," like *The Home*, allows for this crucial recognition at the level of content, it simultaneously evokes at the level of form an uncanniness that tends further to sublimate and complicate rather than clarify such a message. Recent feminist interest in one uncanny genre, the gothic, has highlighted the incipient domestic critique lurking amidst its foreboding depths.[26] As Kate Ferguson Ellis reveals in her *The Contested Castle*, the emergence of bourgeois domestic ideology and the popularity of the gothic novel were simultaneous phenomena. Ellis maintains that the gothic exposes the underside of this ideology, providing a space where the home is unveiled not as a haven from menace but as its very source. Even if so, the genre's critique of domestic ideology is and remains implicit rather than overt. While Gilman may have wanted to draw out this lurking didacticism, other uncanny or gothic elements foregrounded in her story provide compelling diversions. These include the story's setting—not just an ancestral mansion but a nursery room, where the narrator regresses to a near infantile state—and its pacing, which becomes more frantic as more layers are unpeeled. Also diverting are the narrator's and narrative's compulsive return to and reiterative preoccupation with that which will ultimately drive her mad, as well as the seemingly uncanny discovery—compare Freud's—of a dormant meaning, a projection or replication of the protagonist's own situation, therein ("I didn't realize for a long time what the thing was that showed behind, that dim sub-pattern, but now I am quite sure it is a woman" [13]). All of these features have served as indexes of "The Yellow Wallpaper's" uncanniness and as fortification for a psychological hermeneutics.[27] Where they have done so, the tale's literariness has come to eclipse its literalness. Put another way, its classification as uncanny (*unheimlich*) functions not only to repress but to serve as a potentially distracting metonym for the *unhomelike* emphasis of its plot.

The definition of "*unheimlich*" cited by Freud in his essay lists "uncomfortable, uneasy, gloomy, dismal, uncanny, ghastly; (of a house) haunted" (221) among the meanings of the English word. The word's denotation—"(of a house) haunted"—may lie at the bottom of "The Yellow Wallpaper's" uncanniness, but the extent to which the story's mood is set by the other connotative adjectives diverts attention away from this domestic foundation. Thus when Janice Haney-Peritz proposes that "the narrator has turned what seemed to be a real heredity and colonial estate into an uncanny place in which no-body is or can be at home—no matter what s/he might say to the contrary" (265), I would substitute the word "narrative" for Haney-Peritz's "narrator." To my mind, it is the narrative itself, its uncanniness, that distracts from what the narrator might be saying about the origin of her hysteria. The patient's diagnosis of the external cause of her disease notwithstanding, the often fragmented, frenzied, and sublimated form of her story may incline the reader (clinical or critical) to suspect another etiology altogether.

Diane Price Herndl has argued that, for Gilman, writing "The Yellow Wallpaper" was ultimately a curative process, since, once transcribed, the narrative can operate as the formerly hysterical writer's surrogate (68, 74). Yet while writing cures may, like their talking equivalent, have a certain utility, it remains unclear whether this applies to all forms of writing, including uncanny forms. Wouldn't the mode of writing matter as much as the content when it comes to inducing an effective cure, or teaching an effective lesson? Gilman saw all her fictional works, including "The Yellow Wallpaper," as pedagogic in content—as she once avowed, "I wrote it to preach. If it is literature, that just happened" (Black 39). And yet, the sublimation endemic to the uncanny ironically thwarts the possibility of lucid and progressive instruction, of the "truthful re-presentation" Gilman identifies as the essence of her didactic realism. I say ironic because "The Yellow Wallpaper's" horror ought not to distract from its lesson; it *is* its lesson. Ultimately, one of the lessons the story *does* manage to communicate is that pedagogic efficacy depends as much upon the manifest, transparent nature of form as it does upon specific content—a lesson in Gilman's own dictum that "what the thing does makes it what it is" ("Our Excessive" 5).

Evaluating her own tale, Gilman acknowledged that "the story was meant to be dreadful, and succeeded" (*Living* 119). She candidly confessed to her friend Martha Lane in a letter that "it's a simple tale, but highly unpleasant" (qtd. in Hill 186). She even acknowledged that "The Yellow Wallpaper" was "valued by alienists" ("Why I Wrote" 20), as those who studied mental disorders were then called. If this is indicative of the story's "value," however, then its ability to instruct would seem to be one important aspect of its message. The author herself certainly thought so, maintaining in her essay explaining her reasons for writing "The Yellow Wallpaper" that the story "was not intended to drive people crazy, but to save people from being driven crazy, and it worked" (20). But to what extent did it actually work? The story was famously rejected by Horace Scudder of the *Atlantic Monthly*, who returned it with a brief note stating simply, "I could not forgive myself if I made others as miserable as I have made myself!" (qtd. in *Living* 119). This reaction was apparently also shared by Walter Stetson, who told Charlotte that he had "read it *four* times, and [thought] it the most ghastly tale he ever read" (qtd. in Hill 186). One irate reader wrote to complain of the story as "perilous stuff" in the pages of the Boston *Transcript*, arguing that the "graphic" and "sensational" tale had a "morbid fascination" for its readers. This respondent, whose initials were (Gilman believed tellingly) "M. D.," felt that "the story can hardly give pleasure to any reader, and to many ... it must bring the keenest pain" (*Living* 120).

True, several doctors did write to praise the tale for its realism, and several reviewers, including Henry Blackwell, praised its tragically accurate depiction of some marriages and found the story's lessons edifying enough to recommend its wide circulation. Yet Blackwell's comments appeared in the feminist *Woman's Journal*; in general, reviewers for mainstream publications laid stress on the story's horrifying rather than didactic aspects.[28] William Dean Howells, for instance, exemplified such an impulse when he decided to include "The Yellow Wallpaper" in his anthology *The Great Modern American Stories*, some twenty-eight years after its original publication. Although the volume included stories by James, Jewett, Twain, and Wharton, Howells's brief introduction to Gilman's tale highlights its gothic dimensions and, as a result, tends to isolate Gilman from these other realists. Maintaining that he still "shiver[s] over it," Howells foregrounds this "terrible and too wholly dire" story's capacity "to freeze our young blood" (From "A Reminiscent" 55).[29] Howells was not alone in "shivering" over the tale. As Gilman confided to a friend of hers, "I read the thing to three women here however, and I never saw such squirms!" (qtd. in Allen 186). So even if we grant Herndl's contention that writing "The Yellow Wallpaper" may have helped Gilman to arrive at some form of cure for her own "hysterical" symptoms, by the author's own admission it seemed only to induce them in some of the women who heard it.

Conrad Shumaker has argued that "The Yellow Wallpaper's" polemical message failed to reach an audience because the narrative stages a conflict between Gilman's realist and reformist impulses. To be a realist, Shumaker contends, "the writer must respect the conventions that make up a large part of what the audience will accept as 'reality.' Yet if women's role is what the writer wants to reform, then those very conventions are what must be attacked. In effect, the writer must hope that a significant portion of her audience already feels enough doubt about those conventions to accept her unconventional portrait of reality" (87). Many in Gilman's contemporary audience, Shumaker maintains, were not yet prepared for the consequences of accepting her representation as remotely realistic, and would hence have tuned out the story's radical portent as best they could. Shumaker raises important considerations, but I would add that if "The Yellow Wallpaper" does qualify as realistic, it by no means clearly conveys the instructive, truthful re-presentation of human life that Gilman valorizes. Furthermore, the story's inability to communicate its didactic point may have stemmed less from readerly inattention and resistance than from "The Yellow Wallpaper's" uncanny form and the way the sedimentation inherent to the genre functions to obscure Gilman's re-formist appropriation of it.

In a larger sense, it may be the very fictionality of "The Yellow Wallpaper" that allows for this potential obscurity: as Freud himself conceded, "*a great deal that is not uncanny in fiction would be so if it happened in real life*" (249, emphasis in the original). If the story and its stultifying vision of domesticity fail to disturb, in other words, it may be because such harrowing portraits could always be safely rationalized as the stuff of mere fiction or fantasy. If so, this may help to explain why Gilman stopped writing fiction for nearly two decades after publishing "The Yellow Wallpaper." It may also explain why she did not return to the gothic format when she did resume writing creatively, opting instead to expose the haunting, harmful effects of homemaking via more conventionally didactic prose.[30]

Gilman's *Herland* has frequently been read as the flipside of "The Yellow Wallpaper," with Susan Gubar suggesting that the women the short story's narrator espies in the garden prefigure the Herlanders (146).[31] The two narratives do, at least at first glance, seem to be positioned contrapuntally. In contrast to the claustrophobic mansion central to "The Yellow Wallpaper," there is nothing remotely homelike in this utopia: while Herland might, intriguingly, remind the story's male narrator of "an old established, perfectly run country place" (99), "home" is neither a place nor an idea that the Herlanders themselves recognize. When the three American intruders attempt to describe the traditional American domestic scene, the Herland women have to ask "what is home?" (61). Their vocabulary lacking any such word, the Herlanders cannot grasp the concept—especially in its privatized sense—no matter how often their male interpreters try to explain it (94, 96–97). Additionally, and in stark contrast to the detailed domestic setting of "The Yellow Wallpaper," we never get to see inside a single Herland dwelling—in fact, there is little topographical description of Herland at all, unusual for the utopian genre. Clearly, Gilman's two stories are in crucial ways markedly dissimilar. Yet while we have every right to expect *Herland*, *qua* utopia, to enact the genre's governing compulsion *not* to repeat, in many respects Gilman's 1915 novel replicates the "unpleasant" story she composed some twenty-five years earlier. Indeed, I want to suggest that the apparent (but not always actual) differences between their two genres tends to obscure the extent to which the later narrative actually duplicates aspects of the earlier one.

*Herland*'s plot can be quickly summarized: three male Americans, all friends and scientists, join a scientific expedition to a remote and "savage" country, where they hear legend of a land peopled only by women.[32] Though their current voyage allows no time to explore this legend's truth, the three men decide to launch their own expedition at a later date. Upon returning, they do indeed discover such a place, filled with creatures who, while female, bear little resemblance to the women of their own land. Imprisoned when they threaten to tell the world about the country they name "Herland," the Americans are nonetheless treated with kindness. They are also pumped for information about their "bisexual" society, forced to draw comparisons that bathe their own country in a distinctly unfavorable light. Even still, the Herlanders persist in believing that a world with two sexes must surpass their own; thus, there is widespread rejoicing when the Americans eventually marry their Herland girlfriends. The honeymoons have barely commenced, however, when the macho Terry, fed up with his new bride's typically Herlandesque asexuality, tries to rape her, whereupon he is promptly and permanently expelled.[33] The third American, Jeff, opts to stay in Herland, contented with his newfound paradise, but Van (the narrator and most likeable of the Americans) and his wife, Ellador, agree to accompany Terry back to the states (thereby setting the stage for the sequel, *With Her in Ourland* [1916]).

Rather than muddling points Gilman strenuously insists upon elsewhere, *Herland* succinctly encapsulates them. Domesticity is a prime example. For all her confessed suspicions of the domestic, Gilman's stated goal was never to destroy the home but to refurbish it—to transform it into a place of growth and renewal. The poem "Birth," with which Gilman opens her poetry volume *In This Our World*, testifies to this remodeling process. In sharp contrast to the stultifying confinement conveyed in the earlier-cited poem "In Duty Bound," the trope Gilman employs here is a bodily home without boundaries:

> Lord, I am born!
> I have built me a body
> Whose ways are all open,
> Whose currents run free . . .
> . . .
> I am clothed, and my raiment
> Fits smooth to the spirit,
> The soul moves unhindered,
> The body is free . . .
> . . .
> I am housed, O my Father!
> My body is sheltered.
> My spirit has room
> 'Twixt the whole world and me. . . .
> . . .
> And the union and birth
> Of the house, ever growing.
> Have built me a city—
> Have born me a state—
> Where I live manifold,
> Many-voiced, many-hearted. . . . (1–2)

While as in "In Duty Bound" this poem clearly analogizes home and body, here it becomes a liberating versus enshackling metaphor. For Gilman, the ideal home was never some "small dark place" (*Home* 277) associated with and fixed in the past; what she envisioned was always an open-aired, enlightened, future-oriented entity—a structure best exemplified by those the Herlanders construct. Indeed, even though the respective determining processes yield dramatically different outcomes, *Herland* is just as much a document of domestic determinism as is "The Yellow Wallpaper"; in both stories, female identity is structured according to the architectural blueprints of the homes the fictional women inhabit. In Herland, the fact that there is "no place" like home is instrumental to the happiness and healthiness of its inhabitants and hence to its status as a utopia: a "no place" that is simultaneously "a good place."

Significantly, *Herland* diverges from the classic utopian formula in that its founding displacement is not temporal but spatial: that is, it is not as a temporal metonym but via a spatial syllogism that the relation between early twentieth-century America ("Ourland") and Gilman's synchronous utopian society ("Herland") is best understood. In this syllogism, America is to Herland as depth is to surface—in other words, Herland makes manifest the best qualities lurking within "Ourland" yet constrained by prevailing environmental forces from emerging to the surface. Here, Gilman willingly utilizes a surface-depth model but only so as to reinforce the inherent naturalness and health of her utopia.

But this is not the only strategy Gilman deploys to naturalize Herland. As we have seen, Gilman claimed that she wrote "The Yellow Wallpaper" to expose the distorted and detrimental views of womanhood proffered by doctors like Mitchell. *Herland*, I would suggest, is no less informed by biological understandings of female subjectivity. The difference resides in the way it represents reproduction not as potentially *pathogenic* but as *parthogenetic*. For *Herland* constitutes an attempt to "truthfully re-present" the biologistic theories of sociologist Lester F. Ward, whom Gilman identified as the "greatest man" she ever knew (*Living* 187). It may be Ward and his theories that Gilman had in mind when she dismissed Freud's narrow approach to human (sexual) nature with the assurance that "a larger knowledge of biology, of zoölogy is what is wanted to offset this foolishness" (*Living* 323).[34] Gilman met Ward some four years after the publication of "The Yellow Wallpaper" at a Woman's Suffrage Convention, and he soon became a mentor. Besides crediting him as one of two sources for her *Women and Economics* (1898), Gilman dedicates her *Man-Made World* (1911) to Ward, writing of his "Gynaecocentric Theory of Life" that "nothing so important to women has ever been given to the World."[35]

Ward's theory, as its etymology would suggest, posits the female as the race type, the necessary and primary force in evolution, and relegates the male to a secondary role based on his reproductive utility. Life began, Ward contends, in a single fertile organism and that organism was female, leading him to conclude that "life was originally and essentially female"

("Past and Future" 542). It is from Ward that Gilman's Reform Darwinism is largely derived: his evolutionary schema, like Gilman's, emphasized growth and nurturing rather than combat and struggle. Inspired by Ward, Gilman came to believe that once the nonorganic forces responsible for toppling woman from her rightful place as "mother of the world" (*Living* 331) were rectified or removed, the human race could rejoin its path toward boundless improvement. Ward's female-centered theory allowed Gilman to give full voice to her essentialist understandings of women as mother without risk of pathologizing taint. As she wrote in *Women and Economics*, if motherhood were truly valued by the human race, "all its females [would be] segregated entirely to the uses of motherhood, consecrated, set apart, specially developed, spending every power of their nature on the service of their children" (19)—precisely the situation *Herland* depicts.

Ward's self-sufficient organism, capable of sustaining all life, was instrumental in shaping not just Gilman's perception of life's origins but of literature's possibilities. In a 1906 article by Ward found in Gilman's papers, Ward criticizes the recent boom in utopian fiction for its meager prophetic powers. Opposing mere speculation, Ward contends that "the only possible scientific basis for forecasting the future of the sexes is a study of their past history from the very origin of sex" (542). Setting his own example, Ward embarked on such a study and arrived at his Gynaecocentric theory. Similarly, Gilman's deployment of his recommended "cosmological perspective" yields the utopian vision most clearly encapsulated in her fictional *Herland*. Indeed, Gilman's debt to Ward might explain why she chooses a male American sociologist to narrate her tale and to represent a Gynaecocentric worldview plausibly to a potentially skeptical audience.[36] More to the point, Ward's model of the parthogenetic, essentially female original ovum doesn't just provide the microcosm for Gilman's Herland; it also enables her desired confluence of mimetic and didactic modes, as Gilman's fictional re-presentation of Ward's model both reflects and informs about a "prior" reality. In other words, despite utopian fiction's futuristic emphasis, *Herland* could be read as exemplifying Gilman's mimetic didacticism by forging a symmetry between the utopian future perfect and the biologized past unearthed by Ward.[37]

This prerequisite regression to a recessed organicism, combined with the aforementioned reinvocation of a surface-depth model, suggests the extent to which the utopian approximates the uncanny as defined by Freud. Although for Gilman, this re-presented biology was cellular and social, not genital and subjective, and although utopian and psychological fiction are typically perceived as incongruous modes (see Jones, "Gilman" 117), there are actually several significant overlaps between uncanny and utopian genres, and, accordingly, between the uncanny "Yellow Wallpaper" and the utopian *Herland*. Like the uncanny, utopian fiction functions as a literature of estrangement, a mode that re-presents the familiar in such a way as to make it appear strange. According to Jean Pfaelzer, utopian fiction often veers into the uncanny "as the historical determinants of the utopian world are revealed" and we come to sense that this fantastic world may not, but should, be natural, familiar (*Utopian* 16).[38] Yet while both genres achieve their effect through a recourse to the "natural," the uncanny story does its re-presenting to produce chills; the utopian tale does so primarily to promote change. More importantly, while the uncanny's repetition eerily destabilizes the notion of a natural ground, the utopian, on the other hand, begins from a seemingly strange and "unnatural" re-presentation which by the end, when successful, seems to outstrip the "original" in its naturalness (not to mention stripping the "original" of its pretensions to naturalness).

Both the transformative and the naturalizing dimensions of utopian visions are evidenced in Karl Marx's contention that "the productive forces developing in *the womb* of bourgeois society create the material conditions for the solutions of that antagonism" (qtd. in Pfaelzer, *Utopian* 6, emphasis added).[39] Bearing out Marx's implication that there is something distinctly organic and even specifically womblike about utopias, there is, true to form, something distinctly organic and even womblike about Herland. Indeed, its naturalness (and initial uncanniness) is foregrounded from the very beginning: the first chapter of the novel is entitled "A Not Unnatural Enterprise."[40] More to the point, the three Americans are confined within this female yet strangely unfeminine place for approximately "nine months"—a period Van refers to outright as "our confinement" (58). At the end of this gestational period, the insensitive Terry can find nothing familiar about the place, while the always chivalrous Jeff can find nothing strange: "'Home!' Terry scoffs. 'There isn't a home in the whole pitiful place.' . . . 'There isn't anything else and you know it,' Jeff retorts" (98). Van's reaction combines those of his two friends and invokes seemingly uncanny thoughts of mother and home:[41]

It gave me a queer feeling, way down deep, as the stirring of some ancient dim prehistoric consciousness. . . . It was like—coming home to mother. . . . I mean the feeling that a very little child would have, who had been lost—for ever so long. It was a sense of getting home, of being clean and rested; of safety and yet freedom; of love that was always there, warm like sunshine in May, not hot like a stove or a featherbed—a love that didn't irritate or smother. (142)

While Van's "queer feeling" might qualify as a "womb phantasy," couched as it is as utopian, natural, and overt rather than as uncanny and sublimated, it functions ultimately to soothe rather than to unsettle. The homelikeness Van describes here holds none of the connotations of claustrophobia, darkness, or dankness that Gilman associates with the traditional home or that Freud associates with the *unheimlich*. More than simply a "return to latency" (Pfaelzer, *Utopian* 155), Van's "homecoming," at least generically speaking, signifies revision, not regression. The possibility of such renovations in utopias like Herland (both fictional place and text)—combined with a confessed lack of respect for the past (*Herland* 111)—allow both the invocation of the womb-as-metaphor and the site so symbolized to convey what Van describes as an overriding aura of "health" rather than "hysteria" (81). To put it differently, Herland's all-pervasive womblike re-presentation is so thoroughly organicized as to qualify it as mimetic (in Gilman's healthy sense) and to extirpate any lurking suspicion of mimosis.

One way to read *Herland*, then, is as utilizing the utopian form to restage the drama of the uncanny—or, to be more specific, to return to the issues dramatized but ultimately submerged in "The Yellow Wallpaper"—and script alternate conclusions. In content, *Herland* emulates the classic uncanny formula, replete with examples of estrangement, the unhomelike, and even its own version of a "womb-phantasy." But the open-ended, picaresque format, didactic tone, and rational narrative mode of the utopian genre cooperate to remove any vestigial claustrophobic creepiness still clinging to these seemingly uncanny devices, as does what Lewis Mumford refers to as the genre's "externalism," its virtually exclusive preoccupation with surface details (qtd. in Lane, "Introduction" xxi). Above all else, the novel's emphatic and explicit insistence on the organic nature of Herland obviates any possibility of uncanny sublimation or simulation, an insistence matched at the level of form by the naturalizing impulse intrinsic to the utopian genre. In *Herland*, at least, narrative form works to further substantiate rather than distract from the novel's thematic insistence on a maternalistic worldview as both natural and normative.

Given her avowed maternalism, Gilman would no doubt have seen this re-presentation as eminently "truthful." The utopian formula, in fact, provides an ideal forum for Gilman's sociological critique of domestic ideology, while its manipulation of the tropes and devices that also define the uncanny help to bring her point "home," so to speak, all the more effectively. Still, *Herland*'s accomplishments are not without costs. Among them, there is a stasis endemic to the utopian genre reminiscent of the static "unmoving" (*Home* 6) quality Gilman so deplored in the traditional home. As the concluding lines of *The Home*'s chapter on the "Evolution of the Home" avow, "the world does move—and so does the home" (35). Gilman envisioned this dynamism as operating on both spatial and temporal planes, as we see in her celebration of "the home that is coming" (341). To Gilman's mind, so long as the traditional home remained a static entity, so too—in keeping with Gilman's domestic determinism—would the domesticated woman remain. Indeed, one of Gilman's chief critiques of existing gender differences was that the male of our species alone has been allowed to range widely while the female has been forced to become "absolutely static" (*Women and Economics* 65).

However much she regretted motionlessness, it is ineluctably inscribed in *Herland*'s utopian vision, conferred not so much by its content as by its form, as the utopian genre is by definition a static mode.[42] Complaints about the stasis intrinsic to Herland—place and novel—are leveled both within and against the narrative. In the story, even its ardent supporter Van notes that "the years of peace, the unmeasured plenty, the steady health, the large good will and smooth management which ordered everything, left nothing to overcome" (99). Elizabeth Keyser takes such passages as proof for her argument that "Herland, despite its inhabitants' concern for the future, is ... a static society" (167). If Gilman's ideal woman is perpetually in flux, then the statical quality of "Herland" as utopia, despite its utopian content, impedes the achievement of this mobile ideal.

Perhaps more troubling, the stagnant nature of this utopian vision interferes with its potential as praxis. As Ernst Bloch has argued, the revolutionary potential of utopian visions is only capable of being tapped if "this totality appears not as a static, as a finished principle of the whole, but rather as . . . the process of latency of a still unfinished world" (qtd. in Pfaelzer, "Response" 194). Bloch's understanding of utopian "latency" as the site of change qualifies *Herland*'s political aspirations, for in the novel, the latent is presented as not only "finished" but fixed, perfected, affirming the society's health but making transformation appear not too easy but irrelevant, even obsolete.

Finally and ironically, despite Gilman's disdain for psychoanalytic approaches to life and narrative, what she composes in *Herland* actually replicates the classic, coherent, Oedipal linear plot. *Herland*, after all, is a place in which all the fathers (all the men) have been killed off, leaving the three young male outsiders free to marry the(ir?) mothers. In turn, with the intrusion of the male Americans, the imaginary world of female-female nurturance is rather abruptly—we might say phallically—disrupted (a disruption even the Herlanders come to see as necessary for their own survival, maturation, and good). Gilman, who by 1915 had begun her campaign against Freud, ironically duplicates as feminist and utopian the "sexologist's" very formulas for normative development, not to mention his version of the foundational script of patriarchal civilization.

Gilman and Freud did share a belief that for a woman anatomy could prove destiny. But for Gilman, this equation remained a utopian goal, not a mimetic representation of women's lives as already constituted under patriarchy. Turning from human to narrative form, however, the equation between anatomy and destiny does compute for Gilman's two most famous fictional works. For as I have shown, the formal principles or "anatomy" (see Frye, *Anatomy*) of "The Yellow Wallpaper" and *Herland* have proven influential in determining (though in ways that have often been overlooked or repressed) the function, interpretation, and reception of both works.

# 5

## Black Aesthetics

*The Race Novels of Frances E. Watkins Harper, Charles W. Chesnutt, and Pauline E. Hopkins*

A little more than a decade ago, Jane Tompkins—incensed by Ann Douglas's lament over the feminization of American culture—set out to defend sentimental fiction from its detractors. In her *Sensational Designs* (1985), she attempts to answer that perennially disparaging question "But is it any good?" by tackling the broader subject of the "institutionalization of literary value." Bucking tradition and building on the pioneering efforts of scholars including Nina Baym, Annette Kolodny, Paul Lauter, and Lillian S. Robinson, Tompkins offers a revisionist evaluative model, one that displaces the Kantian emphasis on pure aesthetic value and focuses instead on a text's "cultural work," the "sensational designs" it has upon its readers.[1] Or as Tompkins herself puts it,

> when literary texts are conceived as agents of cultural formation rather than as objects of interpretation and appraisal, . . . When one sets aside modernist demands—for psychological complexity, moral ambiguity, epistemological sophistication, stylistic density, formal economy—and attends to the way a text offers a blueprint for survival under a specific set of political, economic, social, or religious conditions, an entirely new story begins to unfold, and one's sense of the formal exigencies of narrative alters accordingly. . . . The text succeeds or fails on the basis of its "fit" with the features of its immediate context, on the degree to which it provokes the desired response, and not in relation to unchanging formal, psychological, or philosophical standards of complexity, or truth, or correctness. (xvii–xviii)

In short, if sentimental writing is ever to be appreciated, the supposed universality and objectivity of aesthetic standards must first be interrogated. In addition to thoroughly re-evaluating hitherto ignored or derided narrative content, Tompkins insists we must reassess the very function of narrative form.

This emphasis on literature's functional rather than aesthetic value has been hailed (with good reason) by a host of critics who have eagerly joined in the effort of rehabilitating hitherto devalued works of literature. Indeed, studies like *Sensational Designs* have helped to usher in a veritable cottage industry dedicated to recovering the formerly uncanonized, bringing to the attention of scholars, teachers, and students alike texts that might otherwise still be prejudicially languishing in some literary wasteland. The reach of this recuperative project quickly extended beyond Tompkins's grasp; for example, while *Sensational Designs* reconsidered previously noncanonical fictions written strictly by white middle-class women and men, a number of subsequent studies have successfully employed this cultural model (with modifications) to reclaim an African-American literary "tradition."[2]

Yet to study the history of African-American literature in this country is to realize that the equation between literary value and utility predates Tompkins by at least one hundred years. In 1895, for instance, Victoria Earle Matthews delivered a speech defining "The Value of Race Literature," which she locates in its potential to provide role models for blacks while simultaneously teaching white readers the true nature and "intrinsic worth" of each of her colored brethren (qtd. in Tate 83). For Matthews, a work's merit is commensurate with its contribution to the politico-evangelical project of racial uplift in an interracial nation. A similar if more assimilative sociological understanding informs the prefatory apologia of Pauline Elizabeth Hopkins's first novel, *Contending Forces* (1900), in which Hopkins maintains that "after all, it is the simple, homely tale, unassumingly told, which cements the bond of brotherhood among all classes and all complexions" (13). Aspiring author Charles Chesnutt voiced less humble motives in an early journal entry (1880), detailing his intent to "write for a purpose, a high, holy purpose.... The Negro's part is to prepare himself for recognition and equality, and it is the province of literature to open the way for him to get it—to accustom the public mind to the idea; and while amusing them to lead them on imperceptibly, unconsciously step by step to the desired state of feeling" (*Journals* 139–40). As Chesnutt's agenda makes clear, even at a young age the writer considered the line between literature and praxis to be irrevocably blurred. This holds true as well for Frances E. Watkins Harper, who at the age of sixty-seven found the segue from uplifting speaker to didactic author a virtually effortless one. Harper's first novel, *Iola Leroy* (1892), includes many of the author's speeches more or less verbatim and concludes with the hope that its "mission will not be in vain if it awaken in the hearts of our countrymen a stronger sense of justice and a more Christlike humanity" (282). Clearly, for all four representatives of W. E. B. Du Bois's "talented tenth," "race literature" ought to manifest an overt didacticism, or, as Claudia Tate puts it, a "pedagogic intentionality" (86). Even more, the value of these works is to be found not in intentions alone but in use—in their pedagogic efficacy.

As Tate maintains in *Domestic Allegories of Political Desire*, to read late-nineteenth-century black-authored novels with our late-twentieth-century eyes, and to judge them unfavorably according to prevailing, supposedly universal aesthetic standards, is to overlook or dismiss their subversive, context-specific political aims. Along similar lines, Susan Gillman, in an insightful article analyzing what she terms "the nineteenth-century American race melodrama," argues against reading such works as "aesthetic forms" since to do so invariably leads to a dismissal of their "lasting literary merit." Gillman promotes instead an ideological model of evaluation, which allows her to circumvent questions of "abstract literary value that so preoccupied an earlier generation of critics" (225).

Gillman's "earlier generation," as with Tate's "twentieth-century eyes," are meant to indicate (and indict) critics inclined to dismiss these works on pure aesthetical grounds alone. Many of these turn-of-the-century African-American novels, however, have also suffered at the hands of those for whom the primary criterion of literary evaluation is politics. Among others, critics who hold with Addison Gayle's definition of a "black aesthetic" have deplored as politically misguided or offensive many of the very works to which Gillman and Tate assign cultural, political value.[3] More recently, Houston Baker in *Workings of the Spirit* (1991) has drawn upon a complex of political and aesthetic standards to reproach late-nineteenth-century African-American women writers for ignoring what he names "black southern soundings"; in the process, Baker chastises modern day critics—he calls them "revivalists"—who to his mind neglect this tonal deafness in order to rain unqualified praise on these texts' "'cultural' merit" (23). This blind spot leads them, in Baker's estimation, to turn "everywhere in their commentary but to the texts themselves as they seek grounds for fulsome evaluations" (23).[4]

Is Baker right? Must we really look elsewhere than to the intrinsic features of nineteenth-century black-authored novels in order to praise them? More broadly, are the aesthetical and ideological really so fundamentally opposed? And is it then necessary for those of us invested in recovery to swap evaluative modes informed by the former for those addressing the latter? Thanks to the rise and spread of the new historicism and other cultural materialist approaches to literature, the value and pleasures of reading texts in context are increasingly appreciated. As a result, many more readers are prepared to acknowledge that rich insights can be gleaned from placing turn-of-the-century African-American works within the specific context of the "racial nadir" in which they were composed. I, for one, am very interested in exploring how these works responded to a climate in which racialized forms—both literary and corporeal—were being held up to "white" aesthetic standards and found inherently inferior, ungainly, and indelicate. But again, does fair treatment require that their responses be assessed through an ideological literary criticism that reads literature as ideological criticism?

No doubt, aesthetic evaluation proper has functioned primarily as an exclusionary force throughout African-American literary history. The 1994 reissue—thanks to the sleuthing efforts of Frances Smith Foster—of three hitherto overlooked novels written by Harper testifies to a history of literary neglect, one which approximates that of Harriet Wilson's earlier *Our Nig* before Henry Louis Gates's 1983 rediscovery, or, for that matter, many of the other more or less "forgotten" texts being reissued in such series as Gates's Schomburg Library of Nineteenth-Century Black Women Writers. Even in those relatively rare instances where works by turn-of-the-century black authors did garner a fairly broad readership, influential literary lions like William Dean Howells sought to set the terms of appreciation, praising writers who captured "the range between appetite and emotion" (damning praise Howells offered Paul Laurence Dunbar in an introduction to the latter's poems [xvi–xviii]) at the same time that he objected to the "bitter, bitter" qualities of Charles Chesnutt's all too realistic *The Marrow of Tradition* ("Psychological" 882).

It was not simply or even primarily black-authored *literary* forms that were being branded aesthetically inadequate, however. The very "appetite and emotion" Howells valued in Dunbar's poems were, in what can scarcely be coincidence, the self-same traits being inscribed within a racialized black morphology.[5] Indeed, a central irony in framing African-American literary works as "aesthetically flawed cultural workers" is that this framework disturbingly evokes minoritizing definitions of African Americans themselves, prevalent throughout this country's divisive racial history. And as this insidious history teaches, whatever value may have been assigned to American blacks' labor has been vastly outweighed by the devaluation of their purported extrinsic and intrinsic qualities. Beginning around the 1830s or '40s but intensifying during the abysmal 1890s, numerous attempts were made to locate justifications for continued oppression and devaluation—to locate racial identity itself, a notoriously slippery concept—in some aspect of anatomy, always through a framework presupposing Caucasoid standards of superiority (see Gossett, esp. 69–83).[6] These efforts often directly involved aesthetic judgments, as evidenced by Havelock Ellis's 1905 contention that, "so far as any objective standard of aesthetic beauty is recognizable, that standard involves the supremacy of the fair type of woman" (177). With characteristic aplomb, Ellis proceeds to apply this Anglophile "standard" to assess various races and nationalities according to their divergence or proximity therefrom. Ellis's aesthetical axiology was, of course, not very original; for the most part, it only elaborated on the earlier work of figures like the skull-collecting Doctor Samuel George Morton, who sought to map out cranially Darwin's Great Chain of Being, placing the Anglo-European as the literal epitome of the formally pleasing "high brow" and the "Negro" of the primitive "low brow" (the implications for literary cultures should be self-evident).[7]

While much of this quasi-science worked to brutalize the pure black figure, other camps were nominating the mulatto as the very emblem of racial degeneracy and bodily impurity—as quite literally, to cite the popular lingo, a "taint."[8] In 1905, for example, William Benjamin Smith published his *The Color Line: A Brief in Behalf of the Unborn*, which draws on popular pseudoscience to posit "*panmixia*" (or the "amalgamation of Black and White") as the "deadly enemy" of the South's and its (Caucasian) people's evolution and preservation (13). In a chapter dedicated to proving the Negro's "inferiority," Smith maintains that to equate the Negro and the European in terms of physical beauty would be like proposing that "the tiger-lily was as beautiful as the rose, the hippopotamus as pretty as the squirrel" (not very decisive examples, in my opinion). Smith goes on to insist:

Does some one say that physical beauty is a poor, inferior thing at best—that beauty of soul is alone sufficient and only desirable? We deny it outright. Beauty of form and colour has its own high and inalienable and indefectible rights, its own profound significance for the history alike of nature and man. Even if the intermingling of bloods wrought no other wrong than the degradation of bodily beauty, the coarsening of feature and blurring of coloration, it would still be an unspeakable outrage, to be deprecated and prevented by all means in our power. Moreover, we hold that every such degeneration of facial type will drag along with it inevitably a corresponding declension of spirit. (38)

For all its "indefectibility," beauty of form and face—the inherent birthright, Smith presumes, of pureblood whites—is perpetually at risk of degradation from "panmixia"; and once this facial degeneration has commenced, the soul can't help but follow. The peculiar logic of Smith's trajectory thus inverts the popular maxim "beauty is as beauty does."

Nor, in such circles, was the impetus solely toward constructing racialized *aesthetic* scales. There were also concerted efforts to differentiate between peoples on the basis of allegedly *anaesthetic* qualities, a not exclusively (although significantly) clinical term for a lack or "defect in physical sensation" (Williams, *Keywords* 31).[9] Italian physician Cesare Lombroso, whose work was well known in this country, was one doctor among dozens to help promulgate the racist view of blacks as insensate: "All travellers know the indifference of Negroes and American savages to pain: the former cut their hands and laugh in order to avoid work; the latter, tied to the torture post, gaily sing the praises of their tribe while they are slowly burnt" (qtd. in Gould 227). Although writing primarily about Native Americans, Charles Darwin, especially in *The Descent of Man*, also connected savagery and anaesthesia: "The American savage voluntarily submits to the most horrid tortures without a groan" (315).

This view of the inherent "anaesthetic" capacity of less advanced types persisted well into the century's final decades, as evidenced by S. Weir Mitchell's 1892 conclusion in the *Journal of the American Medical Association* that "in the process of being civilized we [Anglo-Saxons] have won, I suspect ... intensified capacity to suffer. The savage does not feel pain as we do" (108). Just as "the myth of the loose black woman" worked to justify her rape by white men, this anaesthetic myth helped to rationalize the sustained torture and mistreatment of those considered "primitive."

The damage inflicted from being labeled "unaesthetic" and/or "anaesthetic" is readily apparent. Yet ironically, even the term "aesthetic" when used to describe blacks could prove injurious. Consider, for instance, what we might call the "aesthetic" stereotype—which condescendingly depicts blacks as being sensuously (and sensually) prone to revel in the beautiful. Even W. E. B. Du Bois concedes (while revaluing) this typecasting in his claim that "the Negro is primarily an artist. The usual way of putting this is to speak disdainfully of his 'sensuous' nature. This means that the only race which has held at bay the life destroying forces of the tropics, has gained therefrom in some slight compensation a sense of beauty, particularly for sound and color, which characterizes the race" ("Negro Art and Literature" 311). When I looked up "aesthetic" in my dictionary, I was struck by the word's evocation of the "disdainful" characterizations of African-Americans Du Bois himself disdains. Standard definitions of the word include "having a sense of the beautiful; characterized by a love of beauty; pertaining to, involving, or concerned with pure emotion and sensation as opposed to pure intellectuality" (*Random House*). There is an audible resonance between such definitions and the racist clichés which bestow on blacks an inherent aesthetic sense—a process that, far from indicating refinement, only served to further dissociate blacks from "intellectuality." African-Americans, according to such demeaning accounts, could desire beauty but could not be beautiful, produce the beautiful, or even articulate what the beautiful was.

When we add to the equation the highly charged economic undertones of the very notion of "value" for a people still bearing the visible scars of possession and dispossession, a clearer picture emerges of the hostile, dehumanizing context that shaped when, where, and how these black writers entered the literary marketplace. I suppose it could be argued that the issue of evaluation was so vexatious, so volatile for late-century black writers that they might be exonerated for skirting aesthetics altogether when they sat down to write. Yet such an argument would not only be too reductive, too in itself evasive, but also, quite simply, wrong. For aesthetical issues were absolutely vital to these writers' conceptions of literary form and representations of human form therein, central, that is, to the very political designs and features of their respective texts.[10] Rather than conceiving of art *either* in aesthetic *or* in propagandistic terms, authors including Harper, Chesnutt, and Hopkins deploy aesthetics *as* protest, *as* ideology.[11] By this I mean not only that they thematically explore the nature of beauty as a means of protesting the opposition between a black "nature" and the beautiful, but that they utilize specific idioms—ranging from Harper's simple, direct, and accessible language and dialogue through Chesnutt's complex, amorphous, indeterminate stylistics to Hopkins's melodramatic, excessive, polemical style—all of which, in their diverse ways, serve to accentuate and replicate at the formal level the nexus between aesthetics and politics exemplified and extolled thematically. Or, to put it more simply, what these narratives tell they also, simultaneously, attempt to show. Above and beyond acknowledging their emplotted disquisitions on aesthetic issues, then, we need to consider these works' *structural features* as integral components of their respective strategies for racial uplift and political transformation. Viewing narrative form as an organic extension of narrative content, these authors utilized both in the project of destabilizing reified aesthetic categories. It is all the more ironic, then, that it is largely on the basis of these very categories that their works are still being devalued. It is even more ironic when we consider that these novels effectively syncretize characteristics ("aesthetic" and "cultural") which the present-day critical climate typically dichotomizes.

One problem with an unabashedly functional hermeneutics is a tendency to disregard formal properties through a primary focus on content and hence to slight what Raymond Williams has called the "structure of feeling... demonstrable, above all, in fundamental choices of form" (qtd. in G. Levine 21). To reduce desire to narrative content alone is, in other words, to overlook the feeling in the form. In the ensuing analyses of Harper's *Iola Leroy*, Chesnutt's *Marrow of Tradition*, and Hopkins's *Of One Blood*, I attend to this "feeling" by examining each author's "fundamental choice" of narrative form as what Kenneth Burke would call "a strategy for confronting or encompassing ... [a] situation" (54). Burke insists that beauty's consoling power, its capacity to equip us for living, always implies a larger threat without which there would be no need for comforting. This is precisely how we might discuss the formal properties of these novels, that is, as "*strategic* answers, *stylized answers*" (3) to a situation in which African-American literary and bodily forms and the aesthetically treasured were poised in antipodal relationship.[12] Burke's emphasis on the "style" of these answers reminds us that any fair assessment of the "designs" these works have upon readers requires a consideration of their "design" or form, and not simply their representational content.

All three novels are united in taking up—in order to make over—culturally sanctioned "beautiful" forms, whether bodily or literary; at both structural and thematic levels, they unsettle the notion of a fixed, timeless beauty identified with a fixed, given, Anglo-identified form. But these three novels aren't just exclusively dedicated to deconstructing hegemonic standards. They are equally invested in constructing an alternative aesthetics—one that is, importantly, not necessarily lacking biological import. I say importantly because, even with pseudoscientific attempts to divest black bodies of beauty and feeling and/or prejudicially to locate a passion for them therein, there would have nonetheless remained good reason to articulate a response that maintains a link between aesthetics and anatomy. For the fact that "aesthetics is born as a discourse of the body" can allow for its potential to denote a region beyond the conceptual, a territory that comprises our sensate life and attests to the impingement of the biological upon the world. It is, Terry Eagleton believes, in our "affections and aversions" that we uncover not just the "palpable dimension of the human" but "the body's long inarticulate rebellion against the tyranny of the theoretical" (13).[13] As such, aesthetics becomes a crucial realm for reasserting a denied or suppressed humanity, but only through first acknowledging our indispensable physicality. Indeed, this is the positive side of the dual nature of the aesthetic: while it invariably serves reactionary purposes when it makes monistic claims about beauty, purity, and autonomy, its practical value derives from its insistence on "a vital relation between bodily or material life and the universal level on which questions of reason and justice are raised" (Harpham 126). The body, in other words, may serve as the ground for both aesthetics and political activism simultaneously. The difficulty lies in how to reap this ground—how to incorporate what Eagleton calls "the guts"—without in so doing perpetuating the reactionary, essentializing judgments of "the gaze."

This is the essential conundrum that I explore in the subsequent sections: is it possible for these three authors to minimize the sensate in their compositions in order to contest somaticizing, bestializing devaluations while retaining just enough of its trace to stage an affective, aesthetic protest of the injustices perpetuated in the name of the abstract and impersonal? And how, ultimately, do each's formal strategies and choices—especially when and where they function *organically* to magnify and verify points made narratively—enhance or inhibit such a project?

The most controversial aspect of Frances Watkins Harper's 1892 novel, *Iola Leroy*, has proven to be the eponymous heroine herself, first introduced to us by an admiring character who lays stress on Iola's physical appearance: "My! but she's putty. Beautiful long hair comes way down her back; putty blue eyes, an' jus' ez white ez anybody's in dis place" (38). Iola's conspicuous "whiteness" has been condemned by a number of critics as evidence of mimicry, of her creator's subservience to white norms. Others, most vocally Hazel Carby, defend Iola's appearance as both a metaphoric "vehicle for the exploration of the relationship between the races" and an historically accurate "expression of that relationship" (*Reconstructing* 89).[14] Carby encourages us to read Harper's mulatta creation as "signifyin'" on black-white interrelations and, in particular, on the aesthetic encoding of their offspring.

While I find Carby's approach useful, what I want to emphasize here specifically is Iola's status not as daughter but as potential spouse. At least four novels from this period—*Iola Leroy,* Amelia Johnson's 1890 *Clarence and Corrine,* Chesnutt's 1901 *Marrow of Tradition,* and Pauline Hopkins's

1902–3 *Of One Blood*—employ the recurring convention of a beautiful if not always tragic mulatta coupled with an ambitious mulatto male doctor.[15] Why this persistent repetition? Why this exact pairing quadrupled? As Deborah E. McDowell and Hazel Carby have each noted separately about Harper's novel, the story instantly transforms that which is elsewhere represented (in, say, certain white-authored sensational fictions) as personal into the political, as private into the public, and as individual into the collective (Carby, *Reconstructing* 73, McDowell 97–99). With such transformations in mind, we could read the recurring appearance of this fictional doctor character as gesturing toward a larger anxiety about medico-scientific epistemes. If so, then this mixed blood doctor figure conjoins in an individual body that which the social body charts as an ineradicable divide—i.e., that between scientist and object of "scientific" study. The doctor's marriage to yet another "hybrid" figure extends even as it overdetermines this potential conflict and figures forth prospects for reconciliation, with the relative happiness of the union attesting to the power of this counternarrative to subvert dominant medical-aesthetical hierarchical scales.[16]

Such a reading finds validation within *Iola Leroy*. At one point, Iola's brother Harry pokes fun at the affianced couple's lack of individuation: "Dr. Latimer used to be first-rate company, but now it is nothing but what Iola wants, and what Iola says, and what Iola likes. I don't believe that there is a subject I could name to him ... that he wouldn't somehow contrive to bring Iola in. And I don't believe you could talk ten minutes to Iola on any subject ... that she wouldn't manage to lug in Frank" (277). Yet even while this indivisibility models a desired solidarity, Iola still persists in calling her fiancé "Doctor"—an unnecessary formality which may simply denote Iola's respect for her betrothed but also handily serves to remind readers that this union bears the stamp of medical sanction. Frank and Iola's utterly sanguine courtship, in sum, lends a scientific aura of legitimacy (and healing) to their union even as each's integrity and the couple's promise counters medical horror stories about hybridization and its consequences.

But the pair's debunking role doesn't end there. The symbolic importance of the marriage plot in general to these novels is addressed in two recent studies of black women's fiction. Ann duCille contends that what she calls "the coupling convention" is appropriated in these works for "emancipatory purposes" (3), as a means of critiquing and restructuring gendered relations and generic conventions. Claudia Tate likewise stresses these marriages' allegorical nature, the extent to which they represent the fictional if not actual satisfaction of political and personal desires. Following these two critics' lead, I see Harper's couple as collaborating within her narrative both to condense a whole constellation of mythologies and, ultimately, to displace the very myths they superficially resemble. In particular, they explicitly and emphatically reverse the kind of mythologizing script identified by Roland Barthes, in which complex historic "forms of signification" are transformed into naturalized, depoliticized objects. Intriguingly, Barthes uses as his exemplary myth a picture of a Negro saluting, which, he suggests, can only *qua* myth convey an "impoverished," "distorted" meaning as a result of its conversion into form. The critic who wishes to restore the proper historical and political dimensions to such a myth, Barthes proposes, must begin by looking "from the point of view of the signifier, the thing robbed of its meaning" (110).

Applying Barthes's advice to Harper's novel and attending to the viewpoint of her mulatto characters, we are almost immediately diverted from the superficial aesthetical standards they seemingly embody toward the more nuanced questions these characters pose to the very classificatory apparatus employed to evaluate their aesthetic appeal. For all its didactic, sentimental cast, *Iola Leroy* swerves from generic expectations in one marked respect: it lacks a visibly intrusive narrator. The story thus unfolds largely through dialogue, a narrative structure ideally suited to the project of debunking myths by letting the myths become animated and speak for themselves. Granting her mulatto characters a strong, clear voice and a mobility that defies their static, mythicized status, Harper allows them to debate the value of their own physical beauty, and, in so doing, forestalls the mythmaking process in fiction if not yet in fact by restoring the myths themselves to the dialectical processes of history.

In keeping with Harper's didactic intent, when Frank and Iola speak it is never solely or even primarily to each other; their wooing is always also inflected toward a mixed-race audience with its own preconceived but hopefully not unshakable standards of beauty.[17] True to Harper's own dictate that "marriage should not be a blind rushing together of *tastes* and *fancies*" ("Enlightened Motherhood" 286, emphasis added), the restrained courtship of Iola and Frank comes replete with often pedantic, instructive reflection on the nature of the truly tasteful. Despite their superficially Caucasoid appearances, despite their acknowledged good looks, what attracts Doctor Latimer and Iola Leroy to each other is not that they could pass as white but that they choose not to do so. Nor is this represented merely as a matter of personal taste: as yet another mulatto character insists, to "pass" as white is "a treason, not only to the race, but to humanity" (203). Ultimately, Harper's "mulatto" novel is more concerned with "fairness"—justice—than with "fairness"—light-colored beauty—even though it is often through the latter vehicle that points about the former are made, and made beautiful(ly).[18]

It is by now something of a critical commonplace to identify Lucy Delaney—whose hair and complexion, according to her lover, Iola's brother Harry Leroy, show not "the least hint of blood admixture" (199)—as the novel's aesthetic standard bearer, and hence "black is beautiful" as the narrative's overt message. Yet even Lucy rates as "ideal woman" not because of her looks but because of her behavior; it is not her appearance but how she comports herself, her dedication to the race and its uplift, and the fact that "she is grand, brave, intellectual, and religious" that make her Iola's "ideal woman" (242). In this light, the stereotypical characterizations for which Harper's narrative has been derided can, alternately, be appreciated for their complex, subversive potential, to the extent that these stereotypes are incarnated only so as to implode them from within and to construct a counter-aesthetics that deontologizes and politicizes matters of taste.

From one perspective, the promise of wedded bliss for the ideally matched Iola Leroy and Doctor Frank Latimer (not to mention Iola's rejection of the suit of a white doctor who asks that she "pass" were she to become his bride) might suggest that Harper shares some concerns about the dangers of "panmixia," of marrying outside one's own race. But the impetus behind Frank and Iola's match is less fear of the consequences of intermarriage than a desire to love, honor, and cherish their shared racial heritage.[19] As Iola informs Frank, he instantly qualified as the hero of the book she plans to write the moment she learned of his admirable decision not to "slip out from the race and pass into the white basis" (263). In turn, Doctor Latimer believes that Iola's decision not "to cast her lot with the favored race" makes her "the subject of a soul-inspiring story" (263–64). It is deeds, not looks, which each defines as not just pleasing to contemplate but, significantly, pleasing to narrate. Reflecting this as well, it is in the wake of Iola's more impassioned speeches on behalf of racial uplift, not in the more private moments set aside for wooing, that the narrative pauses to linger on her "beautiful, expressive face" (219), its "rare loveliness" and "etherealiz[ed] ... beauty" (257).[20] Through such passages, Harper's narrative encodes an idealized aesthetics in which the recital of uplifting deeds enhances the beauty of the speaker while simultaneously making the speech act itself both beautiful and beautifying. Extending this standard to Harper's own novel-cum-prolonged-speech, *Iola Leroy* itself merits the descriptive "pleasing" precisely by adhering to its diegetic structure, a structure that critics not attuned to the novel's inherent aesthetics have frequently found to be its chief flaw.

What remains to be addressed is why and how the novel's counteraesthetic, so vitally necessary and useful in Harper's own day, has come to represent for many of Harper's harshest critics her story's primary aesthetic failing. Why have critics so often deployed the very aesthetical standards to castigate the novel that the novel itself deconstructs? Ironically, that which *Iola Leroy* debunks has been remythicized over the course of its critical history—so that, in critical readings of the novel, "fairness's" etymological links to justice have been eroded in the process of its reiteration and concomitant reification as signifier for beautiful form. In specific ways, Harper's adherence to a sentimental mode as the framework through which to convey her idealized aesthetics has only hastened this erosion—this although, in many respects, sentimentalism's central tenets were ideally suited to Harper's dual aims of "soul-inspiring" and debunking.

Whatever sentimentalism's liabilities, there are a host of sound reasons why Harper might have been drawn to this mode. Realism posed its own share of problems. Not only do its mimetic pretensions assume the value of mirroring extant reality, its practice risks reinscribing, even perpetuating a version of the real—specifically, in this case, an aestheticized version—that allowed little room for reform or reinvention.[21] Harper's distrust of mimetic modes may have informed her decision to set her novel in the Reconstruction period rather than her own post-Reconstruction age—although, ironically, doing so allows her upbeat, even utopian depiction to appear more realistic than it would have seemed if set during the racial nadir in which it was written.

By taking the risk of anachronism, Harper can give freer play to her idealistic, moralistic bent. This combined with the novel's initial focus on a beautiful, imperiled, orphaned heroine and its courtship plot lands *Iola Leroy* pretty squarely within sentimental rubrics, a location that would have offered certain irresistible attractions. As Philip Fisher has proposed, before the advent of literary naturalism and the increasingly divisive class struggles of the late nineteenth century, "the liberal humanism of sentimentality was the primary radical methodology within culture" (92). According to Fisher, writers tend to resort to sentimentality at the moments, in the places where subjects previously unrepresented in novel form first make their appearance. As a result of its empathic representational strategies, Fisher maintains, sentimentalism extends not just humanity but normality to its hitherto dehumanized, marginal subjects (98–100). If so, for Harper to adopt a sentimental format for her best-known novel would seem a wise strategic move, its personalizing script conferring as a matter of form the humanity that she and other black intellectuals were elsewhere, in countless hostile interrogations, called upon to verify. Of course, Harper also wanted to exclude that which has previously been included—namely, the minoritizing discourses framing African-Americans as at once aesthetically displeasing and grossly sensual. Here again, the choice of sentimental modes (especially to the extent its conventional characterizations accentuate and valorize spirit over body) would seem not just a wise but an ideal formal choice.[22]

In Harper's case, however, this exclusion should not be seen simply as some incidental generic side effect but, rather, as a central proponent of her plan for racial uplift (a plan that, in turn, informed her formal choices). In speeches on literature's instrumental role in this project, for instance, Harper identifies the goal of both African-American art and the community at large to be transcending what she considered the "sensuous and material" dimensions of everyday life. An artwork, according to Harper, is most elevated and most exquisite when it instills a desire for self-sacrifice on behalf of others, a desire that takes root and precedence as the reader trades physiological for spiritual concerns. As she concludes in her speech-cum-essay "A Factor in Human Progress,"

> however low down a people may be in scale of character and condition, absorbed in providing for their physical wants, or steeped in sensuous gratifications, the moment their admiration is awakened and their aspirations kindled by the recital, or the example of deeds of high and holy worth, and the spirit of self-sacrifice and self-surrender for some good cause is awakened and developed, there comes in that race a dividing line between *the sensuous and material, and the spiritual and progressive*. (278, emphasis added)

To the extent that *Iola Leroy* through "recital" as well as "example" both illustrates and incites the crossing of this line, it eschews the sensuality associated with a more primitive or "low" aesthetics and approaches Harper's paradigmatic uplifting, beautiful literary composition.

While Harper's ennobling motives are without a doubt admirable and compelling, we need to ask whether, where *Iola Leroy* is concerned, the author's strategic investment in enacting this trajectory is so great that she risks obliterating the biological ground that Eagleton considers essential to a humanistic counter-aesthetic. A superficial reading of the novel could very well lead us to just such a conclusion: by focusing so sharply therein on spirituality, by discounting the value of physical appearance and skimming over the pressures of physical existence, Harper risks eliding the particularity of embodied identity and leaves herself open to charges of a naive idealism. But a closer look at the narrative enables us to see how the author ultimately, skillfully averts such dangers. For even as *Iola Leroy* refutes gross depictions of blacks as unfeeling or insensate, it inscribes in their place a sentimental iconography which retains a biology encoded as healing rather than hurtful. The narrative, for instance, accentuates a "sympathizing bosom" (194), a "paroxysm of joy" (182), the caress of "womanly hands" (209). In these and other synecdoches, Harper retains vestiges of the physical but ensures that these traces, feminine and sentimental as they are, could not easily be appropriated for dehumanizing purposes. *Iola Leroy*'s sentimental anatomy highlights the feeling, humane nature of its characters while obscuring a more fully palpable physicality which might bring with it the risk of reactionary expropriation. As such, the narrative's emphasis on emotion, on "natural, spontaneous expression" (Eagleton 9), facilitates Harper's project of defying anaesthetic myths even as it helps to render the novel's own aesthetic priorities concrete, trustworthy, and hence potentially liberatory.

Yet whatever their conceivable power and appeal in Harper's own day, Harper's paeans to sentimental agency have over the course of the novel's literary history often been misconstrued as evidence of a cloying and overblown sensibility. Harper, who desired to write "stirring," "thrilling" "songs for the people" (Foster, *Brighter* 371), meant for these adjectives (as with her "sympathizing bosom") to connote political agency rather than privatized affect. Yet, ironically, the politics of generic classification—at least until recent feminist work revalidating sentimentalism's cultural work and reanimating its concrete dimensions and political intentions—have tended to obscure this political desire even as they helped to divorce the novel's affective dimensions from the public realm where Harper hoped they would most fully resonate. In large part, these classificatory politics have worked to locate sentiment within an isolate body while ignoring or overlooking the possibility that both the body and its feelings might serve as loci of potentially transformative evaluations and revaluations.

Of all the dangers Harper faced while composing her novel during the "nadir," the possible dangers of lending it a sentimental cast were ones she doubtless did not anticipate.[23] Over time, however, its potentially radical and novel blueprint for sentimental agency came to be reinterpreted via modernist aesthetic standards as emblematizing banality and predictability. For example, while one of the first reviews published in the *Independent* praised its "really effective and pathetic delineation" of character (qtd. in Carby, Introduction xi–xii), later critics dropped the "effective" and dwelled on what they perceived to be the narrative's excessive pathos, accusing the author, as did Saunders Redding in 1937, of being "apt to gush with pathetic sentimentality" (40). Elsewhere, via an equivalence which Harper herself would have vehemently protested, Ulysses Lee dismissed the novel in 1941 for being "as dull as it is pious" (qtd. in Carby, Introduction xii). This framing of Harper's work as either excessively maudlin or exceedingly dull, this depoliticizing of the emotions her works encode and arouse, suggests a sustained readerly inability to affectively emulate or appreciate the sentimental aesthetical and agentive lessons *Iola Leroy* values, models, and seeks to implement.

⁂

Charles Chesnutt's *Marrow of Tradition* is yet another novel to use this conventional mulatto couple (here it is Doctor William Miller and his wife Janet) in order to probe and upset governing racialized aesthetic dichotomies. At the time of *Marrow*'s composition, Chesnutt had been brooding over the mulatto's depiction as "an insult to nature, a kind of monster" (qtd. in H. Chesnutt 57). He informed his editor at Houghton Mifflin that the subject of "miscegenation" was begging for "literary treatment" (McElrath and Leitz [M&L] 150)—the kind of treatment that would remove the taint from "taint" ("I hate the word," Chesnutt wrote Cable, "it implies corruption" [M&L 66])—and prove the viability and vitality of miscegenated forms, whether bodily or literary. In *Marrow*, Chesnutt utilizes not just the coupling convention but a Doppelganger effect—Tom Delamere as Sandy Delamere's impersonator, half-sisters Janet Miller and Olivia Carteret as mirror images—to blear the boundaries dividing blacks from whites. The novel is not only about the "fusion" politics of the Reconstruction South but enacts a politics of fusion that continually collapses spaces sharply segregated under post-Reconstruction regimes, establishing in their stead what Eric Sundquist has identified as an "anatomy of miscegenation" (397). Indeed, it is implied that the only promise of a future lies precisely in this collapsing of spatial and physiological barriers: *Marrow* ends with Doctor Miller preparing to cut a white child's throat, but unlike the novel's white-originated bodily violations, this incision represents a healing intervention (it's a tracheotomy), performed just in the nick of time.[24]

Over the course of his career, Chesnutt vehemently sought to disprove the identification of the (always impossibly) pure of form as the incarnation of inherent, lasting appeal. As Chesnutt concluded in the first of a series of three essays he submitted to the Boston *Evening Transcript* in 1900 under the title "The Future American," "the conception of a pure Aryan, Indo-European race has been abandoned in scientific circles, and the secret of the progress of Europe has been found in racial heterogeneity, rather than in racial purity" (August 18, 1900, 20). In *Marrow*, Chesnutt verifies the revised scientific findings he polemicizes in this article by casting the "pureblood" sister, Olivia, not the "hybrid," Janet, as the one who is morally degenerate, who has difficulty reproducing, and who, when she does conceive, gives birth to a frail, perpetually imperiled child aptly named "Dodie" (as an insightful student once pointed out, change the inflection and you get "Do die").

All the same, it is Janet's child that "does die" in the end, killed amidst the fury of the race riots, while the narrative closes on the suggestion that (thanks to Miller's surgical intervention) Olivia's son will survive, at least for a while. Bereft of her own son, *Marrow*'s beautiful "mulatta" heroine qualifies as tragic, albeit as a result of circumstance rather than "nature." Furthermore, Janet's doctor husband, the novel's other prominent mixed blood character, is cast in by no means as unambiguously heroic a light as Harper's Doctor Frank Latimer, for he is flawed if humanized by his accommodationist impulses.[25] Although his mulatto characters vie with, even outshine, their white counterparts in terms of physical beauty, Chesnutt's commitment to verisimilitude apparently prevented him from casting their prospects in a rosier hue. So if *Marrow* does bear out Chesnutt's premise that racial heterogeneity not only ensures but guarantees health and future promise, it seems necessary to look beyond characterization and take narrative expression and form into account as evidence. This expanded focus allows us to circumvent the critical stalemate over who represents the hero or heroine in the piece by acknowledging the central, arguably "heroic" role of both narrator and narration. It is, after all, the story's indeterminate narrator who most closely resembles Chesnutt's amalgamated, formidable "Future American."

In 1889, Chesnutt wrote Albion Tourgée that he was contemplating abandoning his dialect tales: "I think I have used up the old Negro who serves as a mouthpiece, and I shall drop him in future stories, as well as much of the dialect" (M&L 44). By the following year, he was confessing his disgust with the servile "full-blooded" blacks who peopled the magazine pages, declaring: "I can't write about those people, or rather I won't write about them" (qtd. in H. Chesnutt 58). In the manuscript he produced around this time, "Rena Walden" (later revised as *The House Behind the Cedars*), Chesnutt began his experiment with less conventional, more amalgamated forms, only to learn that his editor, Richard Watson

Gilder, found "something wrong" with the "sentiment" produced. To Gilder's charge of a fundamental (and defective) "amorphousness," Chesnutt replied, "I suspect that my way of looking at these things is 'amorphous' not in the sense of being unnatural, but unusual" (qtd. in H. Chesnutt 57). Chesnutt's defense of his "amorphous" point of view is based implicitly on the uniqueness of this perspective, explicitly on its naturalness. In a certain sense, amorphousness was to remain Chesnutt's signature mode, nowhere more firmly etched than in his 1901 fictional masterpiece, *Marrow of Tradition*. For *Marrow* is not merely *about* miscegenation but represents at every level an experiment in sustained indeterminacy, stubbornly resisting dichotomization along conventional racial or generic lines.[26]

In certain respects, it is not just *Marrow*'s tone but its structuring principle (to the extent that there is a singular one) that qualifies the narrative as satirical, in Northrop Frye's sense of the word. Frye notes that the word satire derives from "*satura,* or hash," a derivation that attests to satire's function as a "parody of form" and, in particular, of "the romantic fixation which revolves around the beauty of perfect form, in art or elsewhere" (*Anatomy* 233). Both *Marrow*'s story line and its narrative structure partake of this parodic function. Seen in this light, *Marrow*'s privileging of impurity over purity, pliability over fixity, heterogeneity over uniformity need not signify some aesthetic disorder or flaw; by contrast, it might more profitably be seen as Chesnutt's formal, strategic, satiric response to an aesthetical "fixation" he perceived as aesthetically and morally flawed.

In literature as in life, Chesnutt considered unfixing this fixation to be of the utmost political importance. Believing that "the color line" was a ploy devised by whites to keep blacks sequestered in one claustrophobic space, Chesnutt derided calls for integrity and purity as agitprop of the racist status quo. As Chesnutt argued in 1905: "We are told that we must glory in our color and zealously guard it as a priceless heritage. Frankly I take no stock in this doctrine. It seems to be a modern invention of the white people to perpetuate the color line. It is they who preach it, and it is their racial integrity which they wish to preserve—they have never been unduly careful of the purity of the black race" ("Race Prejudice" 25). Diverging from Harper, Chesnutt proselytizes not on behalf of racial solidarity but instead for the abandonment of overzealous, defensive allegiances to any single color, cause, or creed.

In *Marrow*, Chesnutt employs his own inventive powers to imagine a fictional world which—while graphically documenting whites' carelessness with the integrity of black bodily boundaries—formally experiments with an analogous carelessness, albeit one whose violations yield salutary rather than pernicious consequences. Throughout the narrative, the racial segregation that was the law of the land once Jim Crow was instituted breaks down, not only at such critical moments as Dodie's surgery but via more mundane contact, including jostling on the street, the serving of dinner, peering through peepholes, and so on—and none of these close encounters, despite white panic to the contrary, results in contamination or injury (at least not for the whites concerned).

Amalgamation is not just *Marrow*'s central narrative motif, however; it might also be considered its essential formal device, implemented primarily through narrative voice and viewpoint. For example, the recounting of a train trip taken by Miller and a white medical colleague is interrupted by a meditation on the narrow perspective inculcated by and identified with the nation. Flawed by its dichromatic nearsightedness, the narrowly grounded, tightly blinkered "American eye" can only make broad and gross distinctions between black and white. By contrast, the assessments of the omniscient, depersonalized narrative eye (never an identifiable "I") prove far more insightful. What we might, using Chesnutt's own terminology, call the narrative's "future American" (i.e., amalgamated) eye can discern not only the beauty in a "mulatto's erect form, broad shoulders, clear eyes, fine teeth, and pleasingly moulded features" (49) but also that the differences between this form and the white man's beside him are minimal, ones of degree rather than kind. Significantly, it is a lack of rootedness in a single (national, corporeal) form that affords the amorphous narrative perspective its more discriminating (in its positive rather than pejorative sense) aesthetical insights.

Yet while this narrative digression brilliantly if sardonically illustrates the benefits of indeterminacy, there are several additional unattributable passages whose discriminations come across as less discriminating and more disconcerting. In these instances, *Marrow*'s amorphous structure and amalgamated content seem to work at cross-purposes, so that its narratival indeterminacy seems only to muddy the polemical implications and soften, even deflect the impact of the "anatomy of miscegenation" offered at the representational level. To take an example from personal experience, when I teach *Marrow* to my students, usually at least a half-dozen or so initially come to class angered at my choice of a racist book by a white man.[27] When asked how they arrived at this faulty premise, they indicate that they have been led astray not just by the cover portrait (the light-skinned Chesnutt's picture is imprinted on the cover of the most recent Ann Arbor edition of the novel). They point as well to the narration, to passages including this one about the relationship between blacks and whites: "As theoretical equals,—*practical equality being forever out of the question, either by nature or by law*,—there could have been nothing but strife between them" (241, emphasis added). By law, maybe, but practical equality eliminated by nature? How do we account for such a prejudicial statement without having to apologize for its originator?

*Marrow*'s narrative voice is, in W. E. B. Du Bois's sense, "double": it is dialogized, multivocal, even miscegenated.[28] Sundquist refers to this as Chesnutt's "cakewalking," arguing that the novel resembles this minstrel standard through its simultaneous authentic expression of African-American culture and subversive satire of dominant culture (276ff; see also Knadler). More than merely allowing interplay, however, I believe the narrative often confuses the "authentic" and "satiric," or at least it frequently leaves a reader confused as to whether the unidentified narrative voice believes what is said or is satirizing what others say. Although there are benefits to such disorienting moments—among them, they force us as readers to experience an uncertainty not dissimilar to the one the narrative itself foregrounds and even sanctions—there are also risks, which include blunting the purposefulness of this purpose novel.

Chesnutt once told a friend that *Marrow* was "both a novel and a political and sociological tract—a tremendous combination if the author can but find the formula for mixing them" (qtd. in Render 40). The best way to discern the formula Chesnutt himself arrived at is through rhetorical analysis. In *Marrow*, Chesnutt makes use of free indirect discourse, which Janet Holmgren McKay has shown to be a hallmark of literary realism, a school that held strong attractions for Chesnutt.[29] Free indirect discourse entails the mixing of "directly and indirectly reported discourse" (McKay 17) and hence the entangling of narrator's and character's discourses. The superficially racist passages to which my students objected might thus according to this model be understood as examples of a character's skepticism reported indirectly. At its most subversive, free indirect discourse works in the novel to confirm that "a stream of dark blood [flows] in the veins of Southern whites" (Chesnutt, "Future," August 25, 15) every time the narrative renders Major Carteret's, his wife Olivia's, or other racist whites' thoughts indirectly.

All the same, because free indirect discourse is not an embedded discourse—that is, because by definition no speaker is ever directly identified—the source of many of the narrative's most disturbing, racialized comments ultimately remains ambiguous: even to refer to a narrator is to imply mistakenly that the story personifies such an entity. Nor in the passage cited by my students is there even a remotely proximate character upon whom to pin the sentiments therein expressed. In short, to attempt to assign even an implicit speaker to these narrative comments would be to lend them an air of determinacy that the text itself deliberately withholds. Attributing these disturbing views to a source erroneously naturalizes them where we might instead recognize their strategic, stylized efficacy at calling into question what, precisely, the "natural" consists of.

Still, I'm not entirely certain that this efficacy ought to be so quickly conceded. In such ambiguous, indirect moments, as my students' angry reactions suggest, a little naturalizing might have proven a very good thing. For without it, the palpable force of *Marrow*'s aesthetical protest against the theoretical loses some of its punch, or what Eagleton would consider its "guts." In his articles on "The Future American," Chesnutt belabors the fact that the mulatto is not simply the prototypical future citizen but already an undeniable "corporeal fact" (August 25, 15). Yet *Marrow*'s amalgamated narrative voice (the novel's most potent and resilient amalgamated creation) is less corporeal fact than incorporeal device.

At first glance, it does seem odd that an author so invested in proving amalgamation's "naturalness" would adopt such an abstract, deontologized central consciousness. But there are, in the end, a number of strategic explanations for his choice. First of all, we should note that this relatively diluted presence is nonetheless still a palpable presence. Indeed, the voice and vision that enable the narration could be seen as synecdoches for a physicality that is not so much absent as attenuated. And in so displacing a more full-bodied presence, Chesnutt joins a longstanding African-American literary tradition. As Henry Louis Gates, Jr., has argued, "Black people responded to ... profoundly serious allegations about their 'nature' as directly as they could: they wrote books, poetry, autobiographical narratives. ... The very *face* of the race was contingent upon the recording of the black *voice*. Voice presupposed a face, but also seems to have been thought to determine the very contours of the black face" (Introduction 11). In this sense, *Marrow*'s voice might be conceived as a sanctioned means of depicting the amalgamated visage of the "future American." It may also have served as a safer tactic than would a full-body portrait. For as Raymond Hedin attests, black writers often wisely divested their speech of a highly suspect, even threatening physicality during moments of great emotional intensity in hopes of assuring readers that they were not "in the presence of an uncontrolled beast or savage" (201–2).[30] Clearly, *Marrow* was written at an intense pitch in just such an intense moment. Its narratorial indeterminacy might thus be seen as a strategic device aimed to placate an audience that would not tolerate such views from a more clearly identifiable or more fully corporeal source.

This physical diminishment may represent more than mere safeguard, however. Among other things, it reflects Chesnutt's self-portrait as an artist who "as a matter of personal taste" shrank from "the sordid and brutal" (M&L 214). Here, Chesnutt's "shrinking" from physicality stems more from the author's predilections than from his readers'. While *Marrow* itself depicts the brutality of riot, murder, threatened rape, and lynching, the narrative's omniscient, disembodied perspective places him or her above the fracas. And, as a certain "aesthetic distance" has come to serve as *sine qua non* of both aesthetic composition and aesthetic contemplation,[31] the diminished physicality of *Marrow*'s narrator might thus be understood not merely for its negative function—reassuring the reader that the implied author is no beast—but for its positive role—assuring the reader that the implied author is cultivated, tasteful.

Yet such an interpretation is not without its problems. In particular, it is hard to reconcile the disinterested assessment supposedly requisite to aesthetic appreciation with Chesnutt's conception of the utilitarian value of his own literary output—with, that is, his practical aesthetics. Whatever Chesnutt's similarities with "his high cultural white contemporaries" (Brodhead 178), there were also noteworthy differences. For one thing, the qualities most frequently associated with "highbrow" cultural artifacts include inaccessibility, purity, and disinterest (see L. Levine), whereas what Chesnutt sought to craft in *Marrow* was a work that was readily accessible, thoroughly amalgamated, and profoundly interested.

A better explanation for Chesnutt's choice of an effaced narrator may lie in the author's attractions to literary realism—Chesnutt not only promised Howells in 1900 that he would "endeavor always to depict life as [he had] known it" (M&L 146) but also would later take great pleasure, as he informed his editors, in the fact that none of the reviews of *Marrow* considered the book "at all overdrawn or that [its author had] drawn from any other fountain than the well of truth" (M&L 165). Chesnutt was especially interested in the realism of Henry James, whom he took as technical model for his own experiments with point of view. But before glossing Chesnutt's distanced point of view as realist convention, we need to pause here as well. For his reluctance to embed a narrator in *Marrow* may have had less to do with a desire to explore a Jamesian consciousness without mediation than with his desire to interrogate, even exceed, mimeticism's naturalized representations. After all, while Chesnutt considered it his "rule ... to write for art's sake ... the truth as I saw it, without catering to anybody's prejudices," he also tended to concur with Albion Tourgée's indictment of realism's boundaries as insufficient to contain the "grand truth" of African-American life and to side with Tourgée's enthusiasm for the romance's more capacious frame.[32] Moreover, though he shared with Howells a belief that "the very vitality of art" lies "in its responsiveness to humanity's material needs" (Warren 49), Chesnutt was ultimately less optimistic than Howells about realism's capacity to voice this response.

Clearly, in writing *Marrow* Chesnutt was not wedded to any single literary mode or school but instead practiced fusion here as well, blending historically accurate depictions of time and place with melodramatic story lines and romantic conventions. Desirous as he was of racial uplift and social transformation, Chesnutt no doubt felt the pull of sentimentalism's more sensational designs. Immediately after *Marrow* was published, Chesnutt defined his novel as "the plea of an advocate" (qtd. in Andrews 205); several years later, he confided to a friend that it "was written, as all my books have been, with a purpose—the hope that it might create sympathy for the colored people of the South in the very difficult position which they occupy" (M&L 234).[33] And while it might seem odd that a narrative defined as plea deploys such an indirect voice in which to couch it, in Chesnutt's lexicon, distance does not necessarily entail detachment. As Chesnutt wrote in his journal: "Men are always more ready to extend their sympathy to those at a distance, than to the suffering ones in their midst" (125). Such a claim inverts both sentimental and realist equations between closeness and involvement and offers a final possible explanation for *Marrow*'s narrative depersonalization.

Although it was Chesnutt's hope that his "plea" would reach "an impartial jury" (qtd. in Andrews 205), the response to *Marrow* was nothing if not partial. Indeed, its reception was rather remarkably polarized for a narrative whose fundamental tendency was to deconstruct so as to meld traditional antipodes. On the one hand, some contemporary respondents glossed *Marrow*'s signature aloofness and indeterminacy as signs of aesthetic merit and/or realist intent and glossed over these traits' inextricable sympathetic import. The editors at Houghton Mifflin, for example, praised Chesnutt's "great restraint" (qtd. in Render 143), while Howells, a fan of Chesnutt's "artistic reticence" (*Selected Literary Criticism* 233), would surmise—in direct contradiction to Chesnutt's own perception of his novel—that *Marrow*'s author "did not play the advocate." Yet at the same time, other reviewers complained of the novel's "fierce partisanship" (qtd. in Ellison and Metcalf 48), calling it "less impersonal" than Chesnutt's other works (qtd. in E&M 48), and claiming that "the writer's feelings are neither obliterated nor skillfully hidden" (qtd. in E&M 46). Even as the *Independent* was condemning the novel as a "vigorous and vindictive" work "written apparently by a man with a racial grievance" (qtd. in E&M 54) , the *Nation* was praising its "capacity for cool observation and reflection" (qtd. in E&M 54). These sharply divided, generally one-sided responses suggest an audience ill-prepared to return *Marrow*'s heterogeneous, complex judgments in kind. They suggest as well that—

while there's truth in the statement that "the very survival of black stories depends on their central voices not quite being heard accurately" (Hedin 181)—an accurate hearing can also prove essential to such works' aesthetico-political claims and aesthetico-political viability.

Like Harper, Chesnutt had overt designs upon his reader (evidenced by his distribution of copies of *Marrow* to President Roosevelt and select congressional and cabinet members). Like Harper's, these designs included reconfiguring or at least circumventing prevalent Anglophile standards of beauty and purity as applied to written and bodily forms.[34] Yet also like Harper, Chesnutt's strategic diminishment of the bodily not only complicates the task of communicating these designs but allows for his novel's potentially radical aesthetics to be reinterpreted as mere mimicry of more abstract, disinterested white hegemonic narratives. Hence judgments such as Leroi Jones's (later Amiri Baraka), repudiating Chesnutt's work for its "slave mentality," for what Jones perceives as its message that the Negro "must completely lose himself within the culture and social order of the ex-master" (58–59, 131–32; see also Sundquist 298). Rather than recognizing in this narrative the face of the "Future American," Jones could only discern therein the likeness of that minstrel standard, Uncle Tom.[35]

Such misreadings notwithstanding, we can still concede with Howells that neither Chesnutt's "ethics or aesthetics are false." More precisely, we can conclude that both his ethics and aesthetics are willfully confused—and, what's more, that in this confusion lies *Marrow*'s strongest claim to aesthetic value. For as Eagleton maintains, confusion is central to the concept of aesthetics so long as it is taken to mean "not 'muddle' but 'fusion': in their organic interpenetration, the elements of aesthetic representation resist that discrimination into discrete units which is characteristic of conceptual thought" (15). While both in content and form *Marrow* stages not only this crucial "fusion" but the "resistance" that is its result, its reception testifies that these practices are also perpetually imperiled by segregational impulses and desires, whether literary or extraliterary. We might even see Chesnutt's decision to conclude his novel inconclusively with the words, "there's time enough, but none to spare" (329), as an acknowledgment of such pressures. This tenuous pronouncement provides a provisional epitaph not just for *Marrow* but for the future of the Jim Crow South, not to mention for Chesnutt's project of amalgamation as lifesaver for both the nation and the nation's literature. At the same time, the tentativeness of this conclusion may not, after all, simply signify the author's uncertainty about his project's prospects. It might just as cogently indicate mimetic incompletion, its raggedness the poignant reminder that the author's longed-for "future America"—in which the perfect beauty of amorphous forms would at long last be fully appreciated—was nowhere near realization.

⁊

I want lastly to consider one final novel featuring this coupling convention: Pauline Elizabeth Hopkins's *Of One Blood*, published serially in the *Colored American Magazine* (where Hopkins served as editor and frequent contributor) between 1902 and 1903. *Of One Blood's* mulatta heroine, Dianthe Lusk, is paired with not just one but two doctors, Reuel Briggs and Aubrey Livingston—both, as it turns out, mulattoes, both, as it turns out, not only brothers but *her* brothers. The love-match between Reuel and Dianthe (as with the fated, illicit pairing of Aubrey and Dianthe) doesn't just end unhappily but tragically, suggesting Hopkins's pessimism about the outlook for mixed-race persons in racist America. It also suggests the futility of trying to conjoin a mulatto aesthetics with a medical one—indeed, Aubrey's suggestion that "the results of amalgamation are worthy the careful attention of all medical experts" (451) only bodes ill for those being attended to. Rather than providing a "domestic allegory of political desire," as Tate herself acknowledges *Of One Blood* signifies on the potentially devastating, even lethal ramifications of domestic desire (Tate 206–7). If other black-authored marriage plots at the turn of the century depict "utopian unions" (Tate 31) as allegorical models for national unity, *Of One Blood's* dystopian, sterile matches-made-in-America provide a bleak allegory for the nation's prospects and indeed presage apocalyptic consequences. Unlike in Chesnutt's *Marrow*, the collapse of conventional boundaries in Hopkins's *Of One Blood* generates horror rather than indicating reform.

Also unlike Chesnutt, Hopkins does not pin her hopes for a full appreciation of a mulatto aesthetics on some "future America" but instead largely abandons her investment in our nation and its future. Where she turns instead is not, as with Harper, to a rosier American past, but to an African past glorified as superlative alternative to the racial nadir's classificatory systems—a place and time vital to an identity that African-Americans can take pride in and draw strength from.[36] By rooting her utopian vision in a previously existing, once thriving location, Hopkins puts its imaginary status to the question and lends this "good place" a practical, existential viability.

One impetus behind Hopkins's and Reuel's expatriating (or, more correctly, repatriating) sympathies is our own country's insistence upon biologized understandings of identity. Such understandings are explicitly foregrounded in the novel's title. Even while invoking the "blood" so integral to "one-drop" laws, *Of One Blood* simultaneously nullifies any such legal codifications through blatant reference to the biblical creed: "of one blood have I made all races of men." Understandably committed to monogenetic explanations, Hopkins scripts a narrative climax that reveals, despite racist efforts to prove the contrary, that Americans are indeed all of one blood under the skin, sharing not just the same morphology but in many cases even the same genealogy. In an intriguing twist on white panic, those most traumatized by this revelation are the novel's mulatto characters—defying conventional "wisdom," in Hopkins's rendition it is those legally codified as "black" who suffer the most from the knowledge that white and black blood have been mixed.

In the African section of her narrative, by contrast, this concept of shared blood works to heal the very wounds it invariably inflicted stateside. Through the juxtaposition of two such contrasting situations, Hopkins unmoors blood from its status as essential anatomical substance, allowing it to circulate more freely as a historical sign which, *qua* signifier, derives its meaning in context and in relation.[37] Whether in America or in Africa, history not only confers significance on but alters the significance of biology. Yet in America, history only makes biology hurt (and vice versa),[38] while in Africa the two function symbiotically to restore vitality. The lesson both locales teach is that, when it comes to making sense of biology, context is everything.

Just as essential to Pan-African vitality is an acceptance of the supernatural; indeed, in Hopkins's narrative "supernatural" and "historical" function homologously, each operating to stretch while redefining the seemingly fixed boundaries of "nature." Importantly, in Hopkins's view (a view informed by Pan-African lore), there is no obligatory, inherent separation between the supernatural and the natural or real; rather, all are inextricably bound up together.[39] Hopkins's willingness to entertain the supernatural as a "real" and "natural" if not empirically explicable phenomenon has much to do, as scholars including Thomas J. Otten, Susan Gillman, and Cynthia D. Schrager have recently demonstrated, with the influence of William James and his student W. E. B. Du Bois on her thinking. Indeed, the essay exploring "unclassified residuum" that Reuel is reading when the narrative commences has been identified as an essay of James's.[40] But Hopkins's embrace of the occult is more than merely derivative. Among her more original, strategic intents is her desire to prove the structural and interpretive flexibility of all "natural" constructs.

The supernatural's effect upon and inseparability from the natural—and the reluctance to lend this effect and juncture credence by those aligned with traditional American medicine—is revealed in an incident that occurs early on in *Of One Blood*. After a tragic train accident, Dianthe is pronounced dead by Harvard's medical doctors. The night before, she had appeared to Reuel in apparitional form to plead for his help. When called to the hospital, Reuel is told that the girl—whom he recognizes from the previous night's vision and from having seen her perform once with the Fisk Jubilee Singers—is beyond saving. The head physician, exasperated by Reuel's careful examination of a body without a pulse, proclaims, "rigor mortis in unmistakable form is here. The woman is dead!" (465). All the attendant medical experts concur with this doctor's verdict, based as it is on seemingly irrefutable physiological proof. Reuel, however, remains stubbornly convinced that "the supernatural presides over man's formation always" and that "life is not dependent upon organic function as a principle" (468). Instead, life, as Reuel's study of magnetism has taught him, represents "that evidence of supernatural endowment which originally entered nature during the formation of the units for the evolution of man" (469). Based on this doctrine, Reuel diagnoses Dianthe's condition as suspended animation and attempts to rekindle this supernatural spark within the girl's seemingly inert form. After laying on hands and administering potions, he resuscitates the clinically dead patient by drawing on the "volatile magnetism" which is not a property of our corporeal frames but instead "exists in the free atmosphere" (468). The stuff of life, as Dianthe's successful reanimation proves, is not to be found merely in physiology; it certainly doesn't originate in some internal, organic essence. Rather, life is the result of our sustained and sustaining interaction with the dynamic atmosphere that envelops us, and to attempt to deny this interaction is to suppress the super- in the natural—a suppression that, in Dianthe's case, at least, would have truly proved fatal.

Here and elsewhere, Hopkins's *Of One Blood* strives to show that there is nothing either inherently "unnatural" or merely "magical" about the supernatural. Later in the narrative, while in Ethiopia on an archaeological expedition, Reuel inadvertently stumbles upon the ancient city of Telassar, peopled by the ancient, noble Chaldean tribe, who immediately recognize the intruder as the legitimate and long-awaited heir of their King, Ergamenes. In the midst of a conversation with the Chaldean sage, Ai, Reuel expresses a wish to temporarily revisit "the world [he has] left"; Ai assures him that this is possible with the aid of "occultism." After being instructed to gaze into a mirror-like device, Reuel immediately sees therein the first image that comes to his mind, causing him to cry out in wonder, "It is magical!" Ai's reply is as calm as it is emphatic: "No, no, Ergamenes, this is a secret of Nature" (575). As this exemplary exchange clarifies, the "natural" can explain that which some might believe defies explanation.

What it also makes clear is that the supernatural unveils the truth in ways that the natural—at least, as it is constituted in *Of One Blood*—may not. Within the supernatural realm, at least, appearances are never deceiving. As in that earlier moment when Dianthe was wrongly pronounced dead because devoid of all clinical signs of life, in this later moment before the mirror it is once again Reuel's faith in the supernatural that proves that Dianthe, despite contradictory evidence, is still alive. After wishing to see an image of the woman he thought had drowned in a boating accident "as she last appeared on earth," the mirror remains blank. Contradicting Reuel's assumption that it is an imperfect vehicle, Ai assures him that "the disk cannot err" (576), and from this they both realize that Dianthe must still be among the living. When the search is for truth, the novel suggests that it is not to the natural but the supernatural that we must turn.

It is little wonder that Hopkins devoted so much time to redefining and reshaping the bounds of the natural, given that she was writing in a period in our nation's history when the "nature" of African-Americans was terribly depreciated. Hopkins's celebration of the naturalness of supernatural phenomena might be seen as a strategic reinflection of what counts as natural in order to open up new possibilities for meaning and value; more to the point, this process of reinflection builds into extant understandings of "nature" more room for incorporating and substantiating therein a black aesthetics.

Simultaneously, Hopkins sets out to unveil the extent to which even that which has consistently been taken to be most "natural" or "real" is, despite appearances, still a construct. John Locke's distinction between "nominal" and "real" essences can help us discern the different ways biology may resonate, not only in Hopkins's novel but in general. As Diana Fuss explains Locke,

> Real essence connotes the Aristotelian understanding of essence as that which is most irreducible and unchanging about a thing; nominal essence signifies for Locke a view of essence as merely a linguistic convenience, a classificatory fiction we need to categorize and to label. Real essences are discovered by close empirical observation; nominal essences are not "discovered" so much as assigned or produced—produced specifically by language. (4–5)

One of the central impulses behind Hopkins's *Of One Blood* is to expose how "convenient" some of our "classificatory fictions" have become and to produce in their stead more attractive and contingent alternatives. It's not that Hopkins ignores biology in her novel, but that she proves its fundamental nature to be continually shifting, supple, "nominal," capable of expansion and reformation.[41] For instance, the ambiguous question the narrative poses, "who is clear enough in vision to decide who hath black blood and who hath it not?" (607), doesn't query the existence of corporeal bedrocks; what it does question is the confidence, the certainty with which attempts to determine them decisively are undertaken. What this critical question reveals, furthermore, is that nature is not just *in esse* pliable but that the visual and linguistic mediums through which it is accessed only enhance its fundamental pliability and instability.

In order to illustrate the concept of nominal essence, Fuss revises Shakespeare and allows that there is, in fact, a lot in a name: as she argues, in the constructivist view a rose by any other name "would not be a rose, it would be something altogether rather different" (5). Hopkins's novel bears this supposition out quite literally. As previously mentioned, *Of One Blood*'s plot is divided between two locales: America, where mulattoes are oppressed, and Africa, where they, along with anyone with a drop or more of black blood, are exalted. It is noteworthy that our American hero and heroine assume different names when they resurface in this more liberating environment. In Telassar, Reuel is renamed Ergamenes, while Dianthe is reincarnated as the beautiful, darker-skinned queen Candace (whom Reuel weds thinking Dianthe, his American bride [and sister] is dead). Indeed, a new name is conferred on Dianthe every time she appears in a new incarnation; not only does Dianthe give way to Candace as tragic mulatto is supplanted by proud queen, but earlier on, shortly after her revivification, Dianthe adopts the name "Felice Adams" after losing her memory and being convinced by Reuel that she is white. More than mere aliases, these name changes effect character changes, verifying the nexus between name and identity that defines a nominal essence.

Even beauty (perhaps especially beauty), while still retaining a reference in nature, is shown in *Of One Blood* to be meaningful and accessible only through language. For example, although Dianthe (a.k.a. Felice and Candace) is distinguished by an exquisite "loveliness" (569), the sense of that loveliness—its tragic or, alternately, radiant consequences—shifts according to context. As Reuel confides to Ai about America, "it is a deep disgrace to have within the veins even one drop of the blood you seem so proud of possessing" (560). In Telassar, on the other hand, disgrace is replaced by pride: the Chaldeans "ranged in complexion from a creamy tint to purest ebony; the long hair which fell upon their shoulders, varied in texture from soft, waving curls to the crispness of the most pronounced African type. But the faces... were perfect in the cut and outline of every feature; the forms... were athletic and beautifully molded" (545).[42] In Hopkins's ideal world, beauty is to be found in range, variety, not in any single, irreducible form. Aesthetics, in Hopkins's treatment, could never be mistaken as an inherent, isolatable property of a body, or, analogously, a text. What Hopkins foregrounds in and through *Of One Blood* is the capacity of language to delineate that which can qualify as beautiful, pleasing—indeed, even while identifying this capacity, Hopkins appropriates it as author in order to assign and affirm her own candidates.

Where nominal essences are foregrounded, language is afforded a heady power: the power to create, define, confer, withdraw, instill, unearth, and so on. Hopkins's *Of One Blood* doesn't just acknowledge but exemplifies this power. Contra white-sponsored attempts not just to isolate an anatomy of blackness but to make this a tell-tale anatomy which perpetually testifies to its own status as stigma, Hopkins proves that supposedly biological classifications and categories do not "speak" some irreducible meaning; rather, this meaning is continually being spoken, and with markedly different inflections in different situations. In *Of One Blood*, Hopkins displaces all the conventional anatomical "signs" of racial identity—skin color, hair texture, physiognomy, etc.—leaving as the story's most momentous corporeal signifier a birthmark (not necessarily a clear racial indicator). And, even if we grant Otten's contention that this "birthmark materializes the problem of identity by suggesting that 'what lies inside the person [is] visible on the body'" (249), the interior that the birthmark makes visible is not some stigmatized, ineradicable racial identity lurking in even the palest of forms but is instead, in Hopkins's revisionist tale, the potentially royal blood flowing through African-American veins. More to the point, this birthmark does not inherently signify royalty until someone else has read and identified its import; Reuel, a bearer of the mark, does not fully grasp its significance until told of it by another member of the archeological expedition to Meroe. And this colleague, Professor Stone, has only learned indirectly "that every descendant of the royal line bore a lotus-lily in the form of a birthmark upon his breast" (535). Here again we witness how the natural earns significance through the stories told about it.[43]

The power afforded to storytelling holds true not just within *Of One Blood* but for it. In this novel Hopkins uses story, even or especially when supernatural, not as mere escape or fantasy but as a means of redefining that which counts as real or natural. What Hopkins presents in *Of One Blood* is not simply a narrative about how narrative, the occult, and historical forces can challenge naturalized fictions; it is a narrative that illustrates as a matter of technique its thematic arguments. It is, however, also a narrative whose generic classification can be seen as both enhancing and, simultaneously, hindering the delivery of this polemics.

The generic classification most frequently cited in discussions of *Of*

*One Blood* is melodrama, and in many ways, it is an appropriate one. For melodrama might be considered an ideally democratic form, especially since its scripts virtually guarantee that merit and virtue will prevail over privilege and position—a triumph admirably suited to Hopkins's agenda. Peter Brooks has argued that melodrama enacts a "literary aesthetic of excess—and the coherence and necessity of the excess" (202–3). If so, it is precisely the "necessity of the excess"—evidenced not just by the novel's *super*natural naturalism but by its informing postulate "of a signified in excess of its signifier" (Brooks 199), of a real, a true, a beautiful that exceeds conventional representations of reality, truth, and beauty—that *Of One Blood* zealously documents. What Hopkins's novel illustrates is that melodrama is an "excessive" genre only from certain blinkered perspectives; to the extent Hopkins adopts the form, she takes full advantage of its permissive straining after meaning in excess of representation even while refuting the notion that this excessiveness is inherently irrational or exorbitant.

Still, even when melodrama is reanalyzed and politicized I find myself reluctant to categorize Hopkins's story as such, if only because the genre's sedimented absolutes and Manichean binarisms go against Hopkins's efforts to resist absolutism in all forms. Plus, what's to prevent the excessiveness Hopkins appropriates and politicizes from being misread, as critics of the genre have long been wont to do, as little more than apolitical bombast or implausibility?

A less ideologically and aesthetically fraught way to generically classify *Of One Blood* would be as a "magical realist" work, but only so long as we acknowledge Ai's correction that what may seem "magical" may also be both "natural" and true. As in works of magical realism, *Of One Blood* tells a fabulous story with conviction, combining literary realism with the fantastic without resolving the tension between the two. True to form, the fantastic elements of Hopkins's narrative take their starting point in the real; true to form, these elements are not merely produced within an individual consciousness but are instead products of the collective consciousness of a given culture. As magically realistic political allegory, *Of One Blood*'s partisan agenda draws on real, historical events or figures to question the status of truth vested in official versions of "history" or "nature" and offers itself not just as counterweight but as counternarrative. As a result, writing, words are revealed as indispensable to the act of remembering, to acts of power, and to the discovery of truth. Bucking the constraints of mimetic representation, magically realistic narratives like Hopkins's attempt to enlarge what qualifies as mimesis in order to depict the hitherto undepicted. Like many modern magical realist works, *Of One Blood* negotiates the difference between a hegemonic "first world" people and perspective and the minority whose identity and outlook the narrative seeks to retain and revalue. Forcing representation to be more than representation, magical realist works attempt to show, both in the stories they tell and the stories they are, that fictions of various kinds can have real effects on the world.[44]

Of course, magical realism was not an available rubric in Hopkins's own day. And even this arbitrary classification proves an uneasy retrospective fit for Hopkins's unconventional novel—while *Of One Blood* incorporates gothic, utopian, fantastic, melodramatic, and realist elements, it is, in a sense, as if Hopkins in drafting her last novel invented a new genre—or, at the very least, purposefully exceeds extant generic categories.[45] In so doing, *Of One Blood* exemplifies generically the excess valorized thematically. When we bear in mind that generic categories have "come to be thought of as 'natural' forms" (Jameson, *Political* 145), we can see that Hopkins's challenge to and exceeding of natural frameworks occurs at both thematic and structural levels.

*Of One Blood*'s resistance to generic categorization may provide one explanation for why the story garnered so little critical attention in its author's day (I could find no evidence of contemporary reviews of the novel, nor do any of the extant bibliographies of Hopkins cite any); its unconventionality might also explain why it has earned so much increasing recent attention in our own more experimental, revisionist age. While this initial neglect of *Of One Blood* is disturbing, we might construe it in hindsight as not entirely grievous. One thing it did prevent was the kind of constrictive labeling that so hampered the receptions of Harper's and Chesnutt's novels. Hopkins's *Of One Blood*, at least, has until recently managed to dodge the process of classification that, for all its usefulness and unavoidability, would only rub against the grain of Hopkins's revisionist, polemical project. For above all, what Hopkins attempted in her novel was to refute, alter, and expand pre-existing (natural) categories, to breathe new life into them, to make them not only more expansive and flexible but, as a result, more pleasing to behold and relate.

⸻

Given their collective attention to blackness and aesthetics, it is ironic that Harper's, Chesnutt's, and Hopkins's respective political-aesthetical endeavors have all been found wanting according to the literary standard Addison Gayle christened as a "Black Aesthetic." As Gayle defined it, this aesthetic challenges universal, absolute notions of beauty in favor of beautifying effect: "The question for the black critic today is not how beautiful is a melody, a play, a poem, or a novel, but how much more beautiful has the poem, melody, play or novel made the life of a single black man?" (xxii). Although, ironically, each of these novels does set out to answer Gayle's valorized question, they are just as invested in responding to his first one, as superlative responses to both at once would all the better reinforce projects contesting Anglo-aesthetic standards of beauty.

Yet in the end, if writers like Chesnutt and Harper do rate as aesthetes, we must be very precise in our definition of the word, avoiding as all three authors themselves did any grossly sensual coloring the better to define each as one who, according to the *Oxford English Dictionary*'s definition, has "found out what is really beautiful in nature" and "endeavors to carry his [or her] ideas of beauty into practical manifestation." Like other African-American literary works produced during the racial nadir, these three representative stories serve as profound meditations on the nature of the beautiful, while simultaneously probing the validity and affirming the contingency of all existing classificatory systems. Taking abstract, "disinterested" understandings of the word "aesthetic" and polemicizing them, they make concrete and political the inherent "autonomy" and "self-sufficiency" of aesthetic forms; in the process, they literalize what has traditionally counted as aesthetic value—"the end of a work of art is simply to exist, and to be beautiful"(Abrams 1)—as survival value, or, at the very least, as survival strategy, for both their works and their race.

In so doing, these three writers satisfy their contemporary W. E. B. Du Bois's own "Criteria of Negro Art." I have chosen to quote Du Bois's criteria at length below because his equation of art and propaganda is so often taken out of context and hence removed from its integral connection to beauty. For Du Bois, art is not simply propaganda but propaganda with a specific purpose. To create, promote, and preserve beauty—such are the aims of black American art according to Du Bois, and such are the aims of the three black American artists examined in this chapter. As Du Bois maintains,

[Beauty's] variety is infinite, its possibility is endless. In normal life all may have it and have it yet again. The world is full of it; and yet today the mass of human beings are choked away from it, and their lives distorted and made ugly.... it is the bounden duty of black America to begin this great work of the creation of Beauty, and the preservation of Beauty, of the realization of Beauty, and we must use in this work all the methods that men have used before.... The apostle of Beauty thus becomes the apostle of Truth and Right not by choice but by inner and outer compulsion.... Thus all art is propaganda and ever must be, despite the wailing of the purists. I stand in utter shamelessness and say that whatever art I have for writing has been used always for propaganda for gaining the right of black folk to love and enjoy. (325–38)

Sentiments to which each of these writers would, and in their various ways did, gladly testify.

The artist, suggests Kenneth Burke, might be aptly compared to a "medicine man," and "the situations for which he offers his stylistic medicine may be very real ones" (54). At times, Burke maintains, a writer functions something like a "homeopath," transforming poison into medicine through a strategy of dilution. Other, more "impious" literary practitioners more closely resemble "allopaths," finding cures in "antidote" and antithesis. Whichever therapeutic strategy is deployed, however, Burke stipulates that "it is only in so far as his situation overlaps upon our situation, that his strategy of encompassment is felt by us to be relevant" (54–55).

Each of the authors I've discussed in this book deserves consideration along these lines. Each confronted a "very real" situation via literary means; yet as I have sought to clarify, the "medicine" she or he offered remained no pure elixir but was unavoidably constituted out of and filtered through the mix of generic conventions, rhetorical devices, and the demands of narrative form. So even when artists follow Du Bois and approach literature as propaganda, even when they deeply desire to use art for propagandistic purposes, these intentions do not radiate intact from and through the content of their compositions but are, of necessity, inflected (and at times defused) by the formal structures that both shape and contain meaning. Throughout *Bodily and Narrative Forms*, I have engaged a series of dialogues between informing situations most accurately described as medico-scientific and responsive literary strategies; along the way, I've paid careful attention to the varied mediating processes through which these dialogues might ultimately have come to sound muffled, distorted, alien, even hollow to our ears.

If they do ring hollow, however, the fault may lie less in the texts than in readers' interactions with them; for if, as Burke proposes, the situation a work of art addresses does not "overlap" with "our" own, its relevance as strategy, as cure, may be undermined. This could very well pertain to the situation facing Harper, Chesnutt, and Hopkins; the virtual neglect into which each of their powerful novels has until recently fallen would seem to affirm a lack of "overlap" characteristic of a profoundly segregated society like our own.

And yet, to isolate this lack may be to provide too simple an explanation for neglect and stasis. Judging if only by the alternately misguided, divided, or deficient reception afforded these three works, it does seem necessary to reconsider literature's efficacy as "a strategy for dealing with situations." Especially when forced to grapple with pernicious, pervasive belief systems, to what extent can any literary work—even when packing the combined one-two punch of structural and thematic rebuttals—effectively constitute a potent weapon? In such situations, can it ever really act as potent medicine? This is not to question literature's political value but to question its political significance, its political agency—to question, that is, whether political problems can ever actually be solved by means of literary solutions to aesthetic problems. A text may offer "healing" in many ways, not the least of these being its potential to offer comfort, pleasure, or momentary escape. But to say that literature can effect social transformation is to make claims for literary works that few, if any, of these works can sustain. All the same, this relative impotency of ends has not and should not militate against the use of form as strategic, prophylactic means—it should not, in short, prevent writers from taking up their pens for political purposes, or, at the very least, with healing in mind. It just makes the struggle (for a cause, for a cure) all the more arduous, and, at times, all the more poignant.

My decision to close *Bodily and Narrative Forms* in 1915 represents, in large part, an acknowledgment of the medical profession's hegemony at that time. With each passing year of the new century mainstream medical practitioners found themselves more assured of consensus and authoritative status and less besieged by the skepticism that had been generated in part by the persuasiveness of alternative forms of therapy, in part by their own ineptitudes. I chose to focus on the years of medicine's ascendancy mainly because I thought to find in this less-than-settled period a bit more flexibility as well as greater imaginative possibilities in the construction of forms (though as it turns out, emergent frameworks, in their potential insidiousness and elusiveness, can at times prove more difficult to confront and combat than better established and presumably more commonsensical ones).

And yet, to assert that the profession of medicine achieved a certain authority by the second decade of the twentieth century is not to militate against all future comparisons between literary and medical practice, nor should it rule out studies devoted to assessing how these two at times not dissimilar practices have shaped the ways we continue to think about and represent our embodied lives. The meanings we assign to the body, after and despite all, remain stubbornly open to reinterpretation and rebuttal. It seems to me that many of these meanings might still be advantageously correlated to shifts in medical explanatory frameworks (since, of course, affording medicine a certain authoritative clout is not the same thing as assuming that its practices and beliefs became absolute and fixed at that authoritative moment), as well as to a still lingering faith in narrative's potential as strategic intervention or mimetic site.

There thus remains good reason for the interpretive model exemplified in the preceding close readings to be utilized in discussions of later literary movements and periods. Further research on, say, the influence of William James's principles of psychology upon his student Gertrude Stein's experimentalism, or potential overlaps between the concerns of medicine and literature in the careers of William Carlos Williams or

Walker Percy, or the relationship between Flannery O'Connor's chronic disease and the author's "grotesque narratives," or the healing agendas of medical student turned short story writer Ethan Canin and poet, doctor, and AIDS activist Rafael Campo, would be useful as welcome explorations of the diverse ways in which the bodily and literary forms that served as my focus here continue to intersect and interact.

I started this project believing that the period of medicine's ascendancy lends the comparison of artist to "medicine man" (or woman) a compelling mixture of urgency and uncertainty. While I still believe that this is so, I also believe that writers from subsequent periods (and I would include literary scholars here) can continue to benefit from thinking of their tasks as medicinal, with all the political urgency, historic specificity, and transformative, curative potential the term, as I have used it in this study, seems capable of retaining. What remains for time and future study to decide is whether the stylistic remedies we continue to devise and prescribe will prove not just palatable but effective.

# REFERENCE MATTER

# Notes

INTRODUCTION

1. As medical historians typically agree, it was only relatively late in the nineteenth century that the profession began to make headway in its long struggle for authority. Paul Starr summarizes this slow and relatively uneven process:

> One way of looking at the changes that took place between the 1870s and the early 1900s is that the social distance between doctor and patient increased, while the distance among colleagues diminished as the profession became more cohesive and uniform. The state, which had been indifferent to physicians' claims since the Jacksonian era, finally embraced the profession's definition of a legitimate practitioner. All these developments reflected a movement toward the strengthening of professional status and the consolidation of professional authority. (81)

As Starr's wording suggests, the authority of the medical profession is best thought of as a "movement toward" rather than an already established fact. For further evidence of the complexity of the Victorian era and its medical epistemes, see Degler, who in "What Ought to Be and What Was," argues that the moral and medical treatises of this period have been "taken to be descriptive of the sexual ideology of the time when in fact they were part of an effort by some other medical writers to establish an ideology, not to delineate an already accepted one.... The medical literature ... was really normative or prescriptive rather than descriptive" (40). See also Vance, who maintains that "historical examination of even the most seemingly objective 'scientific' prescriptive material reveals that its messages have not been homogeneous and static, but have changed over time. These fluctuations are traceable to the emergence of different scientific groups; changes in theories about workable solutions to social problems; battles and competition for ideology, professional turf, patients, and money; and the rise and fall of particular scientific paradigms" (12).

2. These debates deserved to be placed in the context provided by Foucault in his *History of Sexuality*, volume I. There Foucault rejects Freud's theory of sexual repression and suggests instead that from the eighteenth century onward there was an increasing tendency to talk, and talk endlessly, about sex and sexu-

ality. We could say that both Freud and Foucault agree that this was a repressive age, but whereas Freud locates repression at the intrapsychic level, Foucault locates it on a social level.

3. On ideological sedimentation, see Jameson, *The Political Unconscious* 140–41.

4. Though I address his theories explicitly only in Chapter 3, my debt to Bakhtin both here in this introduction and throughout the entire project is great.

5. Among the many feminists who adopt formal as well as thematic approaches to literature, I have particularly benefited from the models established by Nancy Armstrong, Nina Baym, Rachel Blau DuPlessis, Anne Cranny-Francis, Cathy N. Davidson, Rita Felski, and Susan Harris.

6. Some of the more recent works to explore links between medicine and literature include Herndl's *Invalid Women*, Poovey's *Uneven Developments*, Rothfield's *Vital Signs*, and Jacobus et al., *Body/Politics*. Many of the most exciting articles in the field appear in the journal *Literature and Medicine*.

7. These histories would include Arney's *Power and the Profession of Obstetrics*, Degler's *At Odds*, Ehrenreich and English's *For Her Own Good*, Laqueur's *Making Sex*, Showalter's *The Female Malady*, and Smith-Rosenberg's *Disorderly Conduct*. Foucault's *History of Sexuality*, volume I, has influenced many subsequent discussions of medico-scientific constructions of gender but is in itself rather disinterested in gender politics.

8. Here my study intersects and benefits from a number of recent feminist works—including those by Riley, Scott, Spelman, and Moraga and Anzaldúa— that acknowledge gender's mutability as well as its integral relationship with the other social factors that shape both identity and difference.

9. I don't mean to imply that the discourse of medicine serves as these texts' sole interlocutor. My focus on the relationship between literary and medico-scientific frameworks is meant to isolate for the sake of sustained analysis one informative strand from the potentially rich weave spun between text and context. It is also meant to serve as a model for future analyses of additional strands in this weave.

CHAPTER 1

1. On this desire for impenetrability, see Foucault, *Discipline and Punishment*. Foucault, who reintroduced Jeremy Bentham's *Panopticon* to modern critics, claims in an interview that he stumbled upon Bentham's text "while I was studying the origins of clinical medicine.... I wanted to find out how the medical gaze was institutionalized, how it was effectively inscribed in social space" ("Eye" 146). I examine the American context of this institutionalization in the next section.

2. The dating of realism has always been problematic: as a formal literary movement, American realism dates roughly from the postbellum period, reaching its peak in the 1880s when William Dean Howells, its "Dean" and initial theorist, began waging his "Realism War." And yet, there are numerous works with elements of realism that appeared prior to the full-fledged realist movement, including Harriet Wilson's *Our Nig* (1859) and three novels featuring doctor characters: Rebecca Harding Davis's *Life in the Iron Mills* (1861), John William De Forest's *Miss Ravenel's Conversion from Secession to Loyalty* (1867), and, the one I address here, Oliver Wendell Holmes's *Elsie Venner* (1861).

3. Discussions of the clinical gaze invariably begin with Foucault even if they take issue with him. Contributors to Diamond and Quinby are among the few who insist upon taking into account the gendered dialectic of the gaze. Among the studies of clinical realism that have influenced my own work are Åhnebrink's, Rothfield's, and Seltzer's. My project differs from these three in that it explicitly places this emergent mode in dialogue with the more sentimental one it sought to displace.

4. Compare Rothfield's definition in his study of the overlapping discourses of clinical medicine and clinical realism within Great Britain: "to see with a medical eye means invoking, however tacitly, a complicated system of techniques, conceptual configurations, presuppositions, and protocols of interpretation that enable one to take signs as symptoms and thereby to impose a particular order on reality" (175).

5. Throughout the nineteenth century, there were distinctions made between "regular" or regulated licensed physicians and "irregulars," the latter including such practitioners of alternative medicine as homeopaths. See Kett, Link, Rothstein, and Starr for helpful overviews of medical practices in this period.

6. See Rosenberg's *The Cholera Years*.

7. For a detailed explanation of the etymology of "science," see Williams.

8. The rise of science as a profession was also informed by gender ideologies and differences, perhaps best evidenced by the fact that when William Whewell coined the term "scientist" in 1834 it was in the same sentence in which he declared that there is a "sex in minds." For more thorough overviews of the professionalization of science, see Bruce, Kohlstedt, and Schiebinger.

9. In an interesting side-note suggestive of the extent to which race and class influenced medical outlooks, S. Weir Mitchell wrote Holmes the year the latter began serializing *Elsie Venner* about their shared interest in presumed physiological differences between the races and socio-economic classes. In this 1859 letter, Mitchell states:

> I have for some time been much interested in the physical statistics of our native born white race. Last summer I submitted to the Biological Depart-

ment of our Academy of Natural Sciences a plan for collecting the required statistics. This scheme, approved of by a committee of the Department, & since actively aided by its members, has lately received the sanction of the Smithsonian Institution, & enlisted its practical assistance.... In a scheme so extended, it is, of course, requisite to seek aid in many directions. Among others, I desire, if possible, to attain the physical statistics of the undergraduates of our principal colleges. If a register of height, weight, etc. etc. could be kept as a permanent record in our college gymnasia, or otherwise this end would be attained. Is this practicable?

Some twenty-five years later, in a letter dated December 21, 1874, Mitchell again wrote Holmes about the difference "blood" makes:

> I think it can be shown—that the descendants of the "signers" we will say or if you like of the class of aristocrats of that date have like those of England preserved an unimpaired physique—Our lower middle class is the one in which we see the worst examples of bad types of both sexes. Most of the families here of historic or social note are healthy & even vigorous. The Biddles, Cadwaladers, Ingersolls & so on are good examples. My own people are singularly healthy—My two boys represent—besides my own blood—Langdons, Elwyns in New England & Butler & Middleton in South Carolina & are sturdy as God makes anybody—Certainly decay is not a law—here—but if there is anything wrong it is with the women.

There is enough provocative material here to warrant lengthy discussion, but as I will be examining Mitchell's views in depth in Chapter 4, suffice it to say for now that Mitchell would have been the first to acknowledge his assumption of elite white male superiority. It also seems worth noting that Mitchell's research interests eerily foreshadow the recently uncovered, longstanding project of taking nude photographs of Ivy League students, including, allegedly, such illustrious graduates as former President George Bush, newscaster Diane Sawyer, and first lady Hillary Clinton.

10. Prior to this time, female midwives usually treated female complaints, illnesses, and pregnancies. In *Uneven Developments*, Poovey traces the anxiety and unevenness produced by British male practitioners' early interventions in female maladies and bodies. See also Ehrenreich and English.

11. For more on this image of administering angel, see Chapter 2, where I discuss Alcott's description of nursing as intervention in *Hospital Sketches*.

12. See Chapter 3 for a discussion of Clarke.

13. See Burbick 286–95.

14. Holmes's enthusiasm for visual metaphors was boundless. To take one last example, in his "Mechanism in Thought and Morals," Holmes analogizes

intelligence and vision:

> The resemblance of the act of intelligence to that of vision is remarkably shown in the terms we borrow from one to describe the other. We *see* a truth; we *throw light* on a subject; we *elucidate* a proposition; we *darken* counsel; we are *blinded* by prejudice; we take a *narrow* view of things; we look at our neighbor with a *jaundiced eye*. These are familiar expressions; but we can go much farther. We have intellectual myopes, near-sighted specialists, and philosophers who are purblind to all but the distant abstract. We have judicial intellects as nearly achromatic as the organ of vision, eyes that are colorblind, and minds that seem hardly to have the sense of beauty. The old brain thinks the world grows worse, as the old retina thinks the eyes of needles and the fractions in the printed sales of stocks grow smaller. (268–69)

15. Bledstein employs the masculine pronoun throughout his treatise. Of course, he had some historic justification in so doing given the time frame of his discussion.

16. See Holmes's essay "Homeopathy and Its Kindred Delusions," in his *Medical Essays*, for his vehement objection to alternative medicine and "irregulars." See also Chapter 3 for a more detailed discussion of homeopathy.

17. See Berger; see Ryan on the perils of public visibility or overexposure for women. Although writing long before Freud, Holmes here replicates the psychoanalyst's famous dichotomy between male scopophilia and female exhibitionism.

18. In a confidential letter, Holmes confided that his views on female practitioners shared an affinity with those of Dr. E. H. Clarke's, which he thought "founded on a wise estimate of the results of a large experience." As Holmes wrote to Elizabeth Blackwell's brother Henry: "Dear Sir, I was entirely satisfied with Dr. Clarke's paper, which appeared to me founded on a wise estimate of the results of a large experience" ("Letter" n.p.). See Chapter 3 for a discussion of Clarke. For more on the advent of female doctors, see Morantz-Sanchez; see also Chapter 2.

19. The title that was given to the serialized version of the novel was "The Professor's Story."According to some critics, Elsie is loosely based on Margaret Fuller, whom by all accounts Holmes did not much care for. Holmes once described Fuller as possessing "a watery aqua-marine lustre in her light eyes" and a "long, flexible neck, arching and undulating in strange, sinuous movements," a description reminiscent of Elsie's own. If true, Holmes was only one of a number of writers who fictionalized Fuller after her untimely death. See Chapter 2 for a discussion of Fuller and others' perceptions of her.

20. In her recent *Healing the Republic*, Burbick reads Holmes's *Elsie Venner* within a bodily discourse of nerves, not, as I do, of vision. Claiming that what ails Elsie is a fatal impairment of her nervous system, Burbick suggests that the novel represents "not so much a treatise on the organic suffering of an individual, as a

directive on the proper relationship between the social classes in America, and how physiology fated the classes to a fixed social order" (242–3).

21. Numerous critical works have addressed visual iconographies of power in nineteenth-century American culture. See, for example, Bell's *Development*, Pease, and Porter.

22. It is interesting, given the heroine's resemblance to a snake, to note that the serpent is the symbol of the American Medical Association. As Holmes once remarked elsewhere on the choice of this symbol,

> I know not whether in adopting the serpent as the emblem of medical art, it was because medicine deals in poisons and knew how to use them to effect its purposes or for what other reason. But there is one which seems to me sufficient. As the snake casts his skin so does medical science excoriate its worn out doctrines from generation to generation. Hard work it often is to wiggle out of its scaly coat of effete and unclear ideas, but it must get rid of them and it does. ("Address")

While medicine's serpentinity enables its practitioners to thrive and change, Elsie's leads only to her degeneration.

23. In *Love and Death in the American Novel*, Fiedler reads the clash between these two characters as representative of the clash between the "Dark Lady" and the "Fair Maiden," which is, he contends, central to American fiction (300–301).

24. Indeed, one of the ways we know that Elsie is threatening is that she knows the power of drugs (or poisons): when Dick sees her with a white powder, he knows to watch his diet and his step.

25. See, for a discussion of sympathy's medicinal force, Morantz-Sanchez's important *Sympathy and Science* and my elaboration on her discussion in Chapter 2. See Mary Douglas for an exploration of analogies between the individual and social body.

26. See Chapter 2 for a lengthy discussion of sentimentalism's manipulations of physical presence and absence.

CHAPTER 2

1. In his introduction to *Medicine Without Doctors*, Risse defines "medical self-help" as "the diagnosis, care, and even prevention of disability and illness without direct professional medical assistance." Because these activities so often take place in the home, the editors alternately refer to these practices as "home or domestic medicine" (2).

2. As Burbick attests, "The language of the heart, still doggedly present in speech, was imagined as a phase of speaking that must die as it was based upon a physiological misperception" (180).

Notes to Pages 50–52

3. Later in the century, S. Weir Mitchell would advise that "To endure without excess of emotion" (90) would save the woman suffering "pain of body, hurt of mind" (89) from "consequent nervousness" (*Doctor and Patient* 89–90). See Chapter 4 for a discussion of Mitchell.

4. See Samuels's *Culture of Sentiment*.

5. My definition is a deliberately narrow and loose one. While, certainly, not all fiction written by women in this period can be classified as sentimental, acknowledging the diversity of women's writing during the supposedly "feminine fifties" (see Pattee) does not automatically entail retiring the rubric "sentimental." Sentimentalism is a vexed term, but I believe it is still a useful one. In general, there are two dominant schools of thought on sentimental writing: one camp, identified primarily with Ann Douglas, bemoans its emotional debasement, compromises, and inherent conservatism; the opposing camp, spearheaded by Jane Tompkins, highlights and applauds the genre's capacity for elevation and change. This chapter starts from the premise that debasement and elevation are themselves intimately connected in some of the classic sentimental novels of the 1840s and '50s. For additional diverse and contradictory definitions of the sentimental novel as a genre, see Baym, Gillian Brown, H. Ross Brown, Davidson, Samuels, and Todd.

6. In a 1997 article I discovered after completing this chapter, Joanne Dobson revisits sentimentalism, arguing that it, as with realism, romanticism, and other literary movements, deserves not just sustained formal analysis but aesthetic evaluation and argues that sentimental writing is as varied in quality as it is in style, motif, and outcome. This variety notwithstanding, Dobson makes a case for a sentimental tradition, defining literary sentimentalism as "premised on an emotional and philosophical ethos that celebrates human connection, both personal and communal, and acknowledges the shared devastation of affectional loss" (267). My definition takes no issue with Dobson's but merely accentuates the ways in which these connections, and these losses, both foreground and downplay a character's physicality, emotionalism, and/or frailty.

7. See, for instance, Tompkins, who defines the word sentimental as stipulating "that all true action is not material, but spiritual" (151). Tompkins also argues that the "language of tears," which might strike modern readers as excessive, may even in Stowe's day have been inadequate to the task at hand: i.e., the task of convincing people that "a change of heart"—a change in the way they *feel*—could change the world (132–33).

8. In her chapter in *Touching Liberty* entitled "Bodily Bonds: The Intersecting Rhetorics of Feminism and Abolition," Sánchez-Eppler has elucidated "the power of sentiment to change the condition of the human body or at least, read symbolically, to alter how that condition is perceived.... Sentiment and feeling

refer at once to emotion and to physical sensation" (26). Sánchez-Eppler locates the convergence of these two versions of sentience in the reader, whose eyes "take in the printed word and blur it with tears. Reading sentimental fiction is thus a bodily act, and the success of a story is gauged, in part, by its ability to translate words into pulse beats and sobs" (26–27).

9. In this introduction, Baym notes that the writers she addresses considered their own work to be anti-sentimental, especially since they associated sentimentality with the scorned seduction novel, which "denotes private, excessive, undisciplined, self-centered emotionality" (xxix). Baym retains the term "woman's fiction" to refer to one type of narrative among the many that women wrote in the antebellum period, an "inspirational plot" (x) centering on "a young woman who has lost the emotional and financial support of her legal guardians—indeed who is often subject to their abuse and neglect—but who nevertheless goes on to win her way in the world" (ix). Although in this new introduction Baym entertains the possibility that woman's fiction is sentimental, it is in a different sense than the one her writers scorn; for Baym, the sentimentality of woman's fiction stems from its emphasis on "public sympathy and benevolent fellow-feeling," as well as its endorsement of "a practical philosophy of community designed to operate in a variety of social contexts to complement or modify social interactions that are otherwise calculating and instrumental" (xxx).

10. See Welter for her classic if dated definition of the "true woman." Baym takes issue with Welter's concept of "true womanhood," citing woman's fiction as counterevidence that, while pious and pure, women were querying the value of submissiveness and reconstituting domesticity "as their ticket to the public sphere" (Introduction xxxix).

11. This chapter focuses in part on the ways invalid writers take up and manipulate conventional generic forms. For an overview of the discourse of invalidism in American literature and medicine from 1840 to 1940, see Herndl, whose *Invalid Women* does not specifically address Alcott, Hunt, or Fuller. Herndl connects the emergence of the "sickly woman" in American society to her appearance as a fictional character in American literature. Dating from around the 1840s, Herndl suggests, the invalid and her disease moved from the margins to a position of "new prominence" in the fictions of the day. However widespread female invalidism actually was, Herndl maintains (with some exaggeration) that literary invalids, at least, were dropping "like flies" (22). Other helpful sources on this topic include Douglas's "Fashionable Diseases"; Ehrenreich and English; Haller and Haller; Leavitt; Smith-Rosenberg's *Disorderly Conduct*; Smith-Rosenberg and Rosenberg; and Verbrugge. By the turn of the century, as fears of what Teddy Roosevelt dubbed "race suicide" mounted and diet and exercise be-

came increasingly fashionable, female invalidism gradually ceased to be epidemic, if it ever was so (see Verbrugge and Cogan for counterevidence).

12. Critical discussions of *Hospital Sketches* include Elbert's, Capello's, Schultz's, and Young's.

13. Elizabeth Young has discussed how Alcott's Civil War fiction homologizes national and individual body through a process of feminization. Young reads this homology as a means for Alcott to comment upon "her own battles against gender propriety" (440) and to construct an alternate, feminized (if problematic) model of national subjectivity. As a result of Young's compelling analysis, I have drastically abbreviated my argument in this section, as it would only reiterate many of Young's central points. For all its emphasis on bodily disorder and disease, however, Young's article only briefly mentions Alcott's own struggles with illness as context for her literary works.

14. Alcott's therapeutics overlaps with those of the AMA's doctors and, in particular, with Holmes's, for in each the proper time for tears to be shed is posthumously. By contrast, Alcott's Concord neighbor, Emerson, rejects just such an approach. As he writes in "Self-Reliance," "Our sympathy is just as base [as our regrets]. We come to them who weep foolishly, and sit down and cry for company, instead of imparting to them truth and health in rough electric shocks" (162).

15. Interestingly, Bronson's cousin and Louisa May's uncle, William A. Alcott, made a similar recommendation in his popular 1850 advice book, *Letters to a Sister; Or Woman's Mission*: "Has woman—even redeemed woman—this willingness to *do*, and *be*, and *suffer*, almost anything which can be laid upon her, for Christ's sake?" (305). In Louisa's case, her willingness to "do, be, and endure" is not explicitly "for Christ's sake" but for her own.

16. For discussions of *Little Women* as Civil War fiction, see both Young and Fetterley, "*Little Women*."

17. In his essay on *Work*, Glenn Hendler explores the paradox of sentimental fiction, wherein assertions of individualism associated with the bildungsroman come into conflict with the effects of sympathy, which are the loss of self, of selflessness. He sees Christie's marriage as an attempt to smooth over this paradox by allowing her to find herself by finding another to fulfill or round out herself. But this solution is only temporal: as Hendler shows, it is not in the heterosexual dyad but a larger community of women that Christie ultimately finds a place for herself as selfless.

18. See Chapter 1 for a discussion of the organization of "regular" American medicine, and Chapter 3 for a discussion of homeopathy.

19. This support was by no means unanimous. There were many who shrank

from the mere idea of a woman amputating, bleeding, and dosing alongside male doctors—one woman going so far as to exclaim of Elizabeth Blackwell, "Oh, it is too horrid! I'm sure I could never touch her hand! Only to think that those long fingers of hers had been cutting up dead people" (Stanton et al. vol. I 94). Further evidence of hostility can be found in a letter Elizabeth wrote to her sister, Emily, from Geneva, New York, where the former attended medical school:

> I sadly want instruction here, & some one with whom to converse, on my readings & observations. ... I get very little from the physicians, they keep aloof, view me with suspicion, think I am stepping out of woman's sphere, have not courage enough to act freely before a lady, have some fear that I shall detect ignorance or malpractice, &c, all which reasons prove complete barriers between us, & I doubt much whether they can be overcome. ... [O]h how different it would be, with intelligent, interested instructors, & companions to share study. ("To Emily" n.p.)

20. This strategy had additional pitfalls: to claim, as Doctor Ella Flagg Young did, that "every woman is born a doctor. Men have to study to become one" (qtd. in Morantz-Sanchez 5) was to risk feeding into professional counternarratives which valorized learned skills over inborn or innate qualities. Even outside the medical profession there were those who seized upon women's "innate" qualifications and used them for conservative ends. For instance, Sarah Josepha Hale, editor of the influential *Godey's Lady's Book*, often shared such thoughts with her readers in her columns. For Hale as for many others at midcentury, healing was simply an extension of women's domestic duties. Women doctors were thus expected to confine their practice to the treatment of women and children and their respective ills—which, in fact, most did. See Bardes and Gossett, Ehrenreich and English, Matthews *Public*, Morantz, and Morantz-Sanchez for further discussions of such views.

21. Holmes himself voted against her admittance. Yet when Hunt tried again three years later, she met with more success. On December 5, 1850, Hunt received a letter from Holmes informing her that she would be admitted to the lectures, making her the first woman granted this privilege. Because Hunt was sick at the time, she was unable to pick up the requisite tickets of admission, and her failure to appear set off quite a controversy in the local papers. See *Glances and Glimpses* 265–72, for Hunt's account of the incident, and Chapter 1 for a discussion of Holmes.

22. As Burbick argues in her discussion of Hunt, "heart language offered a counterpoint to the new physiologies of the body, and restored the voice of the speaking subject. ... to speak from the heart was to speak from a felt interiority of the body, an apprehension of a sensed life different from the causality of physiology" (181).

23. Even the dual dedications of *Glances and Glimpses* bear out Hunt's increasingly impersonal trajectory. Hunt offers two discrete tributes, on two discrete pages—the first a sentimental paean to her sister and maternity, the second a flattering tribute to fellow suffragist and spinster Sarah Grimké. It is significant that the dedication to her sister precedes the one to Grimké because this progression matches the narrative's, as it moves from sentimentalized descriptions of Hunt's upbringing and family life to her career as a doctor "married to humanity" and as a woman's rights activist.

24. Invaluable resources on Fuller and responses to her include Chevigny, Capper, Higginson, Myerson's bibliographies, Russell, and Stern.

25. It is also possible that Hawthorne based Miriam and Donatello, characters in *The Marble Faun*, on Fuller and Ossoli; some have even seen a comparison between Hester Prynne and Fuller. The fact that Fuller may have inspired, to varying degrees, central characters in three of Hawthorne's four published novels suggests that his preoccupation with Fuller bordered on obsession. See Thomas R. Mitchell for a recent rehashing of Julian Hawthorne's revelations of (and reveling in) his father's feelings toward Fuller.

26. Orestes Brownson's review was even more critical, faulting *Woman* for lacking a clear "beginning, middle, [or] end, . . . [it] may be read backwards as well as forwards, and from the centre outwards each way, without affecting the continuity of the thought or the succession of ideas. We see no reason why it should stop where it does. . . . Indeed, we do not know what is its design. We cannot make out what thesis it does or does not maintain. All is profoundly obscure, and thrown together in 'glorious confusion'" (19). In an appendix to *Woman*, Fuller herself acknowledges that she took complaints she had not made her "meaning sufficiently clear" (*Woman* 154) in "The Great Lawsuit" into account as she revised and expanded the essay to make the book-length *Woman*. But even these clarifying attempts failed fully to satisfy Horace Greeley, who while editing the 1855 edition of *Woman in the Nineteenth Century, and Kindred Papers* wrote Fuller's brother Arthur to inform him that he had "carefully revised" the text, making revisions that included "some very slight verbal alterations" in Fuller's prose (Myerson *Descriptive* 51).

27. See Baym's *Novels, Readers, and Reviewers*, in which she argues that male writers were commended by reviewers for using fiction to express their genius, while women writers were praised for "the expression of the sex" (257). Baym also reveals that writers of either sex were applauded not for representing female characters as diverse individuals but as (true) women (97–104). See also Ryan, who skillfully recounts the dangers of the public sphere for bourgeois women. For a more optimistic reading, see Matthews's *Public*.

28. Urbanski, in one of the few critical studies to address *Woman*'s formal

dimensions, claims that "its basic structure is that of the sermon" (161). She also connects Fuller's circular style to Transcendental writing techniques and their belief in the primacy of organic forms (167–68). In a more recent article, Kolodny, "Inventing," maintains that Fuller's rhetorical style represents a strategic application of a book she used while teaching in Providence, Richard Whateley's *Elements of Rhetoric*, which emphasizes in particular the persuasiveness of "rational conversation" (366).

29. In private correspondence, Jeffrey Steele reminded me that Fuller did indeed write fiction, including the story of "Mariana" (embedded in *Summer on the Lakes*), "A Tale of Mizraim" (rediscovered and reprinted in *New England Quarterly*), "Aglaron and Laurie" (appended as a "kindred paper" to *Woman*), "Lost and Won" (recently located by Robert Hudspeth), and several other assorted pieces that can be found in her private papers.

30. While in Italy during its civil war Fuller served for a time as a nurse, a role that might be seen as an extension of her commitment to radiant health as an ideal.

31. See Kolodny's "Inventing" and Urbanski, both of whom discuss the impact of these experiences on Fuller and on *Woman*.

32. Although there are many possible explanations for Fuller's spiritualized portrayal of woman in *Woman*, I am focusing here primarily on biographical possibilities. Among other interpretations, Fuller's portrait could be read as an effective counterattack to conclusions like those of Spinoza, an excerpt from whom Fuller appends to *Woman*. Spinoza maintains in this excerpt that since men and women have never been considered equals, and since what men feel for women is not desire for their souls but lust for their bodies, women's natures must both dominate their lives and define their inferiority to men (Appendix D, 174–76). Fuller's *Woman* represents not only a Transcendental manifesto for women but also a strategic rebuttal of such conventional views.

33. As Packer notes, the male Transcendentalists' obsession with "manliness" is not motivated by a fear of "effeminacy" so much as by a disdain for "servility" or dependence—the ultimate check on self-reliance. In this sense, Fuller's desire to be the man she is "not yet" is not some transsexual longing but a desire for the independence she (quite rightly) associates with men.

34. Some fifty years after Fuller wrote *Woman*, Kate Chopin's Edna Pontellier (an avid reader of Emerson, as was Fuller) would graphically demonstrate the limits of Transcendentalism when its proponent found herself imprisoned in a desired and desiring female body—an imprisonment, moreover, that she finally confronts on a walk with a doctor after both have attended another woman's difficult birth.

35. In the defiant introduction to his early manifesto, "Nature" (1836), Emer-

son succinctly divides the Universe into two parts: Nature and Soul. Defining Soul as "me," Emerson classifies all else, including "my own body," as the "Not Me" (4). For more on Fuller's relationship to Transcendentalism, and in particular to Transcendentalists Emerson and Thoreau, see my "Margaret Fuller, Body and Soul." See also Sidonie Smith's discussion of the "metaphysical self," for whom self-knowledge depends upon transcending "constraining particularities of human existence," including the body, its needs, and desires (77). Smith ranges this "metaphysical self" against the "encumbered self" (81) which demarcates female subjectivity. My point is that Fuller does not necessarily oppose these two concepts but links them in such a way as to interrogate the equation of the body with encumbrance. Her insistence on uniting both body and soul certainly predates Whitman, who is often and perhaps mistakenly celebrated for his originality in conjoining the two.

36. Elsewhere, Fuller lays partial blame on the years she had to take care of her siblings "at a time when my mind was so excited by many painful feelings"; these duties, she claimed in a letter to her brother Arthur dated December 31, 1837, "had a very bad effect upon my health"(Hudspeth 1: 319). While Fuller here acknowledges pain's external source, more often than not she probes its internal origins and its felt, subjective dimensions.

37. See Verbrugge for an elaboration on the theories of stimulation and depletion, esp. 28–48. See Kett as well as Rothstein for representative histories of American medicine. This theory is the predecessor of the theories of organisms as "closed energy systems" popularized in E. H. Clarke's *Sex in Education* (see Chapter 3).

38. Corsets were more than just metaphorically constraining for Fuller: in his biography, Higginson quotes a "venerable Cambridge lady" who disparaged Fuller's figure, claiming that Fuller "was laced so tightly ... by reason of stoutness" (29). Further, Fuller suffered at twelve a suffusion of blood into her head that reportedly "ruined her complexion" and which was very likely the result of the internal pressure applied by her corset (see Higginson 29–30). Fuller herself discusses corsets in *Woman*, celebrating women who give them up as taking one step down the road toward freedom from "all artificial means of distortion" (150).

39. I will return to the underlying biases in Emerson's account and in those of the other compilers of the *Memoirs* at the end of this essay.

40. Gustafson locates Fuller within a sentimental tradition, but the one of sermons, not *Godey*'s. Gustafson maintains that in *Woman* Fuller employs sentimental rhetoric only after radically redefining it so that it is disassociated from the "rhetorical distortion and sentimental manipulation" traditionally identified with feminine speech. Sentimentalism, she contends, is resuscitated in both Ful-

ler's speech and in her classic essay *Woman* as a sincere and transparent language which illuminates the soul (Gustafson 43, 50).

### CHAPTER 3

1. Clarke also cites Weir Mitchell as making similar drear pronouncements about the effects of women's education upon their physiological development (111–12). I will discuss Mitchell in the next chapter.

2. For evidence of Spencer's popularity, see Youmans, comp., *Herbert Spencer on the Americans and the Americans on Herbert Spencer*, the proceedings of a banquet held in Spencer's honor in November 1882. Among the luminaries present were Andrew Carnegie, Edmund C. Stedman, Henry Ward Beecher, Charles Frederic Adams, and Charles A. Dana. Oliver Wendell Holmes, Sr., who was unable to attend, sent a letter singing Spencer's praises.

3. Critics frequently use "Elizabeth Stuart Phelps (Ward)" to distinguish the literary daughter from the mother. Because the works I am discussing here were written prior to Phelps's marriage to Herbert D. Ward in 1888, I have chosen to retain her maiden name here. I feel further justified in so doing by the fact that the author herself used the surname Phelps throughout her professional career.

4. Indeed, Phelps argues that the physician's view of women is further biased by the fact that he "knows sick women almost only. Well women keep away from him, and thank Heaven" (129).

5. See, for example, Blau DuPlessis, Warhol, and Alison introduction and collection.

6. The difficulties women faced juggling professional and domestic duties preoccupied Phelps throughout her career. For instance, in an 1867 piece entitled "What Shall They Do?" published in *Harper's New Monthly*, Phelps attempts to counter the advice offered in a previous column by the editor of the "Easy Chair" (a position, ironically, that Howells would later occupy). The editor was counseling a woman who dreamed of writing, faced rejection, and was at a loss to imagine what else to do with her life. While he encouraged the woman to continue to pursue her dream, Phelps suggests that this rejection might accurately indicate a lack of talent and so lists a host of additional jobs women ought to feel qualified to pursue. Phelps acknowledges that women face greater obstacles because of the need to juggle responsibilities, and acknowledges that "women have died, too, in the struggle to bring the opposing forces into thorough, symmetrical union" (519). This concern with balance and rebuttal is even further pronounced in the works I discuss in this chapter.

7. There are numerous excellent studies of realism as a genre. Among those that directly influenced this chapter are Michael Davit Bell's, Cady's, and Amy Kaplan's.

8. The narratological studies I consulted include those by Booth, P. Brooks (*Reading*), Kermode, Miller, and Torgovnick.

9. All information on Howells's biography is culled from Van Wyck Brooks, Cady, M. Howells, and Lynn.

10. Howells was also no stranger to Clarke's views, as he was still living in Boston when the controversy over Clarke's theories emerged and was still presiding over the *Atlantic* when Holmes published therein his anonymous, overall approving review of Clarke's *Sex in Education*.

11. As Coultrap-McQuin notes, Howells at times pitted his friend James against Phelps. Around the time *Doctor Breen* and *Doctor Zay* were published, Howells asked Phelps to shorten one of her stories to make more room for one of James's, a request to which Phelps vehemently objected (187).

12. Charlotte Perkins Gilman, Stowe's grandniece, shared Phelps's enthusiasm for *Uncle Tom's Cabin*. Gilman argues in *The Man-Made World* that the novel's realism and value lie in its universal appeal and its willingness to marginalize the heterosexual marriage plot to concentrate on greater human concerns (104). See Chapter 4 for a detailed discussion of Gilman's definition of realism.

13. See Chapter 2 for a discussion of the emergence of and reaction to women doctors.

14. The best overview of homeopathy in America is Kaufman's; Starr, Rothstein, and Duffy all include discussions of this alternative form of therapy in their larger histories of U.S. medicine.

15. Oliver Wendell Holmes led the campaign against homeopathy with his "Homeopathy and its Kindred Delusions" (1842), which became the touchstone for homeopathy's opponents and proponents alike. Therein, Holmes objected vehemently to this "delusion's" unscientific nature, claiming that, while due to their impotency homeopathic remedies may not harm the individual, the practice does severe harm by interfering with the regular profession's goal of advancing clinical knowledge and cures. See Chapter 1 for an extended analysis of Holmes.

16. See Chapter 4 for a discussion of Mitchell.

17. In their chapter "The Power of Professionalism," Bardes and Gossett treat the doctor characters in works by Howells and Phelps as well as Jewett, James, and Twain and Warner. Ultimately, *Declarations of Independence* is more helpful as literary history than as literary criticism. This is true as well of Masteller's overview.

18. The sense that heterosexual coupling is the narrative's cure-all is reinforced in the Maynard subplot. Louise Maynard, newly separated from her husband, is suffering from some nebulous illness at the beginning of the story; her health is restored at the end not simply through a "regular" doctor's intervention but, more significantly, through the return of and a reunion with her spouse.

19. Howells and Phelps thus shared a common problem. As already discussed, Phelps, too, tried in the novels written immediately prior to her woman doctor story to avoid or critique the coupling convention.

20. As Kessler maintains, Phelps's intimate contact with the medical community provides important context for her novel. Up to this time, Phelps's "boon companion" had been Mary Briggs Harris, M.D., a female doctor in whom Phelps had the utmost confidence both personally and professionally. In addition, Kessler suggests that "Phelps's increased reliance upon nurses and doctors by this time may have led her to view marriage more favorably: bad health severely limited her own independence" (64).

21. On the other hand, S. Weir Mitchell offered nothing but praise for Howells's portrait, especially in contradistinction to Phelps's:

> I have now beside me Howells's "Doctor Breen's Practice." It is a remarkable attempt to do justice to a very difficult subject, for there are two physicians to handle, male and female, not, I think, after their kind. "Doctor Zay," by Miss Phelps, makes absurd a book which is otherwise very attractive. This young woman doctor, a homeopath, sets a young man's leg, and falls in love with him after a therapeutic courtship, in which he wooes [sic] and she prescribes. The woman doctor is, I suspect, still available as material for the ambitious novelist, but let him beware how he deals with her. (*Doctor and Patient* 82).

See the subsequent chapter for more on Mitchell's views.

22. The inexplicability of this outcome also suggests an "immaturity" that runs counter to Spencer's understanding of realism as a mature and complex form. Given Phelps's admiration for Spencer's literary theory, this inexplicability might constitute an implicit critique of romantic endings at the same time that, for reasons already discussed, she nonetheless scripts such an ending herself.

23. See, for example, Light and Cora Kaplan for their respective discussions of the romance.

CHAPTER 4

1. For consistency's sake, I will refer to the woman born Charlotte Anna Perkins as "Gilman" throughout, even though the name she was using when treated by Mitchell as well as when "The Yellow Wallpaper" was written was still Charlotte P. Stetson.

2. For clarifying definitions of hysteria, see Herndl, Hunter, and the essays collected in Sander Gilman et al., *Hysteria Beyond Freud*, especially Roy Porter's excellent "The Body and the Mind, the Doctor and the Patient: Negotiating Hysteria" (225–85). Markell Morantz, in "The Perils of Feminist History," criticizes Douglas Wood and other feminists—including Ehrenreich and English, Lane, and S. Poirier—for what she considers their overly harsh, oversimplified

representations of Mitchell. Morantz demonstrates that Mitchell's views on women, though quite traditional, were both more complicated and more progressive than these feminist historians have suggested. See Burr, Earnest, and Lovering for essentially flattering biographical portraits of the doctor.

3. Mitchell devoted a great deal of energy to castigating these "charlatans" and expelling them from the ranks of the verifiably hysterical; he referred to them as "the pests of many households, who constitute the despair of physicians, and who furnish those annoying examples of despotic selfishness, which wreck the constitutions of nurses and devoted relatives, and in unconscious and half-conscious self-indulgence destroy the comfort of everyone about them" (*Lectures* 218). Mitchell also fictionalized his clinical encounters with these "despots" in a number of his novels: for instance, his description of a hysterical patient as "an octopus" (*Doctor and Patient* 126) translates literally in the novel *Roland Blake*, where a hysterical character named Octopia nearly sucks the vitality out of her female nurse and cousin. Hysterical females populate Mitchell's novels, in fact. For an overview of several of these novels, see Golden's "Overwriting."

4. Indeed, Freud was already well aware of and quite impressed with Mitchell, having reviewed his *Fat and Blood* favorably in 1887 and having recommended his rest cure as therapy for nervous patients. The admiration, however, was not reciprocated: Mitchell would forcefully distance himself from what he considered Freud's "filthy" views on sex as well as from his emphasis on the psychogenetic origin of diseases (Earnest 227–29). For more on Mitchell's opinions on Freud and vice-versa, see Berman 239–40 n. 21; Golden "Overwriting" 146; and Lane *To Herland* 119–20. Ironically, Mitchell and Gilman shared almost identical views on Freud, with each at one time threatening to burn psychoanalytic works (see Earnest 227–29; Gilman, *Living* 314). I will discuss Gilman's distaste for Freudian theories shortly.

5. See Smith-Rosenberg's important historical analysis of hysteria; see also Herndl's *Invalid Women*.

6. See Butler, who maintains that the materiality of the sexed body does not *precede* representation but is instead the *effect* of a "forcible reiteration of regulatory norms" (Butler, *Bodies* 2). One method of exposing materializing, feminizing bodily narratives as reiterative effects rather than originating causes, then, would be to adopt a strategy that approximates the "mimotic." In the subsequent analysis of "The Yellow Wallpaper," I explore Gilman's adoption of just such a strategy and assess its benefits and pitfalls.

7. Anyone familiar with Gilman's biography would find such celebrations of the maternal instinct puzzling, what with Gilman's infamous "abandonment" of her infant daughter, Katherine, and her unconventional views of mothering even after their reunion. What they do clarify is Gilman's willingness to entertain the

existence of intrasubjective depths, but, as she goes on to argue in the essay, only when these buried instincts constitute the motivating impulse behind female agency rather than the very qualities that fix her in place.

8. This is not to suggest that Gilman's progressive approach is superior; the belief that it is the essence of human nature to prosper and evolve is not without its own share of problems.

9. As the title and subject matter of *Women and Economics* would indicate, Gilman was more than just casually concerned with economic issues. A committed socialist and Nationalist (of the Bellamy stamp), Gilman was attracted to these movements primarily because she saw in their goals the potential fulfillment of her communitarian conception of social relations. For recent readings of Gilman's "The Yellow Wallpaper" vis-à-vis economic, in particular, capitalist, modes of production, see Michaels's "Introduction" (3–28) to *The Gold Standard* and Gillian Brown's chapter, "Empire of Agoraphobia," especially 175–78.

10. Magner's article provides a thorough and lucid synopsis of Spencer's and Gilman's evolutionary views. My aim here is to look at how Gilman's naturalizing, deterministic views informed her fiction even as they marked its difference from the literary naturalism also shaped by such views.

11. See Shumaker, "Realism," and Wilson (278–80) for additional discussions of Gilman's aesthetics. Gilman's emphasis on "the human" rather than "the sex" speaks to her self-definition as a "humanist" rather than a "feminist."

12. It is interesting, in this light, to compare Gilman's literary theories with those of Elizabeth Stuart Phelps, who claimed to be a realist along similar lines. See Chapter 3 for a detailed discussion of Phelps's "realist" aspirations.

13. As Dreiser says of Carrie Meeber, "she was as yet more drawn than she drew" (57).

14. See Gilbert and Gubar, Hedges's "Afterword," and Kolodny's "A Map for Rereading" as representatives of this early feminist criticism.

15. See, for example, Haney-Peritz, Herndl's "The Writing Cure," and Jacobus for exemplary psychoanalytic readings. Other psychoanalytic readings of the story include Berman, Johnson, and Veeder.

16. In addition to Gilbert and Gubar, see also Fetterley, Kennard, and Treichler for examples of critical readings that snatch a feminist victory from the jaws of apparent defeat. Among the many feminist analyses, Ammons and Treichler read "The Yellow Wallpaper" as an analogy for women's writing, while Kolodny, Kennard, and Dimock discuss the story in the context of the reading process. Michaels's essay deploys the kind of New Historicist reading that Dimock both engages and reflects upon. Dimock suggests, in a reading she goes on to critique for its ahistorical tendencies, that a sophisticated, "professional" reader is actually "lurking behind the scene" (89), concealed (both like and un-

like the woman within the paper) within the story itself. See Hedges, "Out at Last?" for a helpful overview of the copious criticism on "The Yellow Wallpaper."

17. In fact, as she makes clear in her autobiography, *The Living*, Gilman suffered from depression for most of her life, and not just postpartum. Thanks to Katy Goelzer for insisting that I clarify this point.

18. In a controversial article published in *PMLA* in 1996, Dock and her undergraduate research assistants argue, among other things, that Gilman's statement of intent in her autobiography both oversimplifies the complexity of the story and contributes to a history of revisionist feminist criticism that has cast the opposition between Gilman and Mitchell as "a dramatic story of Saint Charlotte and the evil Doctor Mitchell" (62). Dock et al. could find no evidence that Mitchell, as Gilman (and recent feminists, citing her) would go on to claim, altered or even abandoned his "rest cure" subsequent to reading "The Yellow Wallpaper."

19. Gilman wrote countless articles on the home, such an extraordinary number, in fact, that an editor of one such essay felt compelled to append a note acknowledging the plethora: "'What?' said Mrs. Gilman; 'another article about the home? Surely we've had enough on that topic. Seems to me I can write 'home' articles with my eyes shut, and as if everybody knew, by this time, that housework must be professionalized.' But we assured her that there were still thousands of intelligent women who were unenlightened on this particular subject" ("Whatever Else We Lose" 72).

20. In her *Building Domestic Liberty*, Allen refers to Gilman's "Architectural Imagination" (83), an imagination clearly on display in these missives. Rather than, as is my aim, documenting and discussing primarily figurative examples of this imagination, Allen's study emphasizes Gilman's "lifelong passion for change in the design of residential buildings" (60) and assesses the extent to which her material feminist domestic and architectural reforms were inspired primarily by communitarian socialists.

21. "Housewife" was a title Gilman abhorred: "why should a woman marry a house?" she asked ("Whatever Else We Lose" 74).

22. See, for example, Berman 223, Lane, *To Herland* 21–65, and Hill 22–43.

23. Ammons argues, by contrast, that "the desired transformation of the narrator has *already been* written on the domestic environment designed to contain her" (37).

24. Jacobus raises similar questions about the disconcerting similarities between narrator and contemporary critics (279).

25. Freud did not publish his essay until 1919, although there is evidence that an earlier draft was composed perhaps even a decade previously. Neil Hertz's "Freud and the Sandman," included in his *End of the Line* (97–121), provides a

provocative explication of Freud's "The Uncanny." Hertz's essay assesses Freud's understanding of the uncanny as a process involving both reminder and repetition, though as Hertz notes, even Freud is unclear as to whether what is being recalled is "the repetition compulsion" itself or "whatever it is that is repeated" (101).

26. I am using the terms "gothic" and "uncanny" more or less interchangeably here, primarily because both share an eerie focus on the homelike. I make more uniform use of the term "uncanny" because of its overt etymological connotations of "the home." Rather than seeking to categorize "The Yellow Wallpaper" definitively, my aim is to probe some of the contradictions in its established generic classifications.

27. In addition to Jacobus, Haney-Peritz also briefly discusses the story's uncanny aspects; drawing on Luce Irigiray's theories, she proposes that the repressed that returns in the story is "the operation of the feminine in language" (265). Richard Feldstein mentions in passing that the story's uncanniness lies in the protagonist's projection of aspects of herself to form "her double(s)" (317).

28. See Golden and Hedges's letter responding to Dock's essay, which also notes Blackwell's strong feminist sympathies. Additionally, Golden and Hedges question Dock's charge against "[p]ioneering feminist critics. " Dock contends that these critics claimed that Gilman's story "was initially received as a ghost story." But as Golden and Hedges point out, Dock cites not one "single early critic who made this claim" (467).

29. See also Shumaker, "Too Terribly Good To Be Printed," for a discussion of the story's reception. See Golden's introduction to *Captive Imagination* for an illuminating discussion of how even the illustrations that accompanied the story in the *New England Magazine* contributed to the sense of "The Yellow Wallpaper" as a horror story (1–23, esp. 4–6).

30. Shumaker makes a similar point in "Realism" (81). The recent release of Gilman's formerly unpublished manuscript, *Unpunished*, a mystery replete with gothic twists and turns, would seem to challenge this point, though her writing in this vein seems to be less a matter of choice than of necessity, a rather poignant attempt to resuscitate her waning popularity in the 1920s with this direct appeal to more popular tastes.

31. Gilman's utopian novel is also indebted to Edward Bellamy's *Looking Backward*, to whose nationalist movement Gilman belonged.

32. See Peyser, who underscores certain (unfortunate) realistic aspects of Gilman's utopia. In particular, he traces the ways in which—especially through the racism and imperialism that inform the three Americans' "discovery" of Herland—the author reinscribes the dominant social order even while trying to reform it.

33. The fact that Terry is a scientist who considers sex "the life force" (134) may be a subtle jab at Freud. See Gilman's "This 'Life Force.'"

34. In addition to Ward, Gilman also admitted her debt to the biologist Sir Patrick Geddes, whose *Evolution of Sex* (1889), she claimed, was the other significant influence on her *Women and Economics* (1898). Geddes "discovered" gendered metabolic distinctions at the level of the cell, arguing that while the passive ovum tended to conserve energy (demonstrating its anabolic nature), the aggressive sperm with its katabolic habit tended to dissipate it. He then took these cellular differences and generalized from them a series of absolute gendered distinctions which only further organicized dominant ideologies. There are traces of Geddes in *Herland* as well, most evident in its maternalism and relative stasis. Ward would no doubt have classified Geddes as one of the biologists whom he believed arrived at a late and profoundly altered stage of cell development and mistakenly assumed this altered state to be both natural and atemporal (Ward 542). See Allen 131–33, and Conway 71–82, for helpful summaries of Geddes's theories.

35. Gilman confessed to having difficulty reading both Ward's *Dynamic Sociology* (1883) and *Pure Sociology* (1903) and seems to have been exposed to his views primarily through an article published in the *Forum* in 1888 titled "Our Better Halves." Hill suggests that there were tensions between the two thinkers about who was indebted to whom. See Hill 265–67n. See Allen 133–34, Hill 264–69, and Magner 123–24 for useful overviews of Ward's influence on Gilman.

36. Of course, the fact that *Herland* is narrated by a man and from memory could merely serve to flag the potential biases and flaws in his report (see Bartkowski 28). See also Wilson, who adds that Van's narration works to illuminate how "Herland" frustrates the dynamics of the male gaze (281–82).

37. In an optimistic reading, Donaldson argues that the novel "neutralizes the patriarchal script" by intercepting the mimetic processes which code this script as at once real and commonsensical. This debate over the novel's mimeticism continues to inform the criticism: for example, while Libby Falk Jones contends that "a utopian work is primarily didactic rather than mimetic" (117), Jean Pfaelzer maintains that in certain cases, "utopian fiction is a mimetic mode" (*Utopian* 15). Gilman's utopian novel, I am suggesting, converges rather than polarizes the two modes.

38. The natural basis of the utopian is also used to differentiate it from the fantastic, as the latter by contrast offers a supernatural explanation for the changes endemic therein. See Cranny-Francis for a discussion of the genre of utopian fiction and, in particular, *Herland*'s estranging effects.

39. Pfaelzer's work has been especially important to my own thinking about utopian fiction. Frye's "Varieties" provides a useful starting point for any study

of literary utopias. Helpful sources on feminist utopias in particular include Bartkowski and the introduction to Donawerth and Kolmerten.

40. The referent here is a vague one; while it might be a description of Herland, it might also simply refer to the American men's interest in a land Terry envisions as a sort of "summer resort" full of "Girls and Girls and Girls" (7)—heterosexuality, after all, is one of the novel's implicit "natural" assumptions.

41. Gough argues that the reader of *Herland*, like the male characters, is also mothered, encouraged to "grow ideologically" (204).

42. See Frye's "Varieties" (31) for a discussion of the utopia as an essentially static society.

CHAPTER 5

1. See, for example, these scholars' essays as collected in Showalter, *The New Feminist Criticism*. See also Gilbert and Gubar's influential *Madwoman in the Attic*. Kant outlined his theory of aesthetics in *Critique of Judgement*. Barbara Hernstein-Smith's important work on literary evaluation provides a touchstone for my own exploration of aesthetics.

2. Critics continue to debate whether works as diverse as those authored by African-Americans can ever approximate a tradition, and whether tradition is an inherently essentializing term. See Bernard Bell, whose title indicates his commitment to the rubric, and Gates's introduction to *Reading Black, Reading Feminist* for a helpful introduction to the debate.

3. *The Black Aesthetic* is the title of a very influential collection of essays edited by Addison Gayle and published in 1971. I will discuss this "black aesthetic" briefly at the end of this chapter. Although Gayle is the principal proponent of the "black aesthetic," other influential African American critics, including Robert Bone, Saunders Redding, and, more recently, Houston Baker, have mounted similar critiques of the politics and the aesthetics of the fiction I discuss here. Thanks to Jim Miller for recommending that I clarify my use of the term.

4. In a well-known debate staged in *New Literary History*, Baker and Gates responded to charges by Joyce A. Joyce that the use of poststructuralist theory to interpret African-American texts entailed catering to the interests of whites rather than to the concerns of blacks. See also Christian, "A Race for Theory," and Valerie Smith, "Black Feminist Theory," for important articulations of what is at stake in this debate. Warren provides a helpful overview of the controversy in the conclusion of *Black and White Strangers*.

5. See also Sander Gilman, who argues that around this time there existed a "synchronic" "web of conventions" informing the world of aesthetics and the world of medicine (224). Gilman exemplifies this synchronicity by studying artistic and clinical portraiture of "loose" female "black bodies" and "white bod-

ies." Aesthetics was by no means the only racialized issue debated in medico-scientific circles at this time. See my "Speaking the Body's Pain" for an elaboration of the ongoing attempts to inscribe racial differences along sexual and sensual lines.

6. See Fredrickson, Gossett, and Stepan for helpful historical overviews of racial ideas in science and Appiah for clarification of the speciousness of these biologizing frameworks. See Ringer and Lawless for a sociological study of the relationality (the "we-ness" and the "they-ness") rather than the ontological nature of racial and ethnic identity in America. Likewise, see Omi and Winant for a discussion of extant paradigms of race, ethnicity, class, and nation and their promotion of a racial formation perspective. Of course, racist ideology neither originated in medico-scientific communities nor utterly saturated them; any full account of racist discourse would also, for example, detail legal conceptions of racialized identity.

7. For more on Morton's hierarchy, see Gossett 74 and Jenkins 244–63.

8. I will discuss Chesnutt's hatred of the term "taint" shortly. Dr. Josiah Nott is among the most infamous of these physicians. His widely touted theory of hybrid degeneration represents one of the most vocal challenges to the old saw that drops of white blood inevitably improved black lineage; it was his assertion instead that racial admixture functioned to hasten the regression and ultimate demise of the Negro even as it imperiled Anglo-Saxon supremacy and purity. Nott's views suffuse such fin-de-siècle racist bestsellers as Thomas Dixon's *Leopard Spots* (1903) and *The Clansman* (1905) and Robert Lee Durham's *Call of the South* (1908); they certainly can be set in disputatious dialogue with the nominally "mulatto aesthetics" (Baker, *Workings* 22) of post-Reconstruction works by writers including Harper, Chesnutt, and Hopkins. See Joel Williamson's *New People*, especially 94–100, for further discussion of "scientific" takes on miscegenation. See also Berzon, whose discussion of the mulatto character in American fiction includes an overview of pseudoscientific views (18–30).

Among the books housed in open shelves at the University of South Carolina's Thomas Cooper Library is Pauline E. Hopkins's copy—embossed with *The Colored American Magazine* stamp and Hopkins's signature as literary editor—of G. F. Richings's *Evidences of Progress Among Colored People* (1904), a book designed to "demonstrate that the color of the skin, the texture of the hair, and the formation of the head, have nothing whatever to do with the development and expansion of the mind" (xii). It is possible, as I hope to show, to read not only Hopkins's but other turn-of-the-century black-authored novels as fictional extensions of this project without ignoring their literary, formal dimensions.

9. Oliver Wendell Holmes claimed to have coined the term in 1846, writing in a letter to W. T. G. Morton that "the state should, I think, be called 'Anæs-

thesia'. This signifies insensibility. ... The adjective will be 'Anæsthetic.'" The *Oxford English Dictionary*, however, cites a 1721 usage of the word to connote a "Defect of Sensation."

10. Critics including Berzon, Carby, Christian, duCille, McDowell, and Tate have discussed the mulatta character in fiction in largely political *or* aesthetical terms. My intent is not to choose one side but to make explicit the fact that within the novels themselves no such division could be upheld, as aesthetical representations were very much politicized and political representations aestheticized.

11. See W. E. B. Du Bois's essays on "Negro Art" from the 1920s for the clearest delineation of this propagandistic aesthetics.

12. For exemplary readings of formal texts in the African-American literary tradition as "socially symbolic act[s]" that encode "the survival strategies ... by which black Americans as an ethnic group came to consciousness of themselves and celebrated their quest for personal and social freedom, literacy, and wholeness" (xi), see Bernard Bell.

13. Eagleton's work has greatly influenced my thinking about aesthetics in this chapter, as has George Levine's collection of essays, *Aesthetics and Ideology*.

14. See, for example, Christian, Baker, and Harris for criticism of Harper's and Iola's white minstrelsy. In addition to Carby, both Tate and duCille argue for historical, political readings and reevaluations of the fictional mulatta. Berzon provides a helpful overview of the mulatta as fictional convention.

15. There are also two white-authored novels, both published in 1892, that employ some combination of mulattoes and doctors: Howells's *Imperative Duty* and Thomas Nelson Page's *The Old South*. Whereas both of these novels, albeit to different degrees, condescend to their mulatto protagonists and suggest that it is the white blood in their veins that singles them out as heroic (Howells) or successful (Page), the three novels I will discuss here interrogate precisely this premise.

16. Christian reads *Iola Leroy* as an attempt to subvert racist medico-scientific codifications of the black woman as lascivious.

17. As Carby and Foster have shown, Harper wrote primarily for a black Sunday school audience, but her books were read by both whites and blacks. *Iola Leroy* was popular enough in Harper's lifetime to be reprinted four times in four years. For more on the novel's literary history, see Foster's compendium of Harper's written and spoken prose, *A Brighter Coming Day*. See also Foster's introduction to the three Harper novels she rediscovered, *Minnie's Sacrifice, Sowing and Reaping,* and *Trial and Triumph*.

18. The novel's emphasis on justice is stressed intratextually, when Doctor Latimer asks his fiancé to "write, out of the fullness of your heart, a book to in-

spire men and women with a deeper sense of *justice* and humanity" (262, emphasis added). One place where the novel "signifies" on the dual meanings of "fairness" occurs near the end of the book, when Aunt Linda, reunited with Iola, confides in her that "I seed in a vision dat somebody fair war comin' to help us." When Iola replies, "I am not very fair," Aunt Linda retorts, "Well, chile, you's fair to me" (275); it is hinted here that fairness (of skin color) is a relative rather than a fixed quality and that being "fair" might have more to do with Iola's treatment of Aunt Linda than her appearance.

19. Indeed, the novel is overpopulated with doctors: in addition to Latimer and Gresham (Iola's white admirer), the narrative also introduces us to Dr. Latrobe, a racist Southern doctor who thinks that people like himself "belong to the highest race on earth and the Negro to the lowest" (227). Latrobe and Latimer debate the principle of hybrid degeneracy, with Latimer arguing against the view that miscegenation represents "a death blow to American [read Anglo-] civilization" by arguing that it has been going on for decades with no sign of Anglo- imperilment to date.

20. See Chapter 2 for a similar discussion of Alcott's potential problems with realist modes. Harper's counteraesthetics is, in part, a reflection of her Christian ethos, which stressed good works as much as faith. For example, in an early essay Harper maintains that literature may bring "her elegance, with the toils of the pen, and the labors of the pencil—but they are also idle tales compared to the truths of Christianity" ("Christianity" 98). Employing literature as the vehicle through which to convey these truths constituted, for Harper, the value of both the work and its author. It's worth noting that her Christian aesthetics had a profoundly political base and import; true believers, she was convinced, would unblinkingly uphold the "Golden Rule" and in so doing cease to participate in all forms of oppression. As Harper wrote Francis Grimké around 1903, the recent, horrific spate of lynching might be explained by "a lack of Christly consecration to the attainment of life's highest excellence and beauty" (qtd. in Foster 323).

21. See Bone 21, Tate, *Domestic Allegories* 109–10, and Warren 3–9, for helpful discussions of the problems realism posed for nineteenth-century black writers.

22. See Chapter 2 for a discussion of the role of the spiritual and physical within sentimentalism.

23. See Still's introduction to the first edition, which begins with a confession of his "doubts" as to the wisdom of Harper's subject matter (1–3).

24. Sundquist explores how the tropes of race, riot, and theft function in *Marrow* to collapse spaces that are elsewhere also being violently reinscribed. See his chapter on Chesnutt in *To Wake the Nations*.

25. In *Domestic Allegories of Political Desire*, Tate has argued that *Marrow* may

represent racial protest, but it does so in terms of "racialized patriarchal desire" (67), distinguishing it from the black female texts that interrogate patriarchal assumptions in the process of constructing their versions of domestic idealism.

26. Recognizing the centrality of amorphousness to Chesnutt's understanding of literary production even helps us to explicate his potentially contradictory understanding of the literary artifact. For it remains unclear whether Chesnutt considered aesthetics or salability the ultimate measure of "betterness." From early on, Chesnutt was very interested in the fact that "literature pays—the successful" and held great hopes "that he will be the successful one" (qtd. in Heermance 111). See also Chesnutt's letter to George H. Mifflin, July 25, 1901, quoted in Andrews, where moments after assessing *Marrow*'s superiority Chesnutt goes on to assure his publisher that "a good sale can be reasonably expected" (176). What Chesnutt desired was to produce literary works that would reap all the benefits associated with two increasingly irreconcilable ways of framing art: as "sacral" and as "commodity" (See Lawrence Levine's discussion of the "sacralization" of art in *Highbrow/Lowbrow* [85–168]). Chesnutt was able to reconcile these seemingly conflicting frameworks by envisioning greatness in terms of rather than in opposition to popularity; one could say that for Chesnutt the utopian element inherent in commodity culture was the ability to sell, sell as many copies as possible, a novel that promoted culturally radical yet to his mind "natural," inevitable, evolutionary progress. For more on Chesnutt's literary and monetary ambitions, see Heermance 36–43, 52–54, and 111–21. See also Andrews, *The Literary Career of Charles W. Chesnutt*, as well as Brodhead's chapter on Chesnutt in *Cultures of Letters*.

27. While Chesnutt early on entertained the idea of passing, and even represented those who pass sympathetically in works like *The House Behind the Cedars*, he was to become an outspoken critic of both passing and the culturally determined preference for lighter-skinned brides, a critique made explicit in his story "Wife of His Youth" and implicit in his own marriage to a darker-skinned woman.

28. I refer, of course, to W. E. B. Du Bois's famous conception of "double consciousness," elaborated in *The Souls of Black Folk*. Henderson, drawing on Gaedemer and Bakhtin, has outlined a dialogic model for black women's writing that seems to me to be applicable to minority writing in general and Chesnutt's in particular. Therein, a work is seen to enter into dialogue not only with some general "Other" but "those aspects of self shared with others" (19). It is in this sense that Chesnutt's narrative voice is dialogized, or to use a term more familiar to Chesnutt, miscegenated.

29. In his formal analysis of Zora Neale Hurston's *Their Eyes Were Watching God*, Gates contends that "it was Hurston who introduced free indirect discourse into Afro-American narration" (147). Certainly, in so concluding, he overlooks *Marrow*.

Notes to Pages 177–82

30. As Hedin suggests, other examples include the narrator of Ralph Ellison's *Invisible Man*, or, even earlier, James Weldon Johnson's *Autobiography of an Ex-Colored Man*.

31. See, for a discussion of "aesthetic distance" or contemplation, Jauss 14 and 31.

32. In 1888, Tourgée claimed that "the richest mine of romantic material" in America was embedded "in the life of the Negro" (qtd. in Warren 4–5). Chesnutt was wont to share with Tourgée a belief that "there is a romantic side to the history of this people" (*Journals* 125).

33. See Warren's introduction (esp. 4–6) for an overview of the debate concerning whether realism or romanticism was the genre best suited for depicting African American life. In fact, Chesnutt envisioned himself in 1880 as providing the realistic underpinning to the romances of Negro life constructed by white writers like Tourgée or Stowe:

> And if Judge Tourgee [sic], with his necessarily limited intercourse with colored people, and with his limited stay in the South, can write such interesting descriptions, such vivid pictures of Southern life and character as to make himself rich and famous, why could not a colored man, who has lived among colored people all his life; who is familiar with their habits, their ruling passions, their prejudices; their whole moral and social condition. . . . why could not a colored man who knew all this, and who, besides, had possessed such opportunities for observation and conversation with the better class of white men in the south as to understand their modes of thinking. . . . why could not such a man, if he possessed the same ability, write a far better book about the South than Judge Tourgee or Mrs. Stowe has written? Answer who can! (*Journals* 125)

34. Carby notes that Harper is responding in *Iola Leroy* to the white supremacist positions of Atlanta *Constitution* editor, Henry Grady; Knadler notes the same thing about Chesnutt. Clearly, both Harper and Chesnutt shared similar interlocutors.

35. Ironically, given the novel's relatively meager sales, Chesnutt and his publishers envisioned *Marrow* as the "next *Uncle Tom's Cabin*," an analogy several of the reviews of the novel mentioned as well.

36. In a recent article (1996), Gillman explores the ramifications of the process of transculturation inscribed in *Of One Blood*. She warns against reductive readings of the novel's reclamation of Africa "either as 'authentic' self-expression or 'inauthentic' assimilation" (64), as these vastly oversimplify Hopkins's complex and nuanced project.

37. Kassanoff also discusses the significance of blood in *Of One Blood*, focusing in particular on four ways the term might resonate; it can justify amalga-

mation and intermarriage; it can justify black nationalism and a pride in black lineage; it creates kinship bonds that raise the threat of incest; and it can highlight black women's role as the "reproductive source of future African American bloodlines" (165). See also Gillman's "Pauline Hopkins and the Occult," which explores Hopkins's transformation of blood "from a biologized term, the staple of nineteenth-century scientific racism, into a multivalent figure of speech capable of generating new meanings" (76).

38. The reference here is to Jameson's definition of history as "what hurts." See *The Political Unconscious* (102).

39. As Ammons has argued, Hopkins does not "use the supernatural as symbol" but rather "asserts the supernatural as reality" (84).

40. The subtitle of Hopkins's novel, "The Hidden Self," has garnered a great deal of recent critical attention. Otten, Schrager, and Sundquist (pp. 569–73) each provide insightful examinations of Hopkins's use of the term, tracing it to William James's 1890 essay. This origin enables a reading of *Of One Blood*'s project as an attempt to elaborate a "surface-depth model" (Schrager 198), a model that, as Otten puts it, reveals "the extent to which the self that lies below the surface is construed neither as wholly abstract nor as racially neutral" (231). These exhaustive analyses enable me to abridge my own discussion of how the idea of "the hidden self" functions in Hopkins's narrative and to concentrate instead on the titular noun, "blood," and on matters of genre. See as well Carby and both Hopkins-related articles by Gillman; both critics also touch, albeit more briefly, on James's and Du Bois's influence on Hopkins.

41. As Kassanoff contends, critics have all too often effaced the body and drained the blood from their analyses of African-American texts; Kassanoff, by contrast, starts from the premise that the body "cannot be easily eliminated from the discourse of race" (164). She goes on to argue that, in Hopkins's novel, "the interconnected corporeal issues of blood and gender ... effectively deconstruct the monolith of the New Negro by questioning its contours and limitations" (160).

42. Carby maintains that in depicting the Chaldeans as the incarnation of beauty, Hopkins invokes a classical rather than African standard. For instance, the narrative compares Candace's beauty to Venus's; this comparison takes on further resonance when we consider, as Carby does, that while *Of One Blood* was being serialized, the *Colored American Magazine* ran an article, possibly written by Hopkins herself, providing scientific proof that "Venus and the Apollo [were] Modelled from Ethiopians." See Carby 159ff. My reading of the novel would suggest that this only further substantiates the power of narrative, whether literary or scientific, to define what is beautiful.

43. By contrast, in the American context of *Of One Blood*, storytelling pro-

duces mainly negative repercussions. For instance, like Reuel, Dianthe, too, is unaware of her heritage until told of it by an older, wiser figure—in this case, her own grandmother, "Aunt Hannah." Learning that she is married to one brother and under the passionate spell of another, she is horrified, driven to attempt murder, and when that fails, to commit suicide.

44. Much of my knowledge of magical realism comes from study of "third world" literature over the course of several years. An essay that has been quite influential to my thinking is Jameson's "On Magic Realism in Film." For an excellent recent anthology devoted solely to the genre, see Zamora and Faris.

45. Gillman, for instance, considers *Of One Blood* an example of what she calls the "American race melodrama." For Gillman, "literary, sociological, and scientific texts" that fit within this rubric attempt dramatically and didactically to negotiate "the social tensions surrounding the formation of racial, national, and sexual identity in the post-Reconstruction years" (222). Tate emphasizes both melodramatic and gothic aspects of the story, while Schrager reads the American half of *Of One Blood* as gothic, the African half as utopian (205 n21).

# Works Cited

Abrams, M. H. *A Glossary of Literary Terms*. 3rd ed. New York: Holt, Rinehart and Winston, 1971.
"Aesthetic." *The Oxford English Dictionary*. New York: Oxford University Press, 1989.
"Aesthetic." *The Random House Dictionary of the English Language*. 2nd ed. Unabridged. 1987.
Åhnebrink, Lars. *The Beginning of Naturalism in American Fiction*. 1950. Excerpted in *McTeague* by Frank Norris. Ed. Donald Pizer. New York: Norton, 1977.
Alcott, Louisa May. *Hospital Sketches*. 1863. *Civil War Nursing: Hospital Sketches; Memoir of Emily Elizabeth Parsons*. The History of American Nursing. Gen. ed. Susan Reverby. New York: Garland, 1984.
———. *Little Women*. 1868–69. New York: Modern Library, 1983.
———. *Work: A Story of Experience*. 1873. New York: Penguin, 1994.
Alcott, William A. *Letters to a Sister; or, Woman's Mission*. Buffalo: Geo. H. Derby, 1850.
Allen, Polly Wynn. *Building Domestic Liberty: Charlotte Perkins Gilman's Architectural Feminism*. Amherst: University of Massachusetts Press, 1988.
Ammons, Elizabeth. *Conflicting Stories: American Women Writers at the Turn into the Twentieth Century*. New York: Oxford University Press, 1991.
Andrews, William L. *The Literary Career of Charles W. Chesnutt*. Baton Rouge: Louisiana State University Press, 1980.
Appiah, Anthony. "The Uncompleted Argument: Du Bois and the Illusion of Race." *"Race," Writing, and Difference*. Ed. Henry Louis Gates, Jr. Chicago: University of Chicago Press, 1986. 21–37.
Armstrong, Nancy. *Desire and Domestic Fiction: A Political History of the Novel*. New York: Oxford University Press, 1987.
Arney, William Ray. *Power and the Profession of Obstetrics*. Chicago: University of Chicago Press, 1982.
Baker, Houston A., Jr. "In Dubious Battle." *New Literary History* 18 (1987): 363–69.

---. *Workings of the Spirit: The Poetics of Afro-American Women's Writing.* Chicago: University of Chicago Press, 1991.

Bakhtin, M. M. *The Dialogic Imagination: Four Essays.* Ed. Michael Holquist. Trans. Caryl Emerson and Michael Holquist. Austin: University of Texas Press, 1981.

Bardes, Barbara, and Suzanne Gossett. *Declarations of Independence: Women and Political Power in Nineteenth Century American Fiction.* New Brunswick: Rutgers University Press, 1990.

Barthes, Roland. "Changing the Object Itself: Mythology Today." *Image— Music—Text.* Trans. Stephen Heath. New York: Hill and Wang, 1977.

Bartkowski, Frances. *Feminist Utopias.* Lincoln: University of Nebraska Press, 1989.

Baym, Nina. Introduction. *Woman's Fiction: A Guide to Novels By and About Women in America, 1820–1870.* 2nd ed. Urbana: University of Illinois Press, 1993.

---. *Novels, Readers, and Reviewers: Responses to Fiction in Antebellum America.* Ithaca: Cornell University Press, 1984.

---. *Woman's Fiction: A Guide to Novels By and About Women in America, 1820–1870.* Ithaca: Cornell University Press, 1978.

Bell, Bernard W. *The Afro-American Novel and Its Tradition.* Amherst: University of Massachusetts Press, 1987.

Bell, Michael Davit. *American Realism: Studies in the Cultural History of a Literary Idea.* Chicago: University of Chicago Press, 1993.

---. *The Development of American Romance: The Sacrifice of Relation.* Chicago: University of Chicago Press, 1980.

Berger, John. *Ways of Seeing.* New York: Penguin, 1977.

Berman, Jeffrey. "The Unrestful Cure: Charlotte Perkins Gilman and 'The Yellow Wallpaper.'" Golden 211–41.

Bersani, Leo. *A Future for Astyanax: Character and Desire in Literature.* New York: Columbia University Press, 1984.

Berzon, Judith R. *Neither White Nor Black: The Mulatto Character in American Fiction.* New York: New York University Press, 1978.

Black, Alexander. "The Woman Who Saw It First." *Century Magazine* 85 (Nov. 1923): 39.

Blackwell, Elizabeth. "To Emily Blackwell." 16 Apr. 1848. Ms. letter. Blackwell Family Papers. Schlesinger Library, Radcliffe College.

---. *The Laws of Life with Special Reference to the Physical Education of Girls.* 1852. New Haven: Research Publications, 1975.

B[lackwell], H[enry] B. Review of "The Yellow Wallpaper." *Woman's Journal* (17 June 1899): 187.

Bledstein, Burton J. *The Culture of Professionalism*. New York: Norton, 1976.
Bone, Robert. *The Negro Novel in America*. Rev. ed. New Haven: Yale University Press, 1965.
Boone, Joseph Allen. *Tradition Counter Tradition: Love and the Form of Fiction*. Chicago: University of Chicago Press, 1987.
Booth, Alison, ed. *Famous Last Words: Changes in Gender and Narrative Closure*. Charlottesville: University of Virginia Press, 1993.
Breuer, Josef, and Sigmund Freud. *Studies in Hysteria*. 1895. Trans. A. A. Brill. Boston: Beacon, 1961.
Briggs, Charles F. Review of *Woman in the Nineteenth Century*. *Broadway Journal* 1 (1, 8, 22 Mar. 1845). *Critical Essays on Margaret Fuller*. Ed. Joel Myerson. Boston: G. K. Hall, 1980. 8–15.
Brodhead, Richard H. *Cultures of Letters: Scenes of Reading and Writing in Nineteenth-Century America*. Chicago: University of Chicago Press, 1993.
Brooks, Peter. *The Melodramatic Imagination: Balzac, Henry James, Melodrama, and the Mode of Excess*. New Haven: Yale University Press, 1976.
———. *Reading for the Plot: Design and Intention in Narrative*. New York: Vintage, 1985.
Brooks, Van Wyck. *Howells: His Life and World*. New York: Dutton, 1959.
Brown, Gillian. *Domestic Individualism: Imagining Self in Nineteenth-Century America*. Berkeley: University of California Press, 1990.
Brown, H. Ross. *The Sentimental Novel in America, 1789–1860*. New York: Pageant, 1959.
Brownson, Orestes A. "Miss Fuller and Reformers." *Brownson's Quarterly Review* 7 (Apr. 1845). *Critical Essays on Margaret Fuller*. Ed. Joel Myerson. Boston: G. K. Hall, 1980. 19–25.
Bruce, Robert V. *The Launching of Modern American Science, 1846–76*. New York: Alfred A. Knopf, 1987.
Burbick, Joan. *Healing the Republic: The Language of Health and the Culture of Nationalism in Nineteenth-Century America*. New York: Cambridge University Press, 1994.
Burke, Kenneth. *The Philosophy of Literary Form: Studies in Symbolic Action*. Rev. ed. New York: Vintage, 1957.
Burr, Anna Robeson. *Weir Mitchell: His Life and Letters*. New York: Duffield, 1929.
Butler, Judith. *Bodies That Matter: On the Discursive Limits of "Sex."* New York: Routledge, 1993.
———. *Gender Trouble: Feminism and the Subversion of Identity*. New York: Routledge, 1990.
Cady, Edwin H. *The Road to Realism: The Early Years 1837–1885 of William Dean Howells*. Syracuse: Syracuse University Press, 1956.

———. *The Realist at War: The Mature Years 1885–1920 of William Dean Howells.* Syracuse: Syracuse University Press, 1958.

Cady, Edwin H., and Norma W. Cady. *Critical Essays on W. D. Howells, 1866–1920.* Boston: G. K. Hall, 1983.

Cady, Edwin H., and David L. Frazier, eds. *The War of the Critics over William Dean Howells.* Evanston: Row, Peterson, 1962.

Cappello, Mary. "'Looking About Me With All My Eyes': Censored Viewing, Carnival, and Louisa May Alcott's *Hospital Sketches.*" *Arizona Quarterly* 50 (Autumn 1994): 59–88.

Capper, Charles. *Margaret Fuller: An American Romantic Life: The Private Years.* New York: Oxford University Press, 1992.

Carby, Hazel V. Introduction. *Iola Leroy; Or, Shadows Uplifted.* By Frances E. W. Harper. 1892. Boston: Beacon, 1987.

———. *Reconstructing Womanhood: The Emergence of the Afro-American Woman Novelist.* New York: Oxford University Press, 1987.

Cheney, Ednah D. *Louisa May Alcott: Her Life, Letters, and Journals.* Boston: Roberts Brothers, 1892.

Chesnutt, Charles W. "The Future American: What the Race Is Likely to Become in the Process of Time." Boston *Evening Transcript* (18 Aug. 1900): 20.

———. "The Future American: A Stream of Dark Blood in the Veins of Southern Whites." Boston *Evening Transcript* (25 Aug. 1900): 15.

———. "The Future American: A Complete Race-Amalgamation Likely to Occur." Boston *Evening Transcript* (1 Sept. 1900): 24.

———. *The Journals of Charles W. Chesnutt.* Ed. Richard H. Brodhead. Durham: Duke University Press, 1993.

———. *Marrow of Tradition.* 1901. Ann Arbor: University of Michigan Press, 1992.

———. "Race Prejudice: Its Causes and Its Cure." *Alexander's Magazine* (July 1905): 25.

Chesnutt, Helen M. *Charles Waddell Chesnutt: Pioneer of the Color Line.* Chapel Hill: University of North Carolina Press, 1952.

Chevigny, Bell Gale. *The Woman and the Myth: Margaret Fuller's Life and Writings.* New York: Feminist, 1976.

Chopin, Kate. *The Awakening.* 1899. New York: Bantam, 1981.

Christian, Barbara. "The Race for Theory." *Cultural Critique* 6 (1987): 51–63.

———. "Shadows Uplifted." *Feminist Criticism and Social Change.* Ed. Judith Newton and Deborah Rosenfelt. New York: Methuen, 1985. 181–215.

Clarke, Edward H. *Sex in Education; or, A Fair Chance for Girls.* 1873. Boston: Houghton, Mifflin, 1892.

———. *Visions: A Study of False Sight (Pseudopia)*. Boston: Houghton, Osgood, 1878.

Cogan, Frances B. *All-American Girl: The Ideal of Real Womanhood in Mid-Nineteenth-Century America*. Athens: University of Georgia Press, 1989.

Conway, Jill. From "Stereotypes of Femininity in a Theory of Evolution." Golden 71–82.

Cott, Nancy F., ed. *Roots of Bitterness: Documents of the Social History of American Women*. New York: Dutton, 1972.

Coultrap-McQuin, Susan. *Doing Literary Business: American Women Writers in the Nineteenth Century*. Chapel Hill: University of North Carolina Press, 1990.

Cowley, Malcolm. *The Portable Hawthorne*. Rev. ed. New York: Viking, 1969.

Cranny-Francis, Anne. *Feminist Fiction: Feminist Uses of Generic Fiction*. New York: St. Martin's, 1990.

Culler, Jonathan. *The Pursuit of Signs: Semiotics, Literature, Deconstruction*. Ithaca: Cornell University Press, 1981.

Cummins, Maria Susan. *The Lamplighter*. Ed. Nina Baym. New Brunswick: Rutgers University Press, 1988.

Dalke, Anne. "Economics, or the Bosom Serpent: Oliver Wendell Holme's [sic] *Elsie Venner: A Romance of Destiny*." *American Transcendental Quarterly* 2 (Mar. 1988): 57–67.

Darwin, Charles. *The Descent of Man and Selection in Relation to Sex*. Chicago: Encyclopædia Britannica, Inc., 1988.

———. *The Origin of Species by Means of Natural Selection*. 1859. New York: Random House, 1936.

Davidson, Cathy N. *Revolution and the Word: The Rise of the Novel in America*. New York: Oxford University Press, 1986.

Davis, Cynthia J. "Margaret Fuller, Body and Soul." *American Literature* 71 (Mar. 1999): 31–56.

———. "Speaking the Body's Pain: Harriet Wilson's Our Nig." *African American Review* (Fall 1993): 391–404.

Degler, Carl N. *At Odds: Women and the Family in America from the Revolution to the Present*. New York: Oxford University Press, 1980.

———. "What Ought to Be and What Was: Women's Sexuality in the Nineteenth Century." Leavitt 40–56.

Diamond, Irene, and Lee Quinby, eds. *Feminism and Foucault: Reflections on Resistance*. Boston: Northeastern University Press, 1988.

Dickinson, Emily. *Final Harvest*. Sel. and Intro. Thomas H. Johnson. Boston: Little, 1961.

Dimock, Wai Chee. "The Economy of Pain: Capitalism, Humanitarianism, and the Realistic Novel." *New Essays on the Rise of Silas Lapham*. Ed. Donald E. Pease. Cambridge: Cambridge University Press, 1991. 67–90.

—————. "Feminism, New Historicism, and the Reader." *Readers in History: Nineteenth-Century American Literature and the Contexts of Response*. Ed. James L. Machor. Baltimore: Johns Hopkins University Press, 1993.

Dixon, Edward Henry. *Woman and Her Diseases, from the Cradle to the Grave*. 1857. New Haven: Research Publications, 1975.

Doane, F. Harrison. *The Young Married Lady's Private Medical Guide*. Trans. P. C. Doane. 1854. New Haven: Research Publications, 1975.

Dobson, Joanne. "Reclaiming Sentimental Literature." *American Literature* 69 (June 1997): 263–88.

Dock, Julia Bates. "'But One Expects That': Charlotte Perkins Gilman's 'The Yellow Wallpaper' and the Shifting Light of Scholarship." *PMLA* 111 (1996): 52–65.

Donaldson, Laura E. "The Eve of De-struction: Charlotte Perkins Gilman and the Feminist Re-Creation of Paradise." *Women's Studies* 16 (1989): 373–87.

Donawerth, Jane L., and Carol A. Kolmerten, eds. *Utopian and Science Fiction by Women*. Syracuse: Syracuse University Press, 1994.

Douglas, Ann. *The Feminization of American Culture*. New York: Knopf, 1978.

—————. "'The Fashionable Diseases': Women's Complaints and Their Treatment in Nineteenth-Century America." *Journal of Interdisciplinary History* 4 (1973): 25–52.

Douglas, Mary. *Purity and Danger: An Analysis of Concepts of Pollution and Taboo*. 1966. Middlesex, England: Penguin, 1970.

Dreiser, Theodore. *Sister Carrie*. 1900. 2nd ed. Ed. Donald Pizer. New York: Norton, 1991.

Du Bois, W. E. Burghardt. "Criteria of Negro Art." *The Oxford W. E. B. Du Bois Reader*. Ed. Eric J. Sundquist. New York: Oxford University Press, 1996. 324–28.

—————. "Negro Art and Literature." *The Oxford W. E. B. Du Bois Reader*. Ed. Eric J. Sundquist. New York: Oxford University Press, 1996. 311–24.

—————. *The Souls of Black Folk: Essays and Sketches*. 1903. Greenwich, Conn.: Fawcett, 1961.

duCille, Ann. *The Coupling Convention: Sex, Text, and Tradition in Black Women's Fiction*. New York: Oxford University Press, 1993.

Duffy, John. *The Healers: A History of American Medicine*. Urbana: University of Illinois Press, 1979.

DuPlessis, Rachel Blau. *Writing Beyond the Ending: Narrative Strategies of Twentieth-Century Women Writers*. Bloomington: Indiana University Press, 1985.

Eagleton, Terry. *The Ideology of the Aesthetic*. London: Basil Blackwell, 1990.

———. *Criticism and Ideology: A Study in Marxist Literary Theory*. London: NLB, 1976.

Earnest, Ernest. *S. Weir Mitchell: Novelist and Physician*. Philadelphia: University of Pennsylvania Press, 1950.

Ehrenreich, Barbara, and Deirdre English. *For Her Own Good: 150 Years of the Experts' Advice to Women*. New York: Anchor-Doubleday, 1989.

Elbert, Sarah. *A Hunger for Home: Louisa May Alcott's Place in American Culture*. New Brunswick: Rutgers University Press, 1977.

Ellis, Havelock. *Studies in the Psychology of Sex: Sexual Selection in Man*. Vol. 4. 1905. Philadelphia: F. A. Davis, 1925.

Ellis, Kate Ferguson. *The Contested Castle: Gothic Novels and the Subversion of Domestic Ideology*. Urbana: University of Illinois Press, 1989.

Ellison, Curtis W. and E. W. Metcalf, Jr. *Charles W. Chesnutt: A Reference Guide*. Boston: G. K. Hall, 1977.

Emerson, Ralph Waldo. "Nature." *The Works of Ralph Waldo Emerson in One Volume: Essays, Poems, and Biographical Sketches*. New York: Walter J. Black, n.d. 1–55.

———. "Self Reliance." *Selections from Ralph Waldo Emerson*. Ed. Stephen E. Whicher. Boston: Houghton, 1960.

Emerson, Ralph Waldo, W. H. Channing, and J. F. Clarke, eds. *Memoirs of Margaret Fuller Ossoli*. 2 vols. 1884. New York: Burt Franklin, 1972.

Farnsworth, Robert M. Introduction. *The Marrow of Tradition*. Ann Arbor: University of Michigan Press, 1995.

Feldstein, Richard. "Reader, Text, and Ambiguous Referentiality in 'The Yellow Wallpaper.'" Golden 307–17.

Felski, Rita. *Beyond Feminist Aesthetics: Feminist Literature and Social Change*. Cambridge: Harvard University Press, 1989.

Fetterley, Judith. "Reading about Reading: 'A Jury of Her Peers,' 'The Murders in the Rue Morgue,' and 'The Yellow Wallpaper.'" Golden 253–60.

———. "*Little Women*: Alcott's Civil War." *Feminist Studies* 5 (1979): 369–83.

Fiedler, Leslie. *Love and Death in the American Novel*. Rev. ed. New York: Stein and Day, 1966.

Fishbein, Morris. *A History of the American Medical Association 1847 to 1947*. New York: Kraus, 1969.

Fisher, Philip. *Hard Facts: Setting and Form in the American Novel*. New York: Oxford University Press, 1987.

Foster, Frances Smith, ed. *A Brighter Coming Day: A Frances Ellen Watkins Harper Reader*. New York: Feminist, 1990.

———, ed. *Minnie's Sacrifice, Sowing and Reaping, Trial and Triumph: Three Rediscovered Novels by Frances E. W. Harper*. Boston: Beacon, 1994.

Foucault, Michel. *The Birth of A Clinic: An Archaeology of Medical Perception.* Trans. A. M. Sheridan Smith. New York: Vintage, 1975.

———. *Discipline and Punishment: The Birth of the Prison.* Trans. Alan Sheridan. New York: Vintage, 1977.

———. "Docile Bodies." *The Foucault Reader.* Ed. Paul Rabinow. New York: Pantheon, 1984. 179–87.

———. "The Eye of Power." *Power/Knowledge: Selected Interviews and Other Writings, 1972–77.* Ed. Colin Gordon. New York: Pantheon, 1980.

———. *The History of Sexuality, Volume I: An Introduction.* Trans. Robert Hurley. New York: Pantheon, 1978.

Fredrickson, George M. *The Black Image in the White Mind: The Debate on Afro-American Character and Destiny, 1817–1914.* New York: Harper & Row, 1971.

Freud, Sigmund. "The 'Uncanny.'" *From the History of an Infantile Neurosis. The Standard Edition of the Complete Psychological Works of Sigmund Freud.* 24 vols. Trans. James Strachey in collaboration with Anna Freud, assisted by Alix Strachey and Alan Tyson. Vol. 17. Hogarth: London, 1953–74. Vol. 17. 217–56.

Frye, Northrup. *Anatomy of Criticism: Four Essays.* Princeton: Princeton University Press, 1957.

———. "Varieties of Literary Utopias." *Utopias and Utopian Thought.* Ed. Frank E. Manuel. Boston: Houghton Mifflin, 1966.

Fuller, S. Margaret. *Woman in the Nineteenth Century.* New York: Greeley & McElrath, 1845.

———. *Woman in the Nineteenth Century and Kindred Papers Relating to the Sphere, Condition and Duties of Woman.* Ed. Arthur B. Fuller. 1874. New York: Greenwood, 1968.

Fuss, Diana. *Essentially Speaking: Feminism, Nature, & Difference.* New York: Routledge, 1989.

Gates, Henry Louis, Jr., ed. Introduction. *Reading Black, Reading Feminist: A Critical Anthology.* New York: Meridian, 1990.

———. "'What's Love Got to Do With It?': Critical Theory, Integrity, and the Black Idiom." *New Literary History* 18 (1987): 345–62.

———. "Zora Neale Hurston and the Speakerly Text." *Southern Literature and Literary Theory.* Ed. Jefferson Humphries. Athens: University of Georgia Press, 1990.

Gayle, Addison, Jr., ed. *The Black Aesthetic.* New York: Doubleday, 1972.

Gilbert, Sandra, and Susan Gubar. *The Madwoman in the Attic: The Woman Writer and the Nineteenth-Century Literary Imagination.* New Haven: Yale University Press, 1979.

Gillman, Susan. "The Mulatto, Tragic or Triumphant? The Nineteenth-Century

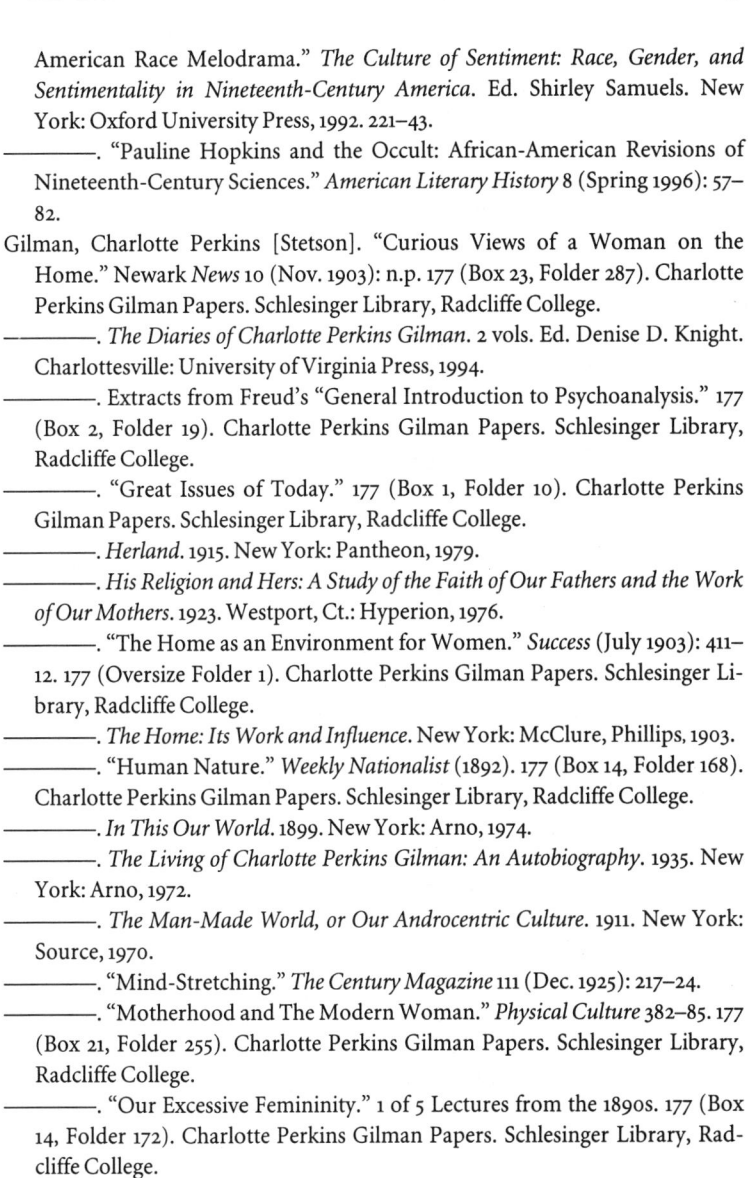

American Race Melodrama." *The Culture of Sentiment: Race, Gender, and Sentimentality in Nineteenth-Century America.* Ed. Shirley Samuels. New York: Oxford University Press, 1992. 221–43.

———. "Pauline Hopkins and the Occult: African-American Revisions of Nineteenth-Century Sciences." *American Literary History* 8 (Spring 1996): 57–82.

Gilman, Charlotte Perkins [Stetson]. "Curious Views of a Woman on the Home." Newark *News* 10 (Nov. 1903): n.p. 177 (Box 23, Folder 287). Charlotte Perkins Gilman Papers. Schlesinger Library, Radcliffe College.

———. *The Diaries of Charlotte Perkins Gilman.* 2 vols. Ed. Denise D. Knight. Charlottesville: University of Virginia Press, 1994.

———. Extracts from Freud's "General Introduction to Psychoanalysis." 177 (Box 2, Folder 19). Charlotte Perkins Gilman Papers. Schlesinger Library, Radcliffe College.

———. "Great Issues of Today." 177 (Box 1, Folder 10). Charlotte Perkins Gilman Papers. Schlesinger Library, Radcliffe College.

———. *Herland.* 1915. New York: Pantheon, 1979.

———. *His Religion and Hers: A Study of the Faith of Our Fathers and the Work of Our Mothers.* 1923. Westport, Ct.: Hyperion, 1976.

———. "The Home as an Environment for Women." *Success* (July 1903): 411–12. 177 (Oversize Folder 1). Charlotte Perkins Gilman Papers. Schlesinger Library, Radcliffe College.

———. *The Home: Its Work and Influence.* New York: McClure, Phillips, 1903.

———. "Human Nature." *Weekly Nationalist* (1892). 177 (Box 14, Folder 168). Charlotte Perkins Gilman Papers. Schlesinger Library, Radcliffe College.

———. *In This Our World.* 1899. New York: Arno, 1974.

———. *The Living of Charlotte Perkins Gilman: An Autobiography.* 1935. New York: Arno, 1972.

———. *The Man-Made World, or Our Androcentric Culture.* 1911. New York: Source, 1970.

———. "Mind-Stretching." *The Century Magazine* 111 (Dec. 1925): 217–24.

———. "Motherhood and The Modern Woman." *Physical Culture* 382–85. 177 (Box 21, Folder 255). Charlotte Perkins Gilman Papers. Schlesinger Library, Radcliffe College.

———. "Our Excessive Femininity." 1 of 5 Lectures from the 1890s. 177 (Box 14, Folder 172). Charlotte Perkins Gilman Papers. Schlesinger Library, Radcliffe College.

———. "A Summary of Purpose." *Forerunner.* Fragment. 177 (Box 18, 240). Charlotte Perkins Gilman Papers. Schlesinger Library, Radcliffe College.

———. "This 'Life Force.'" 177 (Box 15, Folder 181). Charlotte Perkins Gilman Papers. Schlesinger Library, Radcliffe College.

———. "To George Houghton Gilman." 22 June 1897. 177 (Box 3, Folder 42). Charlotte Perkins Gilman Papers. Schlesinger Library, Radcliffe College.

———. "To George Houghton Gilman." 15 Oct. 1897. 177 (Box 3, Folder 42). Charlotte Perkins Gilman Papers. Schlesinger Library, Radcliffe College.

———. "To George Houghton Gilman." 29 July 1898. 177 (Box 3, Folder 42). Charlotte Perkins Gilman Papers. Schlesinger Library, Radcliffe College.

———. "To George Houghton Gilman." 1 Sept. 1898. 177 (Box 3, Folder 42). Charlotte Perkins Gilman Papers. Schlesinger Library, Radcliffe College.

———. *Unpunished*. Ed. Catherine J. Golden and Denise D. Knight. New York: Feminist, 1997.

———. "Whatever Else We Lose, We Must Keep the Home." *The Woman Citizen* 13 (19 June 1920): 72–74. 177 (Oversize Folder 1). Charlotte Perkins Gilman Papers. Schlesinger Library, Radcliffe College.

———. "What the 'Threat of Man' Really Means." ca. 1913. 177 (Oversize Folder 1). Charlotte Perkins Gilman Papers. Schlesinger Library, Radcliffe College.

———. "Why I Wrote 'The Yellow Wallpaper.'" 1913. *The Charlotte Perkins Gilman Reader*. Ed. Ann J. Lane. New York: Pantheon, 1980. 19–20.

———. *With Her in Ourland: A Sequel to Herland*. Westport, Conn.: Greenwood Press, 1997.

———. *Women and Economics: A Study of the Economic Relation Between Men and Women as a Factor in Social Evolution*. 1898. Ed. Carl N. Degler. New York: Harper Torchbook, 1966.

———. "The Yellow Wallpaper." 1892. *The Charlotte Perkins Gilman Reader*. Ed. Ann J. Lane. New York: Pantheon, 1980. 3–19.

Gilman, Sander L., Helen King, Roy Porter, G. S. Rousseau, and Elaine Showalter. *Hysteria Beyond Freud*. Berkeley: University of California Press, 1993.

Golden, Catherine, ed. *The Captive Imagination: A Casebook on "The Yellow Wallpaper."* New York: Feminist, 1992.

———. "'Overwriting' the Rest Cure: Charlotte Perkins Gilman's Literary Escape from S. Weir Mitchell's Fictionalization of Women." Karpinski 144–58.

Golden, Catherine, and Elaine Hedges. Letter. *PMLA* 3 (1996): 467–68.

Gossett, Thomas F. *Race: The History of an Idea in America*. Dallas: Southern Methodist University Press, 1963.

Gough, Val. "Lesbians and Virgins: The New Motherhood in *Herland*." *Anticipations: Essays on Early Science Fiction and its Precursors*. Ed. David Seed. Syracuse: Syracuse University Press, 1995.

Gould, Stephen Jay. *Ever Since Darwin: Reflections in Natural History*. New York: W. W. Norton & Co., 1977.
Greenblatt, Stephen. *Renaissance Self-Fashioning: From More to Shakespeare*. Chicago: University of Chicago Press, 1980.
Gruesser, John Cullen, ed. *The Unruly Voice: Rediscovering Pauline Elizabeth Hopkins*. Intr. Nellie Y. McKay. Urbana: University of Illinois Press, 1996.
Gubar, Susan. "She in Herland: Feminism as Fantasy." *Coordinates: Placing Science Fiction and Fantasy*. Carbondale: Southern Illinois University Press, 1983.
Gustafson, Sandra. "Choosing a Medium: Margaret Fuller and the Forms of Sentiment." *American Quarterly* 47 (1995): 34–65.
Haller, John S., Jr., and Robin M. Haller. *The Physician and Sexuality in Victorian America*. Urbana: University of Illinois Press, 1974.
Hallissey, Margaret. "Poisonous Creature: Holmes's Elsie Venner." *Studies in the Novel* 17 (1985): 406–19.
Haney-Peritz, Janice. "Monumental Feminism and Literature's Ancestral House: Another Look at 'The Yellow Wallpaper.'" Golden 261–76.
Harper, Frances E. W. "Christianity." 1857. Foster, *Brighter* 96–99.
———. "Enlightened Motherhood." 1892. Foster, *Brighter* 285–92.
———. "A Factor in Human Progress." 1885. Foster, *Brighter* 275–80.
———. *Iola Leroy; Or, Shadows Uplifted*. 1892. Boston: Beacon, 1987.
Harpham, Geoffrey Galt. "Aesthetics and the Fundamentals of Modernity." *Aesthetics and Ideology*. Ed. George Levine. New Brunswick: Rutgers University Press, 1994.
Harris, Susan K. *Nineteenth Century American Women's Novels: Interpretive Strategies*. New York: Cambridge University Press, 1990.
———. "Responding to the Text(s): Women Readers and the Quest for Higher Education." *Readers in History: Nineteenth-Century American Literature and the Contexts of Responses*. Ed. James L. Machor. Baltimore: Johns Hopkins University Press, 1993.
Hawthorne, Julian. *Nathaniel Hawthorne and His Wife*. Vol. I. 1884. New York: Archon, 1968.
Hawthorne, Nathaniel. *The Blithedale Romance*. 1852. Ed. Seymour Gross and Rosalie Murphy. New York: Norton, 1978.
———. *Love Letters of Nathaniel Hawthorne, 1839–41*. 1907. Washington, D.C.: NCR/Microcard, 1972.
———. *The Marble Faun*. 1860. New York: Pocket, 1958.
———. *The Scarlet Letter*. 1859. New York: Pocket, 1972.
Hedges, Elaine R. "Afterword to 'The Yellow Wallpaper,' Feminist Press Edition." Golden 123–36.

---. "'Out at Last'? 'The Yellow Wallpaper' after Two Decades of Feminist Criticism." Karpinski 222–33.
Hedin, Raymond. "Probable Readers, Possible Stories: The Limits of Nineteenth-Century Black Narrative." *Readers in History: Nineteenth-Century American Literature and the Contexts of Response.* Ed. James L. Machor. Baltimore: Johns Hopkins University Press, 1993.
Heermance, J. Noel. *Charles W. Chesnutt: America's First Great Black Novelist.* Hamden, Conn.: Archon, 1974.
Henderson, Mae Gwendolyn. "Speaking in Tongues: Dialogics, Dialectics, and the Black Women Writer's Literary Tradition." Wall 16–37.
Hendler, Glenn. "The Limits of Sympathy: Louisa May Alcott and the Sentimental Novel." *American Literary History* 3 (1991): 685–706.
Herndl, Diane Price. *Invalid Women: Figuring Feminine Illness in American Fiction and Culture, 1840–1940.* Chapel Hill: University of North Carolina Press, 1993.
---. "The Writing Cure: Charlotte Perkins Gilman, Anna O., and 'Hysterical' Writing." *NWSA Journal* 1 (1988): 52–74.
Hertz, Neil. *The End of the Line: Essays on Psychoanalysis and the Sublime.* New York: Columbia University Press, 1985.
Higginson, Thomas Wentworth. *Margaret Fuller Ossoli.* Boston: Houghton, 1892.
Hill, Mary A. *The Making of a Radical Feminist, 1860–1896.* Philadelphia: Temple University Press, 1980.
Holmes, Oliver Wendell. "Address on the Opening of the New Building Harvard Medical School." 7 Oct. 1883. bMS Am 1241 (601). Oliver Wendell Holmes Collection. Houghton Library, Harvard University.
---. *The Autocrat of the Breakfast Table.* Boston: Houghton, Mifflin, 1889.
---. *Border Lines of Knowledge in Some Provinces of Medical Science.* Boston: Wm D. Ticknor, 1847. Ts. AC85.18605.Zy 862h. Oliver Wendell Holmes Collection. Houghton Library, Harvard University.
---. *Elsie Venner: A Romance of Destiny.* Boston: Houghton Mifflin, 1891.
---. "Homeopathy and Its Kindred Delusions." *Medical Essays.* Boston: Houghton, Mifflin, 1891.
---. "An Introductory Lecture Delivered at the Mass Medical College, Nov. 5, 1847 By Oliver Wendell Holmes, M.D., Parkman Professor of Anatomy and Physiology." Ms. AC85.H7375.847. Oliver Wendell Holmes Collection. Houghton Library, Harvard University.
---. "Mechanism in Thought and Morals, an Address Delivered Before the Phi Beta Kappa Society of Harvard University, June 29, 1870." Ts. Oliver Wendell Holmes Collection. Houghton Library, Harvard University.

---. *Medical Essays, 1842–1882*. Boston: Houghton, Mifflin, 1891.
---. Notebook incl. clipping. Oliver Wendell Holmes Collection. Houghton Library, Harvard University.
---. "Response to the Toast Given at the Massachusetts Medical Society." *Atlantic Monthly* (July 1867): 3.
---. "To Henry Blackwell." 25 Dec. 1872. Blackwell Family Papers. Schlesinger Library, Radcliffe College. .
Hopkins, Pauline Elizabeth. *Contending Forces: A Romance Illustrative of Negro Life North and South*. 1900. New York: Oxford University Press, 1988.
---. *Of One Blood: The Magazine Novels of Pauline Hopkins*. Intr. Hazel V. Carby. 1902–3. New York: Oxford, 1988. 439–621.
Howe, Julia Ward, ed. *Sex and Education: A Reply to Dr. E. H. Clarke's "Sex in Education."* 1874. New York: Arno, 1972.
Howells, Elinor Mead. *If Not Literature: Letters of Elinor Mead Howells*. Ed. Ginette de B. Merill and George Arms. Columbus: Ohio State University Press, 1988.
Howells, Mildred. *The Life in Letters of William Dean Howells*. Vol 1. Garden City, New York: Doubleday, Doran, 1928.
Howells, William Dean. *Criticism and Fiction*. New York: Harper, 1891.
---. *Doctor Breen's Practice*. Boston: James R. Osgood, 1881.
---. From "A Reminiscent Introduction." *Golden* 54–56.
---. *The Great Modern American Stories*. New York: Garrett Press, 1969.
---. *Heroines of Fiction*. 2 vols. New York: Harper & Bros., 1901.
---. Introduction. *Lyrics of Lowly Life*. By Paul Laurence Dunbar. London: Chapman & Hall, 1897. xiii–xx.
---. *My Literary Passions*. New York: Harper & Bros., 1895.
---. "A Psychological Counter-Current in Recent Fiction." *North American Review* CLXXIII (1901): 882.
---. *Selected Literary Criticism, Volume III: 1898–1920*. Selected and Intro. by Ronald Gottesman. Bloomington: Indiana University Press, 1993.
---. *Selected Letters*. 2 vols. Ed. George Arms et al. Boston: Twayne, 1979.
---. "To E Phelps." 28 Oct. 1881. bMS Am 1784.1 (30). William Dean Howells Collection. Houghton Library, Harvard University.
Hoyt, Edwin Palmer. *The Improper Bostonian: Dr. Oliver Wendell Holmes*. New York: Morrow, 1979.
Hudspeth, Robert N., ed. *The Letters of Margaret Fuller*. 6 vols. Ithaca: Cornell University Press, 1984.
Hunt, Harriot K. *Glances and Glimpses: or Fifty Years Social, Including Twenty Years Professional Life*. 1856. New York: Source, 1970.

Hunter, Dianne. "Hysteria, Psychoanalysis, and Feminism: The Case of Anna O." *Feminist Studies* 9 (Fall 1983): 465–88.

Jacobs, Harriet. *Incidents in the Life of a Slave Girl*. Ed. Jean Fagan Yellin. Boston: Harvard University Press, 1987.

Jacobus, Mary. "An Unnecessary Maze of Sign-Reading." Golden 277–95.

Jacobus, Mary, Evelyn Fox Keller, and Sally Shuttleworth, eds. *Body/Politics: Women and the Discourses of Science*. New York: Routledge, 1990.

James, Henry. "The Art of Fiction." *The Art of Criticism: Henry James on the Theory and the Practice of Fiction*. Ed. William Veeder and Susan M. Griffin. Chicago: University of Chicago Press, 1986. 165–83.

———. "Preface to 'Roderick Hudson.'" *The Art of the Novel: Critical Prefaces*. Intr. Richard P. Blackmur. New York: Scribner's, 1934. 3–29.

———. *Selected Letters*. Cambridge: Belknap-Harvard, 1987.

Jameson, Fredric. "On Magic Realism in Film." *Critical Inquiry* 12 (Winter 1986): 301–25.

———. *The Political Unconscious: Narrative as a Socially Symbolic Act*. Ithaca: Cornell University Press, 1981.

Jauss, Hans Robert. *Aesthetic Experience and Literary Hermeneutics*. Trans. Michael Shaw. Intr. Wlad Godzich. Minneapolis: University of Minnesota Press, 1982.

Jenkins, William Sumner. *Pro-Slavery Thought in the Old South*. Gloucester, MA: Peter Smith, 1960.

Johnson, Barbara. "Is Female to Male as Ground Is to Figure?" *Feminism and Psychoanalysis*. Ed. Richard Feldstein and Judith Roof. Ithaca: Cornell University Press, 1989.

Jones, Leroi. [Amiri Baraka.] *Blues People: Negro Music in White America*. New York: William Morrow, 1963.

Jones, Libby Falk. "Gilman, Bradley, Piercy, and the Evolving Rhetoric of Feminist Utopias." Jones and Goodwin 116–29.

Jones, Libby Falk, and Sarah Webster Goodwin, eds. *Feminism, Utopia, and Narrative*. Knoxville: University of Tennessee Press, 1990.

Joyce, Joyce A. "The Black Canon: Reconstructing Black American Literary Criticism." *New Literary History* 18 (1986): 335–44.

Kahane, Claire. *Passions of the Voice: Hysteria, Narrative, and the Figure of the Speaking Woman, 1850–1915*. Baltimore: Johns Hopkins University Press, 1995.

Kaplan, Amy. *The Social Construction of American Realism*. Chicago: University of Chicago Press, 1988.

Kaplan, Cora. "The Thornbirds: Fiction, Fantasy, Femininity." *Sea Changes*. London: Verso, 1986. 117–46.

Karpinski, Joanne B. *Critical Essays on Charlotte Perkins Gilman*. New York: G. K. Hall, 1992.

Kassanoff, Jennie A. "'Fate Has Linked Us Together': Blood, Gender, and the Politics of Representation in Pauline Hopkins's *Of One Blood*." Gruesser 158–81.

Kaufman, Martin. *Homeopathy in America: The Rise and Fall of a Medical Heresy*. Baltimore: Johns Hopkins University Press, 1971.

Kennard, Jean E. "Convention Coverage or How to Read Your Own Life." Golden 168–90.

Kermode, Frank. *The Sense of an Ending*. London: Oxford University Press, 1966.

Kessler, Carol Farley. *Elizabeth Stuart Phelps*. Boston: Twayne, 1982.

Kett, Joseph F. *The Formation of the American Medical Profession: The Role of Institutions, 1780–1860*. New Haven: Yale University Press, 1968.

Keyser, Elizabeth. "Looking Backward: From *Herland* to *Gulliver's Travels*." Karpinski 159–72.

Knadler, Stephen P. "Untragic Mulatto: Charles Chesnutt and the Discourse of Whiteness." *American Literary History* 8 (1986): 426–48.

Kohlstedt, Sally Gregory. *The Formation of the American Scientific Community: The American Association for the Advancement of Science, 1848–60*. Urbana: University of Illinois Press, 1976.

Kolb, Harold. *The Illusion of Life: American Realism as a Literary Form*. Charlottesville: University of Virginia Press, 1969.

Kolodny, Annette. "Inventing a Feminist Discourse: Rhetoric and Resistance in Margaret Fuller's *Woman in the Nineteenth Century*." *New Literary History* 25 (1994): 355–82.

———. "A Map for Rereading: Or, Gender and the Interpretation of Literary Texts." Golden 149–67.

Lane, Ann J. Introduction. *Herland*. By Charlotte Perkins Gilman. 1915. New York: Pantheon, 1979.

———. *To Herland and Beyond: The Life and Work of Charlotte Perkins Gilman*. New York: Meridian, 1991.

Laqueur, Thomas. *Making Sex: Body and Gender from the Greeks to Freud*. Cambridge: Harvard University Press, 1990.

Larson, Magali Sarfatti. *The Rise of Professionalism: A Sociological Analysis*. Berkeley: University of California Press, 1977.

Leavitt, Judith Walzer, ed. *Women and Health in America*. Madison: University of Wisconsin Press, 1984.

Levine, George, ed. *Aesthetics and Ideology*. New Brunswick: Rutgers University Press, 1994.

Levine, Lawrence W. *Highbrow/Lowbrow: The Emergence of Cultural Hierarchy in America*. Cambridge: Harvard University Press, 1988.

Light, Alison. "'Returning to Manderley': Romance Fiction, Female Sexuality and Class." *Feminist Review* 16 (Apr. 1984): 7–25.

Link, Eugene Perry. *The Social Ideas of American Physicians (1776–1976): Studies of the Humanitarian Tradition in Medicine*. London: Associated University Press, 1992.

"Literary Notes." *New York Times* (1 Jan. 1882): 10.

Lovering, J. P. *S. Weir Mitchell*. New York: Twayne, 1971.

Lynn, Kenneth S. *William Dean Howells: An American Life*. New York: Harcourt, Brace, Jovanovich, 1971.

Magner, Lois N. "Darwinism and the Woman Question: The Evolving Views of Charlotte Perkins Gilman." Karpinski 115–28.

Marcus, Steven. "Freud and Dora: Story, History, Case History." In *Dora's Case: Freud—Hysteria—Feminism*. 2nd ed. Ed. Charles Bernheimer and Claire Kahane. New York: Columbia University Press, 1990. 56–91.

Martin, Emily. *The Woman in the Body: A Cultural Analysis of Reproduction*. Boston: Beacon, 1988.

Masteller, Jean Carwile. "The Women Doctors of Howells, Phelps, and Jewett: The Conflict of Marriage and Career." *Critical Essays on Sarah Orne Jewett*. Ed. Gwen L. Noyel. Boston: G. K. Hall, 1985. 135–47.

Matthews, Glenna. *The Rise of Public Woman: Woman's Power and Woman's Place in the United States, 1630–1970*. New York: Oxford University Press, 1992.

McDowell, Deborah E. "'The Changing Same': Generational Connections and Black Women Novelists." Gates, *Reading Black, Reading Feminist*, 91–115.

McElrath, Joseph R., Jr., and Robert C. Leitz III, eds. *"To Be an Author": Letters of Charles W. Chesnutt, 1889–1905*. Princeton: Princeton University Press, 1997.

McKay, Janet Holmgren. *Narration and Discourse in American Realistic Fiction*. Philadelphia: University of Pennsylvania Press, 1982.

Michaels, Walter Benn. *The Gold Standard and the Logic of Naturalism: American Literature at the Turn of the Century*. Berkeley: University of California Press, 1987.

———. "The Souls of White Folk." *Literature and the Body: Essays on Populations and Persons*. Ed. Elaine Scarry. Baltimore: Johns Hopkins University Press, 1988. 185–209.

Miller, D. A. *Narrative and Its Discontents: Problems of Closure in the Traditional Novel*. Princeton: Princeton University Press, 1981.

Mitchell, S. Weir. "Civilization and Pain." *Journal of the American Medical Association* 18 (1892): 108.

———. *Doctor and Patient*. 1888. New York: Arno, 1972.

———. *Fat and Blood: An Essay on the Treatment of Certain Forms of Neurasthenia and Hysteria*. 3d. rev. ed. Philadelphia: J. B. Lippincott, 1884.

———. *Lectures on Diseases of the Nervous System, Especially in Women.* Philadelphia: Henry C. Lea's Son, 1881.

———. *Roland Blake.* 1886. Author's Definitive Edition. New York: The Century Company, 1915.

———. "To Oliver Wendell Holmes." 23 Mar. 1859. bMs Am 1241.1 (745). Oliver Wendell Holmes Collection. Houghton Library, Harvard University.

———. "To Oliver Wendell Holmes." 21 Dec. 1874. bMs Am 1241.1 (745). Oliver Wendell Holmes Collection. Houghton Library, Harvard University.

———. *Wear and Tear, Or Hints for the Overworked.* 5th ed. Philadelphia: J. B. Lippincott, 1891.

Mitchell, Thomas R. "Julian Hawthorne and the 'Scandal' of Margaret Fuller." *American Literary History* 7 (Summer 1995): 210–33.

Monks, George H. *Selections from the Medical Writings and Sayings of Doctor Oliver Wendell Holmes.* Boston: n.p., 1928.

Moraga, Cherríe, and Gloria Anzaldúa, eds. *This Bridge Called My Back: Writings by Radical Women of Color.* New York: Kitchen Table: Women of Color Press, 1981.

Morantz, Regina Markell. "The Perils of Feminist History." Leavitt 239–45.

Morantz, Regina Markell, Cynthia Stodola Pomerleau, and Carol Hansen Fenichel, eds. *In Her Own Words: Oral Histories of Women Physicians.* Westport, Conn.: Greenwood, 1982.

Morantz-Sanchez, Regina Markell. *Sympathy and Science: Women Physicians in American Medicine.* New York: Oxford University Press, 1985.

Morris, Timothy. "Professional Ethics and Professional Erotics in Elizabeth Stuart Phelps' *Doctor Zay.*" *Studies in American Fiction* 21 (Autumn 1993): 141–52.

Morse, John T., Jr. *Life and Letters of Oliver Wendell Holmes.* 2 vols. Boston: Houghton Mifflin, 1896.

Myerson, Joel. *Margaret Fuller: An Annotated Secondary Bibliography.* New York: Burt Franklin, 1977.

———. *Margaret Fuller: A Descriptive Bibliography.* Pittsburgh: University of Pittsburgh Press, 1978.

———, ed. *Critical Essays On Margaret Fuller.* Boston: G. K. Hall, 1980.

Myerson, Joel, Daniel Shealy, and Madeleine Stern, eds. *The Journals of Louisa May Alcott.* Boston: Little, 1989.

———. *The Selected Letters of Louisa May Alcott.* Boston: Little, 1987.

Omi, Michael, and Howard Winant. *Racial Formation in the United States from the 1960s to the 1990s.* 2nd. ed. New York: Routledge, 1994.

Otten, Thomas J. "Pauline Hopkins and the Hidden Self of Race." *ELH* 59 (1992): 227–56.

Packer, Barbara L. "The Transcendentalists." *The Cambridge History of American*

*Literature.* Sacvan Bercovitch, gen. ed. Vol. 2. New York: Cambridge University Press, 1995. 331–604.

Parker, Gail Thain. "Sex, Sentiment, and Oliver Wendell Holmes." *Women's Studies* (1972): 47–63.

Pattee, Fred Lewis. *The Feminine Fifties.* Port Washington, New York: Kennikat, 1966.

Pease, Donald. *Visionary Compacts: American Renaissance Writings in Cultural Contexts.* Madison: University of Wisconsin Press, 1987.

Peyser, Thomas Galt. "Reproducing Utopia: Charlotte Perkins Gilman and *Herland.*" *Studies in American Fiction* 20 (Spring 1992): 1–16.

Pfaelzer, Jean. "Response: What Happened to History?" Jones and Goodwin 191–200.

———. *The Utopian Novel in America, 1886–1896: The Politics of Form.* Pittsburgh: University of Pittsburgh Press, 1984.

Phelps, Elizabeth Stuart. *Chapters from a Life.* Boston: Houghton, Mifflin, 1896.

———. *Doctor Zay.* 1882. New York: Feminist, 1987.

———. "To William Dean Howells." 11 Aug. 1874. bMS Am 1784 (515). William Dean Howells Collection. Houghton Library, Harvard University.

———. "To William Dean Howells." 10 Mar. 1880. bMS Am 1784 (515). William Dean Howells Collection. Houghton Library, Harvard University.

———. "To William Dean Howells." 2 Nov. 1881. bMS Am 1784 (515). William Dean Howells Collection. Houghton Library, Harvard University.

———. "What Shall They Do?" *Harper's New Monthly* (June 1867): 519–23.

Pizer, Donald. *Realism & Naturalism in Nineteenth-Century American Literature.* Carbondale: Southern Illinois University Press, 1984.

Poe, Edgar A. "The Literati of New York City.—No. IV. Sarah Margaret Fuller." *Godey's Magazine and Lady's Book* 33 (Aug. 1846). *Critical Essays On Margaret Fuller.* Ed. Joel Myerson. Boston: G. K. Hall, 1980.

Poirier, Suzanne. "The Weir Mitchell Rest Cure: Doctor and Patients." *Women's Studies* 10 (1983): 15–40.

Poovey, Mary. *Uneven Developments: The Ideological Work of Gender in Mid-Victorian England.* Chicago: University of Chicago Press, 1988.

Porter, Carolyn. *Seeing and Being: The Plight of the Participant Observer in Emerson, James, Adams, and Faulkner.* Middletown, Conn.: Wesleyan University Press, 1981.

Redding, J. Saunders. *To Make a Poet Black.* Intro. Henry Louis Gates, Jr. Ithaca: Cornell University Press, 1988.

Render, Sylvia Lyons. *Charles W. Chesnutt.* Boston: Twayne, 1980.

Richings, G. F. *Evidences of Progress Among Colored People.* 11th ed. Philadelphia: Geo. S. Ferguson, 1904.

Riley, Denise. *"Am I That Name?": Feminism and the Category of "Women" in History.* Minneapolis: University of Minnesota Press, 1988.
Ringer, Benjamin B., and Elinor R. Lawless. *Race-Ethnicity and Society.* New York: Routledge, 1989.
Risse, Guenter B., Ronald L. Numbers, and Judith Walzer Leavitt, eds. *Medicine Without Doctors: Home Health Care in American History.* New York: Science History, 1977.
Rosenberg, Charles E. *The Cholera Years: The United States in 1832, 1849, and 1866.* Chicago: University of Chicago Press, 1962.
Rosenberg, Charles E., and Janet Golden, eds. *Framing Disease: Studies in Cultural History.* New Brunswick: Rutgers University Press, 1992.
Rothfield, Lawrence. *Vital Signs: Medical Realism in Nineteenth-Century Fiction.* Princeton: Princeton University Press, 1992.
Rothstein, William G. *American Physicians in the Nineteenth Century: From Sects to Science.* Baltimore: Johns Hopkins University Press, 1972.
Rowe, John Carlos. "Swept Away: Henry James, Margaret Fuller, and 'The Last of the Valerii.'" *Readers in History: Nineteenth-Century American Literature and the Contexts of Response.* Ed. James L. Machor. Baltimore: Johns Hopkins University Press, 1993.
Russell, Roberta Joy. *Margaret Fuller: The Growth of a Woman Writer.* Diss. University of Connecticut, 1983. Ann Arbor: UMI, 1985. 8317725.
Ryan, Mary P. *Women in Public: Between Banners and Ballots, 1825–1880.* Baltimore: Johns Hopkins University Press, 1990.
Samuels, Shirley, ed. *The Culture of Sentiment: Race, Gender, and Sentimentality in Nineteenth-Century America.* New York: Oxford University Press, 1992.
Sánchez-Eppler, Karen. *Touching Liberty: Abolitionism, Feminism, and the Politics of the Body.* Berkeley: University of California Press, 1993.
Sartisky, Michael. Afterword. *Dr. Zay.* By Elizabeth Stuart Phelps. New York: Feminist, 1987. 259–321.
Saxton, Martha. *Louisa May Alcott: A Modern Biography.* New York: Farrar, Straus and Giroux, 1995.
Scarry, Elaine. *The Body in Pain.* New York: Oxford University Press, 1985.
Schiebinger, Londa. "Skeletons in the Closet: The First Illustrations of the Female Skeleton in Eighteenth-Century Anatomy." *The Making of the Modern Body: Sexuality and Society in the Nineteenth Century.* Ed. Catherine Gallagher and Thomas Laqueur. Berkeley: University of California Press, 1987. 42–82.
Schrager, Cynthia D. "Pauline Hopkins and William James: The New Psychology and the Politics of Race." Gruesser 182–209.
Schultz, Jane E. "Embattled Care: Narrative Authority in Louisa May Alcott's Hospital Sketches." *Legacy* 9 (Fall 1992): 104–18.

Scott, Joan Wallach. *Gender and The Politics of History.* New York: Columbia University Press, 1988.
See, Fred G. *Desire and the Sign: Nineteenth-Century American Fiction.* Baton Rouge: Louisiana State University Press, 1987.
Seltzer, Mark. *Bodies and Machines.* New York: Routledge, 1992.
Showalter, Elaine. *The Female Malady: Women, Madness and English Culture, 1830–1980.* New York: Pantheon, 1985.
Shumaker, Conrad. "Realism, Reform, and the Audience: Charlotte Perkins Gilman's Unreadable Wallpaper." *Arizona Quarterly* 47 (Spring 1991): 81–93.
───────. "'Too Terribly Good To Be Printed': Charlotte Perkins Gilman and 'The Yellow Wallpaper.'" Golden 242–52.
Sims, J. Marion. *The Story of My Life.* New York: Appleton, 1884.
Smith, Sidonie. "Resisting the Gaze of Embodiment: Women's Autobiography in the Nineteenth Century." *American Women's Autobiography: Fea(s)ts of Memory.* Ed. Margo Culley. Madison: University of Wisconsin Press, 1992. 75–110.
Smith-Rosenberg, Carroll. *Disorderly Conduct: Visions of Gender in Victorian America.* New York: Oxford University Press, 1986.
Smith-Rosenberg, Carroll, and Charles Rosenberg. "The Female Animal: Medical and Biological Views of Woman and Her Role in Nineteenth-Century America." Leavitt 12–27.
Smith, Valerie. "Black Feminist Theory and the Representation of the 'Other.'" Wall 38–57.
Smith, William Benjamin. *The Color Line: A Brief in Behalf of the Unborn.* 1905. New York: Negro University Press, 1969.
Spelman, Elizabeth V. *Inessential Woman: Problems of Exclusion in Feminist Thought.* Boston: Beacon University Press, 1988.
Spencer, Herbert. "The Development Hypothesis." *Essays Scientific, Political, and Speculative.* Vol. I. New York: Appleton, 1892.
───────. *First Principles of a New System of Philosophy.* New York: Appleton, 1864.
───────. "The Philosophy of Style." *Literary Style and Music.* 1852. New York: Philosophical Library, 1951. 1–44.
───────. *Principles of Biology, Volume I.* 1866. New York: Appleton, 1897.
───────. *Principles of Biology, Volume II.* 1867. New York: Appleton, 1897.
Stanton, Elizabeth Cady, Susan B. Anthony, and Matilda Joslyn Gage. *History of Woman Suffrage.* 2 vols. 1881–82. Salem, NH: Ayer, 1985.
Starr, Paul. *The Social Transformation of American Medicine.* New York: Basic Books, 1982.
Stepan, Nancy. *The Idea of Race in Science: Great Britain 1800–1960.* London: MacMillan, 1982.

Stern, Madeleine B. *The Life of Margaret Fuller.* New York: Dutton, 1942.
Stevens, Rosemary. *American Medicine and the Public Interest: A Sociological Analysis.* New Haven: Yale University Press, 1971.
Still, William. Introduction. *Iola Leroy; Or, Shadows Uplifted.* By Frances E. W. Harper. 1892. Boston: Beacon, 1987.
Sundquist, Eric J. *To Wake the Nations: Race in the Making of American Literature.* Cambridge: Belknap-Harvard, 1993.
Tate, Claudia. *Domestic Allegories of Political Desire: The Black Heroine's Text at the Turn of the Century.* New York: Oxford University Press, 1992.
Tilton, Eleanor M. *Amiable Autocrat: A Biography of Dr. Oliver Wendell Holmes.* New York: Henry Schuman, 1947.
"Toast to Oliver Wendell Holmes." 1853. Ts. Clipping. Oliver Wendell Holmes Collection. Houghton Library, Harvard University.
Todd, Janet. *Sensibility: An Introduction.* London: Methuen, 1986.
Tompkins, Jane. *Sensational Designs: The Cultural Work of American Fiction, 1790–1860.* New York: Oxford University Press, 1985.
Torgovnick, Marianna. *Closure in the Novel.* Princeton: Princeton University Press, 1981.
*Transactions of the American Medical Association.* With Appendix including the Committee on Medical Literature Report. May 3, 1848.
Treichler, Paula A. "Escaping the Sentence: Diagnosis and Discourse in 'The Yellow Wallpaper.'" Golden 191–210.
Urbanski, Marie Mitchell Olesen. "*Woman in the Nineteenth Century*: Genesis, Form, Tone, and Rhetorical Devices." *Margaret Fuller: Visionary of the New Age.* Ed. Marie Mitchell Olesen Urbanski. Orono, Maine: Northern Lights, 1994.
Vance, Carole S., ed. Introduction. *Pleasure and Danger: Exploring Female Sexuality.* Boston: Routledge & Kegan Paul, 1984. 1–27.
Veeder, William. "Who Is Jane? The Intricate Feminism of Charlotte Perkins Gilman." *Arizona Quarterly* 44 (Autumn 1988): 40–79.
Verbrugge, Martha H. *Able-Bodied Womanhood: Personal Health and Social Change in Nineteenth-Century Boston.* New York: Oxford, 1988.
Wall, Cheryl A. *Changing Our Own Words.* New Brunswick: Rutgers University Press, 1989.
Ward, Lester F. "The Past and Future of the Sexes." *The Independent* (8 Mar. 1906): 541–45. 177 (Box 21, Folder 267). Charlotte Perkins Gilman Papers. Schlesinger Library, Radcliffe College..
Warhol, Robyn. *Gendered Interventions: Narrative Discourse in the Victorian Novel.* New Brunswick: Rutgers University Press, 1989.
Warren, Kenneth W. *Black and White Strangers: Race and American Literary Realism.* Chicago: University of Chicago Press, 1993.

Welter, Barbara. "The Cult of True Womanhood, 1820–1860." *American Quarterly* 18 (1966): 151–74.

Wexler, Laura. "Tender Violence: Literary Eavesdropping, Domestic Fiction, and Educational Reform." Samuels 9–38.

Williams, Raymond. *Keywords*. Rev. ed. New York: Oxford University Press, 1985.

Williamson, Joel. *New People: Miscegenation and Mulattoes in the United States*. New York: Free, 1980.

Wilson, Christopher P. "Charlotte Perkins Gilman's Steady Burghers: The Terrain of *Herland*." *Women's Studies* 12 (1986): 271–92.

Woodson, Thomas, et al., eds. *Nathaniel Hawthorne: The Letters, 1853–1856*. Vol. XVII. *The Centenary Edition of the Works of Nathaniel Hawthorne*. Columbus: Ohio State University Press, 1987.

Youmans, Edward L., compiler. *Herbert Spencer on the Americans and the Americans on Herbert Spencer*. 1882. New York: Arno Press, 1973.

Young, Elizabeth. "A Wound of One's Own: Louisa May Alcott's Civil War Fiction." *American Quarterly* 48 (Sept. 1996): 439–74.

Zamora, Lois Parkinson, and Wendy B. Faris, eds. *Magical Realism: Theory, History, Community*. Durham: Duke University Press, 1995.

# Index

In this index an "f" after a number indicates a separate reference on the next page, and an "ff" indicates separate references on the next two pages. A continuous discussion over two or more pages is indicated by a span of page numbers, e.g., "57–59." *Passim* is used for a cluster of references in close but not consecutive sequence.

Advice books, 50, 205n15
Aesthetic, 3f, 10–11, 116–17, 154–94 *passim*
African-American literature, 10–11, 154–94. *See also* Chesnutt, Charles W.; Harper, Frances E. Watkins; Hopkins, Pauline E.
Agassiz, Louis, 18–19
Åhnebrink, Lars, 15
Alcott, Louisa May, 8, 53–54, 55–63, 73, 79, 87–88, 205nn12–17; *Hospital Sketches*, 55–62 *passim*; *Little Women*, 55, 61–62; *Work: A Story of Experience*, 55, 62–63; *A Long Fatal Love Chase*, 56; *Moods*, 56; *On Picket Duty, and Other Tales*, 56; *The Rose Family*, 56
Amalgamation, *see* Miscegenation; Race
American Institute of Homeopathy, 108
American Medical Association (AMA), 2, 7, 16–25 *passim*, 107–8, 202n22, 205n14
Ammons, Elizabeth, 138
Anatomy, 13, 26–27, 153
Anesthesia, 19, 159–60, 169, 219n9
"Anna O." (Breuer), 136
"Art of Fiction, The" (James), 98–99
*Atlantic Monthly*, 24, 32, 94, 104, 107, 143
Autobiography, *see* Memoir
"Autocrat of the Breakfast Table, The" (Holmes), 16, 24, 28

Baker, Houston, 156–57
Bakhtin, Mikhail, 4, 92–93, 198n4
Balance, 8–9, 93–121 *passim*, 210n6
Baraka, Amiri (Leroi Jones), 180
Barthes, Roland, 165
Baym, Nina, 52–53, 54, 154, 204n9
Beauty, 10–11, 158–72 *passim*, 181, 186, 190–91. *See also* Aesthetic; Black aesthetic
Beecher, Catharine, 50–51
Bell, Michael Davitt, 102–3
Bersani, Leo, 101
Bichat, Marie François Xavier, 26
Bildungsroman, 70–71, 95, 135
"Birth" (Gilman), 147
Black, *see* African-American literature; Black aesthetic; Miscegenation; Race

Black aesthetic, 10–11, 154–94 *passim*
Blackwell, Elizabeth, 20, 50, 205–6n19
Blackwell, Henry, 144
Bledstein, Burton J., 27
*Blithedale Romance, The* (Hawthorne), 73
Bloch, Ernst, 153
*Bodies and Machines* (Seltzer), 15
Body: as closed energy system, 3, 8–9, 90–94, 108; of doctors, 22, 28–29, 38–39, 44–48. *See also* Aesthetic; Beauty; Balance; Black aesthetic; Gender identity; Hysteria; Transcendence; Vision, clinical; Vision, female; Womb; Women
*Body in Pain, The* (Scarry), 83
Boone, Joseph Allen, 119
Booth, Alison, 121
Breur, Josef, 123, 136–37; "Anna O.," 136. *See also* Freud, Sigmund
Briggs, Charles F., 73
Brooks, Peter, 99, 188
Brownson, Orestes, 85, 207n26
Bruce, Robert V., 19
Burke, Kenneth, 4, 162, 191f
Burr, Anna, 122–23

Cady, Edwin H., 102f
Campo, Rafael, 194
Canin, Ethan, 194
Carby, Hazel, 163–64
Channing, William Henry, 75, 81f, 86
Chapman, Nathaniel, 18
*Chapters from a Life* (Phelps), 104f, 109
Chesnutt, Charles W., 10–11, 155–64 *passim*, 171–81, 190–92, 222; *The Marrow of Tradition*, 10–11, 158–64 *passim*, 171–81; *The House Behind the Cedars*, 172–73; "The Future American," 176
"Christianity" (Harper), 221
Civil War (U.S.), 19, 34, 55, 61, 100, 122, 205n

Clarke, Dr. Edward H., 9, 26, 89–96, 100, 106, 113, 115ff, 201n18, 211n10; *Sex in Education*, 9; *Visions: A Study of False Sight (Pseudopia)*, 26
Clarke, James Freeman, 86
Closure, 9, 95–100, 104, 109–21, 130. *See also* Marriage plot; Narrative form
*Colored American Magazine*, 181
*Color Line: A Brief in Behalf of the Unborn, The* (Smith), 158–59
*Contending Forces* (Hopkins), 155
*Contested Castle, The* (Ellis), 141–42
Corsets, 80–81, 209n38
"Criteria of Negro Art" (Du Bois), 190–91
Criticism, 5–6, 157
*Culture of Professionalism, The* (Bledstein), 27
*Culture of Sentiment, The* (Samuels), 51
Cure, 43–44, 47–48, 55, 58, 60–61, 65–70, 80–81, 87–88, 130–32, 142–44, 191–94

Dalke, Anne, 34
Darwin, Charles, 19, 34, 36, 125, 127, 149, 158f; *Origin of the Species*, 36; *The Descent of Man*, 159. *See also* Determinism (biological)
Davis, Nathan, S., 19–20
Davis, Rebecca Harding, 17, 59, 199n2
Degler, Carl, 197n1
*Descent of Man, The* (Darwin), 159
Determinism (biological), 9, 125–41 *passim*, 148. *See also* Darwin, Charles; Spencer, Herbert
Determinism (domestic), 9–10, 126–41 *passim*, 147–48
Dickinson, Emily, 49–50
Didacticism, 16, 128, 141–50 *passim*, 156. *See also* Idealism; Morality and literary representation
Dimock, Wai Chee, 5, 214n6

# Index

Dirix, Dr., 123
Disease, *see* Illness; Invalidism
Disembodiment, *see* Transcendence
Dissection, 32, 38
*Doctor Breen's Practice* (Howells), 94, 100, 107–17 *passim*, 211n18, 212n21
Doctors: "regular," 18–24, 64–65, 107–8, 211; "irregular," 17–18, 27–29, 64–65, 96, 107–8; relationship with patients, 16, 22–23, 34f, 43, 46, 55, 64–67, 122, 134–35. *See also* Homeopathy; Women, as doctors
*Doctor Zay* (Phelps), 9, 94–97, 106, 113–21, 212n21
*Domestic Allegories of Political Desire* (Tate), 156, 165, 181
Domesticity, 10, 21–24, 93, 132–48 *passim*, 151f. *See also* Determinism (domestic)
"Dora's Case" (Freud), 136–37
Douglas, Ann, 154, 203n5
Dreiser, Theodore, 130
Du Bois, W. E. B., 156, 160, 175, 183, 190–91
DuCille, Ann, 164–65
Duffey, Eliza Bisbee, 91
Dunbar, Paul Lawrence, 157–58
DuPlessis, Rachel Blau, 95

Eagleton, Terry, 3, 162–63, 169–70, 176, 180
Ehrenreich, Barbara, 50
Ellis, Havelock, 158
Ellis, Kate Ferguson, 141–42
*Elsie Venner* (Holmes), 7–8, 16f, 29–48, 199n2, 199–200n9, 201n20
Emerson, Ralph Waldo, 59, 78ff, 205n14
Emotion, *see* Heart as metaphor for womanhood; Sentimentalism; Sympathy; Tears
English, Deirdre, 50

Equilibrium, *see* Balance
Evolution, *see* Darwin, Charles; Determinism; Spencer, Herbert
Excitement and disease, 50–51

*Fat and Blood* (Mitchell), 123, 213n4
Female, *see* Gender identity, Vision, female; Womb; Women
Femininity, *see* Gender identity; Women
Feminism, 114, 124–29
Feminist criticism, 5–6
Fiction and healing, *see* Writing and healing
*First Principles* (Spencer), 90, 94, 97
Fisher, Philip, 168
Flaubert, Gustave (*Madame Bovary*), 15
*Foregone Conclusion, A* (Howells), 112
Form (definition), 4. *See also* Aesthetic; Body; Narrative form
Formalist criticism, 5
Foster, Frances Smith, 157
Foucault, Michel, 13–14, 23, 27, 197–98
Free indirect discourse, 175–76
Freud, Sigmund, 9–10, 123, 131, 136–45 *passim*, 151, 153, 197–98, 213n4; "Dora's Case," 136–37; "A General Introduction to Psychoanalysis," 137–38
Frye, Northrop, 153, 173
Fuller, Arthur, 86
Fuller, Margaret, 8, 53–54, 55, 72–88, 201n19, 207–10 *passim*; *Woman in the Nineteenth Century*, 73, 79–88 *passim*, 209; "The Great Lawsuit," 75, 79
Fuller, Timothy, 79
Fuss, Diana, 185–86
"Future American, The" (Chesnutt), 176

Gates, Henry Louis, Jr., 157, 177, 222n29
Gayle, Addison, Jr., 156, 190

Gaze, *see* Vision, clinical; Vision, female
Geddes, Sir Patrick, 217n34
Gender identity, 6, 21–22, 72–97 *passim*, 125–28, 132–53, 199n8; and doctors, 15, 34–44, 63–68, 110–21; "true woman," 22, 41, 52, 74, 204n10, 207n27. *See also* Women
"General Introduction to Psychoanalysis, A" (Freud), 137–38
Gilder, Richard Watson, 173
Gillman, Susan, 156, 183, 225n45
Gilman, Charlotte Perkins, 9–10, 122–53 *passim*, 211–18 *passim*; *Herland*, 10, 124, 129, 145–53, 216ff; "The Yellow Wallpaper," 10, 124–53 *passim*, 213n6, 214n16, 216; *His Religion and Hers*, 126; *Women and Economics*, 126, 148–49, 214n9, 217n34; *The Home: Its Work and Influence*, 132, 141, 152, 215n19; "In Duty Bound," 133–34, 147; "The Falsity of Freud," 137; "The Freudian Fallacy," 137; "What the 'Threat of Man' Really Means," 137–38; "The Home," 141; "Birth," 147; *In This Our World*, 147; *Man-Made World*, 148
Gilman, Houghton, 133
Girl watching, 28
*Glances and Glimpses* (Hunt), 66–72, 206n21, 207n23
Gothic literature, 141–45 *passim*
"Great Lawsuit, The" (Fuller), 75, 79
*Great Modern American Stories, The* (Howells), 144
Greeley, Horace, 86
Grimké, Sarah, 207n23
Gubar, Susan, 145
"Gynaecocentric Theory of Life" (Ward), 148–49

Hahnemann, Samuel, 108
Haney-Peritz, Janice, 142

Harper, Frances E. Watkins, 10–11, 156f, 162–71, 172f, 180, 189–92, 220–21; *Iola Leroy*, 11, 156, 162–71, 189–92, 220–21
Harris, Mary Briggs, 212n20
*Hawthorne* (James), 87
Hawthorne, Nathaniel, 59, 73, 86, 207n25
Healing, *see* Writing and healing
Heart as metaphor for womanhood, 8, 49–50, 65–72, 76–78, 206n22. *See also* Sentimentalism; Sympathy; Tears
Hedges, Elain, 130, 214n16
Hedin, Raymond, 177
Hendler, Glenn, 205n17
*Herland* (Gilman), 10, 124, 129, 145–53, 216ff
Hermaphrodite, 28–29
Herndl, Diana Price, 131, 142, 144, 204n11
Higginson, Thomas Wentworth, 86, 91, 205n38, 209n38
*His Religion and Hers* (Gilman), 126
*History of Sexuality* (Foucault), 13–14, 27, 197–98
Holmes, Oliver Wendell, Sr., 7–8, 13–48 *passim*, 65, 72, 108, 199–202 *passim*, 206n21; *Elsie Venner*, 7–8, 16f, 29–48, 199n2, 199–200n9, 201n20; "The Autocrat of the Breakfast Table," 16, 24, 28; *A Moral Antipathy*, 29f
Home, *see* Domesticity
*Home; Its Work and Influence, The* (Gilman), 132, 141, 152, 215n19
Homeopathy, 27, 64, 96, 107–9, 110, 116, 201n16, 211n15. *See also* Doctors; Women, as doctors
Hopkins, Pauline E., 10–11, 155, 161–71, 181–92; *Of One Blood*, 10–11, 162f, 181–90, 223ff; *Contending Forces*, 155

# Index

*Hospital Sketches* (Alcott), 55–62 passim
*House Behind the Cedars, The* (Chesnutt), 172–73
Howe, Julia Ward, 91
Howells, Elinor Mead, 112
Howells, William Dean, 8–9, 94, 96, 100, 104, 107–19 passim, 128, 144, 157–58, 178ff, 211; *Doctor Breen's Practice*, 94, 100, 107–17 passim, 211n18, 212n21; *The Rise of Silas Lapham*, 100, 104; *A Modern Instance*, 100, 112; "What Should Girls Read?" 102; *A Foregone Conclusion*, 112; *The Great Modern American Stories*, 144
Hoyt, Edwin, 41
Hunt, Dr. Angenette A., 64
Hunt, Dr. Harriot K., 8, 53–54, 55, 63–72, 73, 87–88, 206n21, 207n23; *Glances and Glimpses*, 66–72, 206n21, 207n23
Hunt, Sarah, 65
Hysteria, 10, 37, 41, 50–51, 123–24, 129–45 passim, 213. See also Womb

Idealism, 74–75, 101, 103–7, 112. See also Didacticism; Morality and literary representation
Illness, 8, 43, 54–69 passim, 79–84, 100–101, 130–31, 134. See also Hysteria; Invalidism
"In Duty Bound" (Gilman), 133–34, 147
*In This Our World* (Gilman), 147
Invalidism, 10, 50–54, 57, 67, 71, 89–90, 93–94, 117–18, 123–24, 204n11. See also Hysteria; Illness
*Invalid Women* (Herndl), 204n11
*Iola Leroy* (Harper), 11, 156, 162–71, 189–92, 220–21

Jacobs, Harriet, 70–71
Jacobus, Mary, 131, 139–40
James, Henry, 87, 98–103 passim, 107, 178; *Hawthorne*, 87; *William Wetmore Story and His Friends*, 87; "The Last of the Valerii," 87; *The Bostonians*, 98; "The Art of Fiction," 98–99
James, William, 183, 193
Jameson, Frederic, 4, 225n4
Johnson, Amelia (*Clarence and Corrine*), 163–64
Jones, Leroi (Amiri Baraka), 180

Kaplan, Amy, 100f
Kermode, Frank, 99
Keyser, Elizabeth, 152–53
Kolb, Harold, 102–3
Kolodny, Annette, 154

Lane, Ann J., 137
Lane, Martha, 143
Language, 23–26, 30, 186–89. See also Speech and pain
Lauter, Paul, 154
Lee, Ulysses, 170–71
*Letters to the People on Health and Happiness* (Beecher), 50–51
*Life in the Iron Mills* (Davis), 17, 59
Literature as medicine, *see* Writing and healing
*Literary Realism and Naturalism* (Pizer), 102
*Little Women* (Alcott), 55, 61–62
Locke, John, 185
Lombroso, Cesare, 159
*Long Fatal Love Chase, A* (Alcott), 56
Love, 62, 109–10

McDowell, Deborah E., 164
McKay, Janet Holmgren, 175–76
*Madame Bovary* (Flaubert), 15
Magical realism, 188–90
Magnetism, 183–84
Mann, Mrs. Horace, 91

Marcus, Steven 131
Marriage plot, 9, 95–98, 109–21, 164–65, 166f, 181, 211n12. *See also* Closure; Narrative form
*Marrow of Tradition, The* (Chesnutt), 10–11, 158–64 *passim*, 171–81
Marx, Karl, 150
Matthews, Victoria Earle, 155
Mead, William B., 112
Medicine, 3–4, 13–29 *passim*, 50–51, 64–67, 89–94, 122–24, 197. *See also* Doctors; Homeopathy; Vision, clinical; Women, as doctors
Melodrama, 187–90, 225n45
Memoir, 55–72 *passim*
Michaels, Walter Benn, 124
Miller, D. A., 99–100, 120–21
Mimesis, 10, 16–17, 30, 98–101 *passim*, 124–31 *passim*, 140, 153, 167–68, 181; and the limits of realism, 31–32, 58, 94, 149, 151, 178, 189. *See also* Mimosis; Realism
Mimosis, 124, 129, 135, 140, 151, 213n6. *See also* Mimesis; Realism
Miscegenation, 159, 166, 171–78, 181–82. *See also* African-American literature; Race
Mitchell, Dr. S. Weir, 9, 30, 122–23, 125, 130–39 *passim*, 148, 160, 199–200n9, 212n21, 213nn3–4; *Roland Blake* 122, 213n3; *Fat and Blood* 123, 213n4
*Modern Instance, A* (Howells), 100, 112
*Moods* (Alcott), 56
*Moral Antipathy, A* (Holmes), 29f
Morality and literary representation, 30–32, 57–61, 105–6, 128–29, 154–94 *passim*. *See also* Didacticism; Idealism
Morantz-Sanchez, Regina, 21, 64
Morris, Timothy, 114–15
Morton, Dr. Samuel George, 158
Mulatto, *see* Miscegenation; Race

Mumford, Lewis, 151–52
Munn, Orson, 18

*Narrative and Its Discontents* (Miller), 120–21
Narrative form, 1–7, 12, 25–26, 54, 66, 70, 74, 154–63, 174–80 *passim*, 191–94; and compensatory theory, 3, 99–100, 102, 106, 117ff. *See also* Closure; Marriage plot
Narrator, 16–17, 44–48, 59–61, 68–72, 84–85, 112–13, 124–53 *passim*, 172–81 *passim*
Naturalism, *see* Determinism; Realism
New historicism, 5, 157
*No Sex in Education* (Duffey), 91
Norris, Frank, 127
Nott, Josiah, 219n8
Nursing, 55–62 *passim*

O'Connor, Flannery, 194
*Of One Blood* (Hopkins), 10–11, 162f, 181–90, 223ff
*On Picket Duty, and Other Tales* (Alcott), 56
Organicism, 128–29, 150
*Origin of the Species* (Darwin), 36
Otten, Thomas J., 183
*Our Nig* (Wilson), 157

Pain, 51–63 *passim*, 79–88 *passim*. *See also* Anesthesia; Transcendence
Panmixia, *see* Miscegenation
Parker, Gail, 34
Patients, 16, 22–23, 34f, 43, 46, 55, 64–67, 122, 134–35
Percy, Walker, 194
Pfaelzer, Jean, 150
Phelps, Elizabeth Stuart, 8–9, 91–100, 104–7, 108f, 113–21, 210, 212nn19–22; *Doctor Zay*, 9, 94–97, 106, 113–21, 212n21; *The Silent Partner*, 95; *The*

*Story of Avis*, 95; *Chapters from a Life*, 104f, 109
"Philosophy of Style, The" (Spencer), 98
Pizer, Donald, 102
Poe, Edgar Allan, 73–74, 86
*Principles of Biology* (Spencer), 90

Race, 10–11, 34, 41, 75, 154–91 *passim*. See also African-American literature; Black aesthetic; Chesnutt, Charles W.; Harper, Frances E. Watkins; Hopkins, Pauline E.; Miscegenation
Reading, 43, 52–53, 56, 66–72, 87–88, 111, 118, 143–45, 154–63. See also Aesthetic; Black aesthetic
Realism, 7–12 *passim*, 94–106, 128, 144–45, 167–68, 175–79 *passim*, 199n2, 223n33; and medicine, 7–8, 14–17, 30–35 *passim*, 45–48, 58f. See also Mimesis; Mimosis
Reconstruction, 168ff
Redding, J. Saunders, 170
*Rise of Silas Lapham, The* (Howells), 100, 104
Robinson, Lillian S., 154
*Roland Blake* (Mitchell), 122, 213n3
*Rose Family, The* (Alcott), 56
Rothfield, Lawrence, 30f

Samuels, Shirley, 51
Sánchez-Eppler, Karen, 52, 203n8
Sartisky, Michael, 114–15
Satire, 173
Scarry, Elaine, 83–84
Scudder, Horace, 143
Seltzer, Mark, 15
*Sensational Designs* (Tompkins), 154–55, 203n5
Sentimentalism, 7–16 *passim*, 32, 40–48 *passim*, 51–88 *passim*, 103–4, 154–56, 203–5; as narrative strategy, 11, 56–63, 68–69, 104, 114–15, 167–71, 178–81. See also Heart as metaphor for womanhood; Hysteria; Idealism; Marriage plot; Melodrama; Sympathy; Tears
Sentimental novels (definition), 51. See also Sentimentalism
*Sex and Education* (Howe), 91
*Sex in Education* (Clarke), 9, 89–91, 113, 211n10
Sexuality, 34, 75, 137–38, 197–98
Shumaker, Conrad, 144
*Silent Partner, The* (Phelps), 95
Sims, Dr. J. Marion, 17–18
*Sister Carrie* (Dreiser), 130
Smith, Sidonie, 208n35
Smith, William Benjamin, 158–59
Social Darwinism, 127. See also Darwin, Charles; Determinism (biological); Spencer, Herbert
Soul, 8, 51–55 *passim*, 59, 62, 66–68, 74–87 *passim*, 159. See also Transcendence
Speech and pain, 84
Spencer, Herbert, 9, 90–98 *passim*, 102, 114, 127, 212n21; *First Principles*, 90, 94, 97; *Principles of Biology*, 90; "The Philosophy of Style," 98
Spirituality, *see* Soul; Transcendence
Staël, Madame de, 74
Starr, Paul, 2, 18, 197n1
Stein, Gertrude, 193
Stetson, Charles Walter, 134, 143
Stillé, Alfred, 107
*Story of Avis, The* (Phelps), 95
Stowe, Harriet Beecher, 52, 105, 211n12
Suffering, *see* Pain
Sundquist, Eric, 171, 175
Supernaturalism, 11, 182–90
Surgery, 142–44, 171, 205–6n19
Symmetry, *see* Balance

Sympathy, 21–48 *passim*, 52–60 *passim*, 64–72 *passim*, 179–86 *passim*, 205n17. *See also* Heart as metaphor for womanhood; Sentimentalism; Tears
*Sympathy and Science* (Morantz-Sanchez), 21, 64

Tate, Claudia, 156, 165, 181
Tears, 7–8, 29, 33, 44–48, 52, 57–62 *passim*, 67, 104, 203–4. *See also* Heart as metaphor for womanhood; Sentimentalism; Sympathy
Tompkins, Jane, 154–55, 203n5
Tourgée, Albion, 172, 178
Transcendence 8, 52, 57–58, 66, 74–86 *passim*
Transcendentalism, 75–76, 78, 207ff
*Transcript* (Boston), 143
"True woman," *see under* Gender identity

Uncanny, the, 10, 129, 139–45 *passim*, 150, 151–52, 215n25. *See also* Freud, Sigmund
*Uncle Tom's Cabin* (Stowe), 52, 105, 211n12
*Unheimlich*, *see* Uncanny
Utopian fiction, 10, 129, 148–53, 181–82, 217n37–39. *See also* Idealism

"Value of Race Literature, The" (Matthews), 155
Vance, Carol, 197n1
Vision, clinical, 7–8, 13–49 *passim*, 71–72, 185
Vision, female, 28–29, 35–48 passim, 138
*Visions: A Study of False Sight (Pseudopia)* (Clarke), 26
*Vital Signs* (Rothfield), 30f

Ward, Lester F., 148–49
Ware, John, 64–65
Weeping, *see* Tears
"What Should Girls Read?" (Howells), 102
Whewell, William, 199n8
Williams, Raymond, 161
*William Wetmore Story and His Friends* (James), 87
Wilson, Harriet, 157
*Woman in the Nineteenth Century* (Fuller), 73, 79–88 *passim*, 209
*Woman's Fiction* (Baym), 52–53, 54
*Woman's Journal*, 144
Womb, 123–24, 140–41, 150–52. *See also* Hysteria
Women: as doctors, 8, 21, 27–29, 50–51, 63–67, 94–97, 107–21, 205–6; frailty of, 8, 51–54, 62, 64, 75; sexual development and education, 67, 89–95. *See also* Gender identity; Heart as metaphor for womanhood; Vision, female; Womb
*Women and Economics* (Gilman), 126, 148–49, 214n9, 217n34
*Work: A Story of Experience* (Alcott), 55, 62–63
*Workings of the Spirit* (Baker), 156–57
World's Fair (Chicago, 1893), 132–33
Writing and healing, 54ff, 61–63, 68–72, 79–88, 142–43, 191–94

"Yellow Wallpaper, The" (Gilman), 10, 124–53 *passim*, 213n6, 214n16, 216
Young, Elizabeth ("A Wound of One's Own"), 61, 205n13

Zola, Emile, 15